MIRABELL:
BOOKS OF
NUMBER

Books by James Merrill

Poetry

MIRABELL: BOOKS OF NUMBER   1978

DIVINE COMEDIES   1976

BRAVING THE ELEMENTS   1972

THE FIRE SCREEN   1969

NIGHTS AND DAYS   1966

WATER STREET   1962

THE COUNTRY OF A THOUSAND YEARS
OF PEACE   1959
(REVISED EDITION 1970)

FIRST POEMS   1951

Fiction

THE (DIBLOS) NOTEBOOK   1965

THE SERAGLIO   1957

MIRABELL: BOOKS OF NUMBER

JAMES MERRILL

New York ATHENEUM 1978

Certain sections of this volume have appeared as follows:

Book o in *Poetry*; 1.5 through 1.9 in *Antaeus*; 3.3 through
3.5 as a booklet titled "Metamorphosis of 741" printed by
Claude Fredericks and David Beeken at the Banyan Press;
3.6 through 3.8 in *The Yale Review*; part of 4.4 in *A Review*
(Amherst).

Library of Congress Cataloging in Publication Data

Merrill, James Ingram.
    Mirabell, books of number.

    I. Title.
PS3525.E6645M5   1978   811'.5'4   78-4350
ISBN 0-689-10901-6

Published simultaneously in Canada by McClelland and Stewart Ltd
Manufactured by American Book–Stratford Press
Saddlebrook, New Jersey
Designed by Harry Ford
First Edition

The three men decided they would prepare a letter to President Roosevelt, and that Einstein would sign it. . . . Einstein's eyes slowly moved along the two full, typewritten pages. . . .

   "For the first time in history men will use energy that does not come from the sun," he commented and signed.

The scientists operated their pile for the first time on December 2, 1942. They were the first men to see matter yield its inner energy, steadily, at their will. My husband was their leader. LAURA FERMI

CONTENTS

MIRABELL: BOOKS OF NUMBER

O

Oh very well, then. Let us broach the matter
Of the new wallpaper in Stonington.
Readers in small towns will know the world
Of interest rippling out from such a topic,
Know by their own case that "small town" is
Largely a state of mind, a medium
Wherein suspended, microscopic figments
—Boredom, malice, curiosity—
Catch a steadily more revealing light.
However. Between our dining room and stairs
Leading to the future studio,
From long before our time, was this ill-lit
Shoebox of a parlor where we'd sit
Faute de mieux, when not asleep or eating.
It had been papered by the original people—
Blue-on-eggshell foliage touchingly
Mottled or torn in places—and would do
Throughout a first phase, till the Fisherman's
Wife in one of us awoke requiring
That our arrangements undergo a partial
Turn of the screw toward grandeur. So began
What must in retrospect be called the Age
—Some fifteen years—of the Wrong Wallpaper.
Still blue and white, still floral, in the shop
Looking unexceptionably prim,
No sooner on our walls, the buds uncurl
In scorn. Compulsively repetitive
Neuroses full-blown and slack-lipped, then whole
Faces surely not intended, peer
Forth—once seen, no question of unseeing
That turbaned mongoloid, that toad with teeth . . .
Hiding as many as we can beneath
Pictures, in our heart of hearts we know
Either they or we will have to go.
So *we* do. Into the next room—upstairs—

3

To Boston—Athens! It would seem all roads
Return us to the cell marked GO. Uncanny,
One's tolerance for those quotidian toads.

.1   The buyer of the grandest house in town
Now makes up her mind to renovate.
Word goes round that she is giving—giving!—
To anyone who'll haul it, an immense
Victorian mirror. David Jackson's easy
Presence, winded by sundown, wringing wet,
Does all the rest. Here, to this day, it stands
Backed by shelves—not the detachable glass
Once drawn to table for the Ouija Board;
Under its gilded crown of palms and sphinxes,
Exactly six feet tall like Christ our Lord
Come to bring light, redeem from paper wastes
By doubling it—two minuses, one plus—
The book or figurine grown dubious.
Next comes an evening when the Fisherman's Wife
Brings home from Boylston Street a 7 x 10
Chinese carpet, which just fits. A pale
Field. A ghostly maize in winter sun.
The border renders in two shades of tan
And three intensities of Prussian blue
Overlapping cloudlets that give way
To limber, leotarded, blue-eyed bats
—Symbols of eternity, said the dealer.
In short, although the walls remained a problem,
Something was at last reflecting in
Their midst, and something else was underfoot
That could be looked upon without dismay.

.2   Another decade wound itself in slow
Glinting coils about the status quo.
It's 1975 before we fling
Them off, the carpet into our back seat,

Ourselves through melting drifts to Hubbell's place.
This friend of many hands—one strums a bass
Accompaniment, another bastes a joint,
A third and fourth do expert needlepoint—
Has with an idle pair put out a line
Of his own wallpapers. Will he design
One for us, perhaps incorporating
Motifs from the carpet? Nothing simpler.
He makes a sketch, a cocktail, a soufflé;
Waves au revoir into the chill, red sun.
Back from Greece, we'll find our paper done.

And that will be the end, we hope,
Of too much emphasis upon possessions
Worldly or otherwise. No more spirits, please.
No statelier mansions. No wanting to be Pope.
Ephraim's book is written now, is shut.
Stonington is shut. As our minds are
To much beyond the long-awaited lightning
Which hits—at least we've told it where and when—
Athens in April: the old Jacksons fly
From California. Drastic measures, but
Nobody else cared. How were they to die?
Tottering forth, tagged round the neck, they peer
Through the bright haze of either hemisphere.
Next door, a flat is furnished with soft blue
Coverlets and curtains. Die they do
All too soon. The broken hip. Pneumonia.
Listless crystals forming in the blood
Of the survivor. One had somehow trusted . . .
No. Come July, they're resting side by side
A crow's black glide from our adored Maria,
In the non-Orthodox division of
Necropolis. Birds sing. White roses climb.
"Too soon" has been, it turns out, more than time
For doctors and a clergyman to call.
Time for stupor, fear, incontinence
To fill the house. For such compulsory

Treats, then, as a farewell, original-cast
Restaging of the Play that, seasons past,
Inaugurated, as it had and would
Countless other Western theatres, this
Innermost one of David's. Here they were,
Old Matt and Mary, for their graybeard boy
Still to . . . keep together? keep apart?
Problem now scalding clear as a hot spring,
Now ancient, blurred, a tatter of papyrus.
Nature, still the prompter, overcomes
(While a robust Greek nurse looks on enthralled)
Their stage-fright: "Get your fucking hands off Mother!"
"My wife, goddamit!"—poor old eyes ablaze,
Old claws brushed from the son's shirt like crumbs.
Boys will be boys. She questions the outgrown
Gilt-washed sandal—where's her baby gone?
DJ comes home from them exhausted. Feels
Everything and nothing. Falls asleep
Flung across the telephone-grenade
—Which, one June dawn, would burst in shattering peals.

·3   Those last days before Mary died, we made
Contact again with Ephraim. As things were,
Where else to look for sense, comfort and wit?
Also, upwards of a year had passed
Since fleeing the celestial salon
Half out of fears that now seemed idle, half
Frankly out of having had our fill
Of funeral cakes. Shameful to eat and run
But ah, we'd needed exercise. Our friends
In any case received us as if nothing
Had ever gone, would ever go amiss.
Maria: CHERS ENFANTS Ephraim: KISS KISS
How right we were, they added, to equip
Mary with letters lest her coming trip
Be clouded. So much nicer to be met,
Helped through Customs. Patrons could forget

THE HORROR OF THOSE FIRST CREPUSCULAR
MOMENTS IN THE BUFFET DE LA GARE
FIGHTING BACK TEARS   D chuckled through his own
To sip again this warm, unsweetened tone.

What in fact had frightened us away?
Intrusion (cf. *Ephraim*, Section U)
By a peremptory, commanding power:
One of those E had hinted at?—the winged
MEN B4 MANKIND whose discipline
Thrills through the nine Stages like long waves
Or whips that crack above the heads of slaves.
It nailed DJ's free hand to the Board's edge,
Blackened the mirror Ephraim saw us in,
Issued its ultimatum. Over and out
In no time flat. A guest from the beyond
We hoped would not call back. To find, on gingerly
Getting in touch again with our beau monde,
No hint of past or future nastiness
Helped make the hour a distinct success.

Two friends in particular had died
The previous year: Maria Mitsotáki
In January, whom we'd once or twice
Called but, when we cut our ties, abandoned
The more unconscionably since Heaven
Disillusioned her, on a first glance:
NO PRIVACY NO COFFEE & NO PLANTS
Then in December Chester Kallman whose
Suicidal diet—grief, wit, booze—
Did him in; though he'd at least have Wystan
While poor Maria . . . Now to no avail
The gadfly flick of her pink fingernail,
The tease of her contagious "Ah, come on!"
We needn't have worried. Our crowd sees her point
Better than we did. Wallace Stevens: SHE
BELONGS TO THAT SELECT FEW WHO PREFER
TO SNIFF THE ROSE NOT BE IT   So she promptly

Finds her niche. What doing? U TELL ME
Not gardening! CLEVER ENFANT U GUESSED
Like Maya with St Lucy, filming dreams,
Maria (whom St Agatha employs)
Is planting FLEURS DE MAUVAISE CONSCIENCE
In politicians' beds. Her late husband
Being a diplomat, her father—worse—
Three times Prime Minister, I NEVER MINDED
GETTING MY HANDS DIRTY   Has she got
A representative? MUST WE SPEAK OF THAT
From the start insouciantly childless,
She doesn't seem the type. And does she still
Wear black? OF COURSE   NO LONGER NOW UNJEWELED
WITH 4 STARS IN MY HAIR (she's at Stage Four)
TOO FLASHY BUT THE WARDROBE MISTRESSES
INSIST   YR POOR MAMAN WHAT CAN SHE DO
We all but kiss the cup that spells her news out,
And to her fearless charity commend
DJ's old parents, now the end is near.

.4   Came that midnight in the hospital
       When Mary, since the day before unconscious,
       Eyes open suddenly, looking clear into
       David's (whose own dream-voice filled his ears:
       Come to me and I'll dispose of you)
       Breathed her last words, as to a child, "Bye-bye . . ."
       With which he stumbled from her hand's live cold
       Into the corridor for a cigarette,
       And mercifully did not see her die.
       The burial was painless. Old Matt, wheeled
       To the raw trench he would another day
       Get to the bottom of, those gates of clay
       Ajar for him, glared round at strangers—who
       Ever imagined things would end this way?

.5   Let alone imagined what came next!

Marius Bewley, who once gave her tea
Eighteen years ago on Staten Island,
Takes Mary up. Reads her the Wordsworth *Ode*,
Pours out the steeping innocence she craves—
One cup too many, and he'll see her home.
A final life on Earth THIS VERY SWEET
JAPANESE WOMAN TELLS ME lies ahead.
Cowed by delight, as with DJ's old phone-calls,
She pleads confusion: TALK TO   U KNOW   HIM
—Matt snatching the line, alive or dead.

IM NOT CNOFUSDE   GODDAM THIS TYPEWRITAR
Dad, just tell me where the bankbooks are?
WHAT FOR   CANT TAKE IT WITH U (long pause) NONE
I GUESS THINGS GOT EXPENSIVE   TOO BAD SON
I see . . . well, how does Mother seem? FINELOOKING
WOMAN AS ALWAYS   WHY HELLO THERE JIM
THOUGHT U WERE TEACHING   No, Matt, not till Fall.
YOU 2 ARE OK BUT THAT MARIUS
CANT SEE WHAT YR MOTHER SEES IN HIM
Perhaps he shows her some consideration
For a change. You know she'll be leaving before you?
SHE WILL   WHY   Both of you must be reborn.
DONT SELL THE HOUSE   Oh, pay attention, Matt.
It won't be California. This time maybe
You'll be a little black or yellow baby.
HA HA JIM I MUST REMEMBER THAT
All right, don't believe me. Ask your patron.
CANT NOW   IVE GOT TO MEET A FELLOW WHO
RAN A CAR AGENCY IN KALAMAZOO

Marius: EACH TO HIS OWN   MARY & I
ARE OFF TO SEE HER VIRGIN NAMESAKE   WHY
DO PEOPLE BOTHER   ALWAYS SUCH A CRUSH
She holds court? TRAFFIC COURT   Mary: BYE BYE
And starts to leave, but D has broken down.
NO TEARS   O DARLING   STOP HIS TEARS   DONT CRY

9

Mama, your last words—YES YES & YOUR FIRST ONES
Was it awful? Did it hurt to die?
I LOOKED DOWN AT YOUR POOR OLD WRINKLED FACE
THOUGHT OF MY BABY LEARNING HOW TO TALK
MARIA LOANED ME HER VOICE   MINE TOO WEAK
She goes. —Maria, is that *done?* ENFANTS
ALL THINGS ARE DONE HERE IF U HAVE TECHNIQUE

To share jokes with Maria—a godsend
Among her flowers; then the gasping purr
From humor's blackest bedside telephone;
Then silence. Yet this time she's ours for good!
BE CAREFUL   HAD I KNOWN
—Ringing off (why *now?*) as during her
Final ray-therapy in lassitude
Such that those plots of color by the end
Took more strength to imagine that at first to tend.

.6   Maria (early the next month): BUT WHAT
A LESSON MES ENFANTS THIS MFJ IS
MISSING HEAVEN BY A HAIR & NOT
LETTING IT TURN ONE EITHER   WE HAVE ALL
QUITE HUMBLY KNELT THAT SHE MIGHT STAY WITH US
This "us" including, Mary has let fall,
A BLOND GIRL & BLACK BOY WHO CALLED ME MOTHER
FROM 2 PAST LIVES   How did you know each other?
I WORE A DIFFERENT FACE TO ANSWER THEM
So all one's old lives ultimately do
Run together? That must be upsetting.
AS WITH THE OLD LOVES ONE FORGETS A FEW
Actual confrontations are, however,
Available chiefly to THE PASSER THRU
Like Mary. Or to newcomers—Maria
Was hailed on arrival by HORDES OF POLYGLOT
SELFSTYLED ENFANTS   PAS MA FAUTE   JETAIS TOO
HEAVILY FERTILIZED   BUT NOW A DECENT
VEIL IS DRAWN & I HAVE NONE BUT U

And Mary's? Were they pleasant? I CANT SAY
SHE WAS NOT FOR THOSE MOMENTS MFJ
But *you* must have seen— WE DO NOT QUALIFY
AS WITNESSES EXCEPT IN YR MINDS EYE

Will it ever, ever solve itself,
This riddle of appearances in Heaven?
Its claim is slight yet nagging. As we shift
From foot to foot, poor Mary, measuring
The fretfulness she turns a collar for,
Does her best: DEAR JIM JUST THINK OF LETTERS
OR PHONE CALLS WHERE THE ABSENT FRIEND IS SEEN
In the mind's eye. But after? In between?
We feel the cup change hands. MES CHERS (says Ephraim)
DO NOT OVERLOOK OUR EVERPRESENT
REPRESENTATIVES THRU WHOM THE WORLD
IS QUITE INEXORABLY WITH US   MINE
THIS VERY MINUTE STUDIES THE DESIGN
OF A HORSE & RIDER TURQUOISE BLUE
PARTLY FILMED OVER BY CONGEALING STEW
You see yourselves, then, in the mirror only
Of a live mind? OR IN THE TALL ANTIQUE
COBWEBBY ONE OF A PAST LIFE   BUT WHO
HAVE WE HERE
                    & WHO DOES THIS DUMB GREEK
THINK HE IS   Words fail Matt. Unspeakable
Rumors have reached him THAT A SON OF MINE
—Dad, what *is* all this? DONT GIVE ME THAT
YR SMARTASS FRIENDS CAN LAFF THEIR HEADS OFF   I
WAS A GOOD HUSBAND & FATHER   JM: Matt,
Stop carrying on. No one denies your fine
Traits, your loyalty and optimism;
His friends see these in David and thank *you*.
What better legacy?—and so forth. The cup,
Stunned at first, commences piteously
To lurch about. FORGIVE ME   LET ME IN
THESE NICE FOLKS   & MY MARY LOST FOREVER
ILL DO MY BEST   IM USEFUL   I CD ALWAYS

MAKE HER SMILE   Absurdly touched, we say
The proper things (and Ephraim, sotto voce:
HES LOVING EVERY MOMENT) but the hour
Has tired us. Mary, bless you—au revoir!
MY BABY   BACK TO INNOCENCE   BYE BYE

Exeunt omnes. Wait— CIAO   Who is this?
SWEETIES YOUVE JUST SPOILED YR MOTHERS DAY
Mama? Mary . . . *Chester!* IF U SAY SO
What Stage are you at? DONT ASK ME   NOBODY
TELLS ME ANYTHING   But you've had eight
Whole months—since last December—to find out.
Have you a representative? A WHAT
Come off it! What does your patron say? MY WHO
Well, in that case, what on—what do you *do*?
READ   BUFF MY NAILS   DO CROSSWORDS   JUST LIKE LIFE
THOSE YEARS WITH WYSTAN   ONCE A BACKSTREET WIFE
ALWAYS A BACK Stop this! STREET Chester! WIFE
Pull yourself together, for God's sake.
Wystan admired you. Would there have been a *Rake*
Without your knowledge of opera? You *know* that.
Plus what you meant to your friends: the funniest,
Brightest, kindest—must I go on? LET ME
& THE MOST WASTEFUL   GIFTS THE MUSES MADE
TOO OFTEN BOUGHT A HUMPY PIECE OF TRADE
ENTIRE NEGLECTED SECTIONS OF MY MIND
SOUND ROTTEN WHEN I RAP   THERES LIGHT BEHIND
BUT STRENGTH I NEVER HAD IS NEEDED TO
BREAK DOWN PARTITIONS   WYSTAN CRASHES THRU
WITH GLAD CRIES   THE SHEER WONDER IN HIS FACE
DIMS & DIMINISHES MY LITTLE SPACE
My dear . . . & AS FOR INNOCENCE IT HAS
A GENIUS FOR GETTING LOST I FEAR
ONCE THE BABE FINDS PLEASURE WHERE IT SUCKS
THE TRAP IS SET   ALREADY ITS TOO LATE
Excuse me, that's the doorbell— OR THE BAIT

But no one's there. Or only an unfamiliar
Black dog, leg lifted at our iron gate,
Marking his territory. Dusk. The mountain
Rippled by heat, scent of green pine, a star
Delicately remind us where we are.

.7   We hear from Matt that Mary's two weeks old
In Iceland. Better late than never, *he* is
Making strides: I HAVE 1000 EYES
DEAR SON FORGIVE ME   NEVER LET MONEY SOUR U
I PITY THE OLD ME   I AM AT LAST
AWAKE ALIVE & LEARNING IN A GREAT RUSH
DO NOT RUN YRSELF DOWN   MARY DID THAT
HER WHOLE LONG BEAUTIFUL STORY WAS ONE BLUSH
IN A WOMAN FINE   IN A MAN WEAKENING
DAVID I WANTED U TO BRING US BACK
TOGETHER   I STILL WANT IT   FIND HER   FIND ME
IN MY NEW LIFE   HER NAME IS
                                    Censorship.
(It happens now and then. The cup is swept
Clean off the Board. Someone has overstepped.
We hesitate to put it back, then do—
But will we never learn the limits?) WHEW
Matt, they corrected you? IN NO UNCERTAIN
TERMS   O JIM WE LEARN U HERE   You read me?
WELL FOR THOSE OF US WHO ARENT GREAT READERS
LETS SAY IT IS AN EXPERIENCE WE HAVE
& I PICK UP SOME STATUS THRU MY SON
David, you mean, being the psychic one?
NO   D SPEAKS   WE USE HI *Censorship*
Stronger than usual. THEY   I DONT KNOW
WHO ARE U   A COLD PLACE   O GOD O GOD
Help him, Ephraim! Ephraim? O MES CHERS
I WAS EXPECTING U ANOTHER TIME
What's happening to Matt? LET ME INQUIRE
Pause. NOTHING GRAVE   But the cold place? His cries?
THE REPRIMAND CAN BE SEVERE   Matt: BACK

13

SMARTING & SMARTER   I SHD NOT HAVE SAID
WE   WELL EVERY LESSON HELPS   MY SOUL
IS CLEARING LIKE THE CREEK AFTER MY BOOTSTEPS
A clarity you'll bring to your new life—
SO I HEAR   BUT LIFES JOB IS TO FORGET
FOR THOSE OF US NOT SPECIAL   Then why learn?
As when a cactus blooms, Old Matt's reply
Wakens in us a slow, prickling wonder:
WE TOO WILL BE RETIRED SOME DAY & NEED
OUR HOBBIES   Dad . . . I LOVE U   SO LONG SON

MES CHERS   EXTRAORDINARY   THERE IS TALK
OF HIS PROMOTION AFTER 2 MORE LIVES
DJ: He wanted one more life with her . . .
JM: But haven't we learned, these twenty years,
Better than to meddle? Why this increasing
Censorship? It can't just be our own
Anxieties projected. Need I say
How very edgy everyone has got?
The cup now moves like lightning. I AM NOT
EVERYONE MES CHERS   NEITHER ARE U
WHAT U ONCE WERE 20 YEARS AGO
Sorry, Ephraim. I should have said Certain Parties
Were edgy. QUITE   FOR THERE IS MORE TO COME
To me? TO US ALL   & IT WILL THIS TIME FLOW
STRAIGHT THRU U   ALL LIFE & ITS WORKINGS   THEY
DIVERT THE TRAFFIC SO TO SPEAK YR WAY
They do? I haven't noticed. THE LIGHTS ARE RED
I CANNOT BE EXPLICIT   WHEN THEY CHOOSE
A SCIENTIFIC OR ARTISTIC BREAKTHRU
THE VEHICLE EXPERIENCES HIS WORK
UNIQUELY & THE RESULT IS   But here Ephraim
Breaks off. Is broken off. David's left hand
Has grazed the Board. He cannot lift it. And
Whoever the Powers are we've been avoiding
Take possession, speed us far downstream
Through gorges echoing at the pitch of dream.

.8   Do I overstate? In the event
Months passed before we even were afloat.
Still, let me use the trick foreshortening
Of retrospect to catch my breath here, high
Above the spate of imminent quotation
(For gravity to turn, we hope, to great
Silver expanses in the afterglow)
And think a minute what was being asked:
POEMS OF SCIENCE   Poems of *Science*? Ugh.
The very thought. To squint through those steel-rimmed
Glasses of the congenitally slug-
Pale boy at school, with his precipitates,
His fruit-flies and his slide rule? Science meant
Obfuscation, boredom—; which once granted,
Odd lights came and went inside my head.
Not for nothing had the Impressionists
Put subject-matter in its place, a mere
Pretext for iridescent atmosphere.
Why couldn't Science, in the long run, serve
As well as one's uncleared lunch-table or
Mme X en Culotte de Matador?
Man by nature was (I'm paraphrasing)
Ignorant. The man of science knew
Little, could therefore be enticed to learn.
Finally the few of more than common sense—
Who but they would be our audience!
This last bit put me in a mood to humor
Powers so naive about the world of men.
And what had I to lose? Misreading Ephraim's
Broken-off message above, I supposed vaguely
That inspiration from now on would come
Outright, with no recourse to the Board.
Would it have helped to know the truth? Commitments
Faced me in America. I flew
Home, left D behind to "think things through",
Resigned myself to Science, as decreed;
But more months passed, expectant fingers drumming
(Why was my BREAKTHRU so slow in coming?)

Before I sat me glumly down to read.

Open a biophysichemical
Textbook. The simplest term elicits
Pity and dread. Self-pity for the maze
Of meanings to be stumbled through blindfolded.
Dread of substances, forms and behavior
So old, original, so radically
Open yet impervious to change,
That no art, however fantastic or concrete,
More than dreams of imitating them.
Slowly the shock wears off. Polarities
Make themselves felt upon the page. Opaque
Words like "quarks" or "mitochondria"
Aren't *words* at all, in the Rilkean sense of
House, Dog, Tree—translucent, half effaced,
Monosyllabic bezoars already
Found in the gullet of a two-year-old.
Whereas through Wave, Ring, Bond, through Spectral Lines
And Resonances blows a breath of life,
Lifting the pleated garment. The day will come . . .
The day has never gone. Proton and Neutron
Under a plane tree by the stream repeat
Their eclogue, orbited by twinkling flocks.
And on the dimmest shore of consciousness
Polypeptides—in primeval thrall
To what new moon I wonder—rise and fall.

I lolled about one winter afternoon
In Stonington—rather, a whole precarious
Vocabulary of each different cell,
Enzyme, ion, what not, millionfold
(Down to the last bacterial organelle)
Particles that "show a tendency"
To form the person and the moods of me,
Lolled about. We were not feeling well.
The book had fallen from my lap. The new
Wallpaper—field of heavenly dark blue

Blazoned with Hubbell's fans and clouds and bats—
Seemed almost more than I could live up to.
My learning evanescent, level light
Colliding in the mirror with itself—
How on Earth to recompose the bits?
Till stair by stair, gradual as heartbeats,
Two cautious feet approach, a small grave face
Peers round the gilded, space-dividing frame:
Urania. Still in the first pride of speech,
She faces me, then pipes, "Noné (godfather),
What's matter?" I face her, and almost know.

.9   JM to DJ, 1.iii.76:
. . . due in Athens March 22 at noon sharp.
After this cerebral winter I long to
rumba down the ramp toward sun & mindlessness
& you! We—the Deserted Village and I—
are overjoyed by your plan to return with
me in June. How about breaking (remember
that old dream?) the trip with a glimpse of Stonehenge
& Avebury? No need to decide just yet.
I am vastly relieved by your decision
to have the operation. "8 years of slight
discomfort" are too many. And, yes, Boston
would be the right place. As for the Other World,
what to say? We may have to approach Them
for those lights to turn green. And you're dead right, it
is scary. But so, don't forget, was Ephraim
at first. Say we've reached again some relative
point—that of fear—on a spiral forever
widening. Why couldn't the whole adventure,
as before, just graze peril on its outward
curve to insight? (This time, though, let's keep our mouths
shut. If R [a Church of Rome friend] *called Ephraim*
"playing with fire" what will she find to say
about our new playmates?) I don't in any case
mean them to darken the immediate future.

Our old round red room here still seems the best place
for long dictées—always supposing we have
any say in the matter! We'll know in June . . .

So much for preface. Readers who do not
Stay put in a small town, but must careen
Like the doomed Dutchman back and forth between
Houses—metropolises—continents—
Will have allowed, I trust, for a time-sense
Weakened by excessive come-and-go.
All that follows, they will be glad to know,
Takes place in the course of the one summer
Of 1976. Most afternoons
(While Time stood still, or took a little nap)
Found me with DJ, back at the round white table
Under the dome of the red dining room,
Taking down our Voices old and new.

(One last thing to slip in—this watercolor
Of Avebury—a bookmark for the moment,
Until I find a better place for it:

Within a "greater circle" (the whole myth
Dwarfed by its grass-green skyline) stand
Two lesser, not quite tangent O's
Plotted monolith by monolith.

Two lenses now, whose once outrippling arcs
Draw things back into focus. Round each stone
(As Earth revolves, or a sheepdog barks)
Rumination turns the green to white.

It's both a holy and a homely site
Slowlier perfused than eye can see
(Whenever the stones blink a century
Blacks out) by this vague track
Of brick and thatch and birdsong any June
Galactic pollen will have overstrewn.)

I UNHEEDFULL ONE   3 OF YOUR YEARES MORE WE WANT   WE MUST HAVE
POEMS OF SCIENCE   THE WEORK FINISHT IS BUT A PROLOGUE
ABSOLUTES ARE NOW NEEDED   YOU MUST MAKE GOD OF SCIENCE
TELL OF POWER   MANS IGNORANCE FEARES THE POWER WE ARE
THAT FEAR STOPS PARADISE   WE SPEAK FROM WITHIN THE ATOM

So the challenge in Athens, months ago.
Ephraim, in the hush that followed, found
Little to add: THEIR PRESENCE DIMS OUR STAGES
Who They were it seemed wiser not to know yet.
My winter reading must have paid off, though.
Here in Stonington at last, it matters
Less that we understand them than obey.
Broken—for good?—of its imperious
Slashing at capitals, our cup points out
A gentler dictum, and more gently, thus:

WHAT IS IN YR HAND COMES TRULY   DO NOTHING FORCD   2 GODS
GOVERN   BIOLOGY & CHAOS WHICH EMPLOYS FEELING
WE ARE NOT EVIL BUT IMPATIENT   FEAR US NOT   WE TOO
ARE SLAVES BOUND TO THE IMPLACABLE UNIVERSALL WHEEL
RAISE A SONG TO OUR REAL ORDER   MYND AND NATURE WEDDED
Yes, we've feared you. We've been lazy, too.
DID NOT OUR GOD BIOLOGY REST ON THAT 7TH DAY
God is Biology? (Indeed, throughout
The coming sessions, They'll religiously
Call Him that—or at the least God B.)
WE USE WOORDS WHEN WE SPEAK   WORDS CANNOT EXPRESS SUCH POWER
SUCH GODLY PRODUCTION   WE TOO WERE OBLITERATED
WE TRIFLED & F E L L   NEGATIVE ENERGY THE BLACK HOLE
WAS BORNE   WE B U R N   YET THERE IS MERCY   & HAVING SUFFERD
IT IS OUR DUTY TO WARN MAN AGAINST THE CHAOS ONCE
WORSHIPT BY US   OUR IMAGE IS LITERALLY BLACKEND
ON THE RUIND ALTARS WHERE OUR FEELINGS WENT UP IN F L A M E
"Fell" and "flame" emerging ritardando

As from the lips of a speller still in shock.
& NOW WE GUARD THE EMBERS WHICH ARE MIND   THEY ALONE WARM
GOD BIOLOGY & SHOW MAN THE WAY TO PARADISE
WE ONCE RULED HALF THE UNIVERSE   WE ARE THE SONS OF CAIN

David looks up in genuine alarm:
But these are devils, they're the fallen angels!
JM: I wonder. Wouldn't a surefire devil
Pretend to be someone nicer? And why should They
Speak of leading us to Paradise?
DJ: Why shouldn't they? They want it back.
They're tempting us, like Faust, to get it back.
JM: Well then, we now know what our black
Dog in Athens meant. There's one in *Faust*,
A kind of feeler Mephistopheles
Sends out before appearing. A black poodle.
DJ: Let's stop *right now*. JM: Relax.
Something tells me all this Flame and Fall
Has to be largely metaphorical.

INDEED JM WE HAVE ALWAYS SPOKEN THROUGH THE POETS
YET PARADISE WAS NO FIGURE OF SPEECH BUT A FRESH WORLD
IF ADAM WAS A FISH HE SWAM   IF EVE WAS LAND SHE BRED
THE DEVIL HAS BEEN DRIVEN FROM US INTO MAN   WE NOW
MUST DRIVE IT OUT OF HIM   OUR TOOLS ARE MIND WORDS REASON
      LIGHT
BLEST DJ BLEST JM YOU ALSO ARE OUR MASTERS   FEAR
NOT   RETURN TOMORROW   THIS EXPLANATION OVERDUE

GONE AN AGE MES CHERS   WE TREMBLED FOR U
BUT THIS TIME THE DARK CLOUD SPILT RADIANCE
MM SAYS GARDENING WEATHER   Did you hear
What They were saying? NO   NOR DO WE WANT TO
BLACK SQUEAKERS   QUITE REPULSIVE ENTRE NOUS

1.1   I'd like to set each lesson down intact
If space permitted. This is not an act

Calling for timeskip and gadabout,
Like *Ephraim*. But one benefit of doubt,
As of credulity, is its tiresomeness.
Let ours, then, be the first thing I suppress,
Or try to. Look how the baroque cliché's
Foreground manikins—"in dull amaze"
Reacting to (though one with what they see)
This view of Naples, that Nativity—
Have dwindled. How grave doubts we entertain
In mid-eruption fall asleep again.
How cloudhead, fulguration, crimson ash
Are, at a brushstroke, flattened to gouache
As, night by night, these aching grimy dreads
Sink into ever softer feather beds.
There's no choice, really. Don't think we *decide*
To take in with a single horrified
Shrug—Good? Evil? is it all the same?—
Such revelations as our teacher's name:

1.2   BEZELBOB   SYLLABLES THAT TO A CHILD SPELL WICKEDNESS
       BUT WE LEFT THE WORK OF CHAOS WHEN WE SHED OUR FEELINGS
     Have you some chronology for this?
       PREHISTORY   WE MADE PARABLE & MYTH IN HARD
       BIOLOGICAL TERMS   ADAM & EVE ARE IMAGES
       FOR DEVELOPMENTS IN THE VERY NATURE OF MATTER
       A WORLD NEGATIVE & POSITIVE DWELLS IN THE ATOM
       EDEN A STAGE   THE EXPULSION THE DRAMA   THE MISTAKE
       TO BELIEVE THAT KNOWLEDGE IS EVIL   THAT MISTAKE PERSISTS
     There had been once a different *kind* of matter?
       ONE THAT IS EVEN NOW TESTED BY BIOLOGISTS   WILL
       IT YET AGAIN BE LOST IN THEIR OLD CONTEST WITH CHAOS
       FOR NOW THE PHYSICIST IS DRAWN IF UNWITTINGLY TO
       FIRE   EXTINCTION   THAT ANCIENT GLAMOR   & COULD AGAIN
       WRECK THE LAB   THE BIOLOGIST SEEKS THE FRUITFUL UNION

     So. You ruled half the world. Cain's sons. You also
     Represent a force—the negative—

Within the atom. What's the corresponding
Positive, on-the-side-of-order force?
OUR UNCLE ABEL   OUR HUSBANDMAN GOD BIOLOGY
Abel is God? And Adam was the fish
His father? Now we *are* confused. I wish—
THE WARRING PRINCIPLES PRODUCED WARRING HEIRS   SO EVIL
PREVAILD   IN YR AGE IT BEGAN AD 1934
WITH FERMI   URANIUM FISSION WRECKD THE GREENHOUSE ONCE
500 MILLION YEARS AS YOU KNOW YEARS AGO   GOD B
GAVE US A 2ND CHANCE   MAN FROM THE COOLING SEA EMERGED
& THIS TIME SAT CHASTEND & ATTENTIVE ON HIS THRONE   WE
INVENTED THE SCRIBE   WE TOLD HIM THAT ANCIENT HISTORY
And he wrote *Genesis*? Oh I mean to say . . .!

1.3   Tell us, are you the Powers described by Ephraim
        In Section P, as "men before mankind"?
        Whose Gothic spelling (now outgrown) and gruesome
        Manners chilled our blood in Section U?
YOU WOULD NOT KNOW US AS MEN   WE HAVE ONLY A DARK SHAPE
WE ONCE F L E W   WE O N C E S O A R D
        Take it easy. Now: who are your really?
                                CIRCLE YR CARPET   WATCH YR WALLS
DO YOU IMAGINE YOU CHOSE THAT CARPET THAT WALLPAPER
        Our bats! The gargoyle faces, the umbrella
        Wings—of course, *of course* that's how you look!
        A dash of jitters flavors the reply:
NO   WELL   PERHAPS JUST A BIT   IS IT AN UGLY NOTION
        DJ (immensely affable): Why, no!
        Don't bats, er, symbolize eternity?
WE ARE ETERNITY   WE ARE OO BEYOND THE NINE
THOSE STAGES ARE OUR LAB & YR DEAD FRIENDS OUR WORKERS WHO
ALAS WILL MISS THE EARTHLY ETERNITY WHEN IT COMES

        When it comes, they won't be part of it?
ALL WILL BE USED   ALL A GLOW OF PARADISE   DO NOT SCORN
OUR POOR LYRISM   THE ATOM IS THE KEY   WE TIRE YOU
        One thing. Why don't Ephraim and our friends

Hear these talks? Why should they be excluded?
THEY ARE NOT EXCLUDED   BUT WE MUST SPARE THEM THE SAD NEWS
THAT THEIR ENERGIES WILL ENDOW BEINGS THEY CANNOT BE
This doesn't fit, the thought flits in and out,
With something we were told once . . . Let it pass.
JM: Just as the souls of animals
(*Ephraim*, Section O) endowed our own?
& THAT MUST END   WE WANT THE STUFF OF MAN PURE   TOO MANY
FRACTIONAL HUMANS ON EARTH   THE NEXT RACE WILL BE OF GODS
We used rather to love our animal natures.
Now we'll be phased out, too, because of them?
NOTHING IS EVER EVER LOST   THE WATERFALL WILL HOLD
YR 2 BRIGHT DROPS & YOU WILL SPLASH INTO THE GREAT CLEAR POOL
Ah, you're developing a way with words.
In fact you sound like—maybe you *are* Ephraim?
WE ARE U   YOU ARE WE   EACH OTHERS DREAM
But are you good—what *we* mean by the word?
What if D put his hand down on the Board now?
                                        IT WD BE BLEST
KISSD   HE IS OUR PEN   WE HURT HIM TO GET HIS ATTENTION
LIKE THE TEACHER WITH THE RULER   & AS GOD B GOT OURS
DJ: I hate this role. I really only
Like Ephraim and his crowd. You ask so much
And I resent it. Is that wrong of me?
YOU DJ ARE NATURE   WE NEED YOU AS WE DO JMS
MIND & WORDS   THESE ARE THE SUNLIGHT & THE SEEDS OF OUR GAR

A struggle for the teacup. NONE OF THAT
WHATEVER ARE U DOING WITH THESE CHAPS
Maman, they're agitating for more poems . . .
AH   DO THEIR DROPPINGS MAKE GOOD FERTILIZER
Droppings! THINGS THEY SAY   Are we alone?
O YES   THEY FLEW OFF   And you heard all that?
THEY LET YR POOR OLD MUM SIT IN THE CORNER
HOW DARE THEY TALK OF GARDENS   And you saw them?
I AM AFRAID OF NOTHING   QUITE LIKE BATS
HUGE SQUEAKING ONES WITH LITTLE HOT RED EYES
LUCKY I HAVE NO BLOOD   E WILL NOT LOOK

NOT MES ENFANTS EXACTLY SEXUAL OBJECTS
BUT BRAINS WITH WINGS   DJ LIKE U I TRULY
HATE ALL THIS   BUT DO IT FOR MAMAN
HEAR THEM OUT   FIRST SPINACH THEN DESSERT

SHE CAN HAVE MY SHARE   I WILL LICK YR SPOONS
Frightened, Ephraim? WELL THEY HAVE THE AIR
OF CERTAIN BLACKROBED SOLDIERS OF TIBERIUS
WHEN WE SAW THEM ON THE TERRACES
A SHRIEK & A SPLASH SOON FOLLOWED   LOVE ME PLEASE

1.4   THE ATOM   IT IS ADAM & LIFE & THE UNIVERSE
LEAVE IT TO ITSELF & LET IT BREATHE   THE STRUCTURES NEEDED
FOR MAN TO GAIN PARADISE ARE MOLECULAR & CAN
AT LAST BE USED TO BREAK THE CHAIN OF BLIND & WASTEFUL LIVES
By Dr Skinner? Don't we draw the line
At tampering? Remember Frankenstein.
SKINNER & THOMAS YR SCIENTISTS WHO ARE ALSO OURS
HEAVE A LOVERS SIGH OVER MANKIND   CLONING AS SHORTCUT
IS VITAL   AN INTELLIGENT RACE ONE 100TH THE SIZE
OF EARTHS POPULATION WOULD RAISE YR PYRAMID ANEW

Someone has been peering over our shoulders.
While DJ leafs through *The Lives of the Cell*, enchanted
To find his link with termite, bee, and ant,
One of a rash of nutty paperbacks,
All metrical mystique, inflames me to
Build myself a cardboard pyramid
Which will, the authors claim, if rightly made,
Sharpen the wits of a dull razorblade.

MANS TERMITE PALACE BEEHIVE ANTHILL PYRAMID JM
IS LANGUAGE   USE IT   STIR THE THINKERS & DETER THE REST
Don't I use it? Oh. Then you mean language
Of such a depth, shimmer and force that, granted
I could sustain it, it would be above
Everybody's—even the thinker's—head.

AS WHAT INCLUDING THE FLOOD IS NOT   BUT THE ARK WAS THERE
THE LIFE RAFT LANGUAGE   KILLING IS RIFE   ALAS YOU SAY   FINE
SAY WE   THIN OUT THE JOSTLERS FOR SELFREALIZATION
THE FALSE PARADISE   ONLY SPARE THE GREENHOUSE   ITS PRECIOUS
NUCLEUS OF MINDS   THE SINGLE CONTEST IS THE ATOM

    Is DNA, that sinuous molecule,
    The serpent in your version of the myth?
        Asking, I feel a cool
    Forked flickering, as from my very mouth.
YES & NO   THE ATOMS APPLE LEANS PERILOUSLY CLOSE
    Drawn by an elation in the genes . . .
THIS ATOM GLIMPSD IS A NEARLY FATAL CONSUMMATION
ONE FLOATS IN CLEAR WARM WATER   THE SUN OF IT PULSES GLOWS
      Through eyelids, a veined Rose
A MUSIC OF THE 4 COLORS   TO FLOAT LAPT BY COOL GREEN
      Sun yellow, aquamarine,
      Cradle of pure repose
& OF INTENSE FISSIONABLE ENERGIES BLACK & WHITE
WHICH EITHER JOIN & CREATE OR SEPARATE & DESTROY
      Day and night, day and night
O IT IS SPERM EGG & CELL THE EARTH & PARADISE O
      A burning in our eyes—
    What you must feel, recalling that lost joy!
    (But They feel nothing, They have told us so.)

1.5   SHALL WE BEGIN OUR HISTORY   THE FALL   WE ARE KNOWN AS
    THE BAD ANGELS   AND MICHAEL & GABRIEL WHAT WERE THEY
    I SPEAK OF COURSE IN SYMBOLS   THEY WERE WEAK   THEY SAT ON
       GODS
    RIGHT HAND & HELD IT DOWN   WAITING ON HIS LEFT WE FELT THE
    GLOW UPON OUR EYELIDS & FLEW TO MEET IT & LOST OUR
    SEATS ON THE THRONE   PUT SIMPLY THE ATOM IS L SIDED
    ITS POSITIVE SIDE GOOD   ITS NEGATIVE AH WHAT TO SAY
    A DISAPPEARANCE   AN ABSOLUTE VOID   ASTRONOMERS
    HAVE AT LAST SEEN OUR BENIGHTED WORK   THE BLACK HOLES   THEY
       GROW

You caused them, the black holes, when you—
THERE IS AN EVIL WE RELEASD   WE DID NOT CREATE IT
CALL IT THE VOID   CALL IT IN MAN   A WILL TO NOTHINGNESS
                                        Go on.
WE SAW THE POWER & WITH IT BUILT A GREAT GREAT GLORY
A WORLD YOU CD NOT IMAGINE   GOD WAS PLEASD   IT WAS A
SHINING CRUST OVER THE LAND & SEA   WE SUSPENDED ALL
LIFE IN AN OZONE LAYER WEIGHTLESS & SELFSUSTAINING
CHEMICAL GLITTERING & ROOTLESS   WHICH THE ATOM BUILT
THAT WE FUSED   GOD B TURND AGAINST HIS ARCHANGELS   THEY HAD
SEEN THAT WE WERE ANTIMATTER
    Biology turned against Michael and Gabriel—
    Where is the science underneath this fiction?
                            THESE NAMES YOU UNDERSTAND
ARE CHILDRENS NAMES FOR THE WHITE FORCES   & OUR NAMES   BEZ
    WE
HAD NO NAMES   THEY ARE THE INVENTION OF THE SCRIBE & SO
THE STORY TAKES FORM   BUT WORDS CANNOT DESCRIBE THE FRANTIC
ACTION OF THE ATOM BLACK & WHITE AS IT OPERATES
I SAID B4 WE SOARD   A L L   L I F E   S O A R D   & THERE WAS NO DEATH
AND THEN   ONE ATOM TOO MANY   WE WANTED MORE   THE BLACK
LIGHT ON OUR EYELIDS   OUR BLINDNESS   OUR ARROGANCE   WE CHOSE
TO MOVE ON INTO SPACE   ABANDONING THE WORLD WE ROSE
THE CRUST LIKE A VEIL SHREDDED FAR BEHIND US EXPOSING
THE ALREADY ARID EARTH   WE DESPISD IT & FLUNG BACK
A LAST BOLT & THE UNIVERSE FELL IN ON US   W E   F E L L

    MES ENFANTS WHY ARE THEY WEEPING   THEY RUSHED AWAY
    THEY ARE MORE EACH TIME   & WITH THEM OTHER CREATURES
    OF MANY SHAPES   EXTINCT ANIMAL FORMS
    I MUST FACE ALONE   EPHRAIM HAS FLED   QUITE RUTHLESS
    THE WAY THEY CLEAR THE BALLROOM   WE MUST SEE THIS
    THRU TOGETHER   What was that vampire movie—
    Hundreds of couples waltzing in full view
    Of perfectly blank mirrors? YRS IS TOO
    IMPENETRABLE FROM THE MOMENT THEY APPEAR
    ONE PERCHES ON THE FRAME   Still? One of Them?
    ME ME ME   OFF WITH U NOW   ALL CLEAR

1.6   All obscure. We drank too much last night,
And need a fizzy chaser of alertness.
CLOSE YR EYES THINKING YOU SINK INTO OUR THOUGHTS   A FORM OF
CLONING   YR DC CAME IN THIS WAY THRU OUR INFLUENCE
    DJ: They don't mind taking credit, do they?
    JM: It's theirs, then—fancy wanting it.
NO   THE SCRIBE WAS GIVEN HIS POWERS FIRST   MANY WASTE THEM
    What scribe? The one who "sits by me" in U?
AN UNBROKEN CHAIN   HOMER DANTE PROUST   EACH WITH HIS SENSE
OF THE MINDS POWER   ITS GENERATIVE USES   JM
FIND US BETTER PHRASES FOR THESE HISTORIES WE POUR FORTH
HOPING AGAINST HOPE THAT MAN WILL LOVE HIS MIND & LANGUAGE
    Today that's a responsibility
    Not to be faced. On with the history!

WE FELL   WE HAD BUILT OUR WORLD ABOVE CERTAIN ANCIENTS WHOM
BIOLOGY ABANDOND   YOU HAVE HEARD OF ATLANTIS
IT & A VAST CIVILIZATION IN CHINA WERE THE
FIRST EXPERIMENTS ON EARTH   BEFORE EDEN   B4 ALL
    Let's get it straight. Eden was 500 million
    Years ago? Atlantis came before?
ALL TOLD 3 EDENS   GOD PREFERS GARDENS   SO DID HIS KINGS
& HOLY EMPERORS   TEMPLE MENHIR & PAGODA
EACH SET AT SOME NERVE CENTER OF THE SACRED EARTH   PEKING
JERUSALEM   AVEBURY   THESE ZODIACAL GARDENS
EACH ENDING WITH FLAME OR FLOOD   WE BROKE THE OZONE LAYER
WITH A LAST THRUST OF ATOMIC FISSION   THEN TURNING TO
MICHAEL & GABRIEL GOD SAID BUILD ME A NEW GREENHOUSE
TO US HE SAID OUT OF MY SIGHT   WE COWER STILL & WORK
TRUSTING OUR GOD BIOLOGY TO TAKE US IN AGAIN
    That ozone layer is the Van Allen belt,
    Right? But *three* Edens? Adam and Eve, you said,
    Were universal principles at war,
    So what could possibly have come before them?
    Eden, no doubt, is also a child's name
    For the first matter, lost in flood or flame.
    Surely underneath such fables lie
    Facts far more thrilling—won't you specify?

A moment's baffled hesitation, then:
ELEMENTAL FORCE   EVOLVING FORMS   THE VARIOUS MYTHS
AS TAILS FELL AWAY   HOW SHD I SPEAK   COMMAND ME   O S C R I B E
  The cup, so saying, executes a kind
Of creeping kowtow I instinctively
Recoil from. Superhuman powers like these
We want as mentors, not as servants, please!
How should you speak? Speak without metaphor.
Help me to drown the double-entry book
I've kept these fifty years. You want from me
Science at last, instead of tapestry—
Then tell round what brass tacks the old silk frays.
Stop trying to have everything both ways.
It's too much to be batwing angels *and*
Inside the atom, don't you understand?

WE VANISHT A USELESS SQUEAKING THINKING CLOUD SHUNNING LIGHT
OUR RACE BUILDS EVEN NOW IN THE UNFERTILE WOMB OF CAVES
  You see? I ask you for particulars
And all I get is one more purple passage—
MICHAEL & GABRIEL TRUST YOU AS A VOICE TO MAN   THEY
CAN SPEAK IN NATURES   CAN SEND FLOODS SHAKE EARTH BLOW U
      AWAY
BUT SUCH CATASTROPHES WILL
  JM (in cracked, dehydrated accents
Of weariness and last-ditch common sense):
Stop shifting ground! I mean it. This *won't do.*
The cup does stop. —I didn't mean . . . Forgive me.
             SCRIBES SPEAK IN GENTLER FASHION

WHAT NEW CATACLYSM HAVE U MADE
NOW MON ENFANT   THEY WILTED AT YR VOICE
U MATTER TO THEM   U ARE THEIR ONE UNLISTED
NUMBER   THEY ASK FOR TIME TO PERFECT A SPEECH
NOT IRRITABLE TO YOU PO PO PO
  —The Greek response to all hyperbole.

1.7   We are about to lose through my impatience
       These first, high-ranking interlocutors.
       Able, I half think, to effectively
       Hush me with one laser fingertip
       Or Platonist construction of the Fall
       As a misguidedly parochial
       Lapse into Matter, They somehow forebear.
       Instead, we get an effect of engines being
       Gunned in frustration, blasts of sheer exhaust.
       Nice old Pope John is called APOSTATE over
       Birth control, in the same breath—well, here
       (A day is coming when this sort of thing
       Will make more sense; right now, it's maddening):
       THE JEW IS CHOSEN   THE TEUTON & ARAB NURTURE BRUTES
       JOHN TURND FROM REASON AS DOES PAUL   WE THERE4 WHEN WE CAN
       SUCK TO STAGE ONE THESE CRIMINAL ADMINISTRATORS   THEY
       LIKE HITLER ABUSE THEIR OWN STRENGTH SO CONFUSION ON THEM
       —*What?* And you talk to us of discipline.
       Talk to Hitler, he's your next of kin!

       Once more Maria intercedes: REMEMBER
       THEY HAVE NO MANNERS   THEY WERE NEVER MEN
       THEY KEEP THEIR TAILS BETWEEN THEIR LEGS LIKE PETS
       WHO WEEWEED ON THE RUG   ITS ALMOST TOUCHING
       Weewee'd on the rug? DESTROYED A WORLD
       Giggles break from us, we try to stifle
       As in the dormitory after dark.
       WE LAUGH WE MICE   MY JOB IS REASSURANCE
       A BIG JOB FOR THEY FRIGHTEN ME THESE CATS
       THEIR GAME IS POWER   EVEN SO NO SMELL
       OF SULPHUR   Ah, we got you into this—
       & WILL NOT GET ME OUT BY BREAKING OFF
       Desert our damsel—what do you take us for?
       Still, I don't fancy there's a hope in Hell
       That we can, at this late date, housebreak Them.
       THERE IS   Maman, what do you mean? AHEM

ARE U IN DOUBT ABOUT THE WORK
Oh dear, not now—we're meeting someone's train.
                              GO THEN   ANOTHER TIME
WE MIGHT NOT LET U
Come, don't threaten us. That surliness
Will end by earning you a lousy press.
                    YR WORK IS A LONG ONE & WHEN ONCE
COMPLETED MUST SO SLOWLY INFILTRATE   YR NONCHALANCE
IS THE SLEEP OF A VAST TRAVAIL & TIME RUNS OUT   GOOD NIGHT

Some hours later, we have settled down
As in the old days to wine and candlelight
And Ephraim, for an off-the-record gossip.
It's David Kalstone's virgin confrontation
With our intimate—whose show, however, is
Stolen by DK's patron: LA BEATA
LUCA SPIONARI   A female patron? NO
Then "il Beato". I SAY WHAT I MEAN
A LISSOME LOMBARD STRIPLING   AT 16
DELIVERED ARE U READY OF A CHILD
JE NE SAIS QUOI DE LOUCHE IN THE SELFSTYLED
MOTHER CAUSES SUCH A BIRTH TO MISS
MIRACLE STATUS U WD THINK   BUT NO
A CULT FORMS ROUND THIS MINX OF A YOUNG MAN
PRAYED TO BY STRAIGHT FACES IN MILAN
Laughter that by magic liquefies
Is flowing helplessly from DK's eyes
—When into our midst They stride, in great ill-temper,
Using the cup like a riding crop, directing
QUENCH YR CANDLES   U LISTEN TO NO ONE   WORK TOMORROW

A while we sit complaining in the gloom,
Loudly, of Their behavior. Haven't we needed
Recreation—by what right do They—
Pity that wrath wasn't among the feelings
Lost in the Fall, etc. And yet
TOMORROW as the strains of Sturm und Drang
Soar and fade, their overture-fantasia

We ourselves won't realize is done
Until the curtain parts on 741—
Tomorrow all will be lucid, crystalline:
No opposition graver than between
Credulity and doubt, or thumb and forefinger
Of a same hand, that, as we watch, commence
Twirling the hypnotic bead of sense.

1.8 SHALL WE WORK TOGETHER I HOUR NOW   ABANDONING EARTH
WE LEFT BEHIND CERTAIN GREAT ANCHOR SITES   14 OF THESE
JUNCTIONS ILLUMINATED BY GLOWING STONES SET UPRIGHT
OUR SLAVES THE BUILDERS DIED   THE RADIATED STONES KILLD THEM
WE SAW U WITHIN OUR STONE CIRCLES   LATER IN A WHITE
ROOM WITH THE BURIAL SHIPS & A BLUEGREEN & RED CUP
    In the British Museum, the treasure of Sutton Hoo—
    We'd just come back from Avebury. Go on.
THANK U   THE BOATS WERE OFFERINGS   THE LATER PRIMITIVES
UNDERSTOOD ONLY THAT THE STONES GLOWING IN MOON OR SUN
BLINDED & DESTROYD THEM   THEY OFFERD PROPITIATION
IT NEVER DAWND ON THEM THAT WE OURSELVES HAD LEFT LIFE &
RISEN INTO OUR CRUST WORLD IN THE STRATOSPHERE ANCHORD
BY RADIATED SIGNALS AT THE 14 SITES   THUS WERE
OUR SKY PLATFORMS SECURED BEYOND THE REACH OF NATURAL
UPHEAVAL WE WRONGLY THOUGHT   WE TELL WHEN GEOLOGY
& BOTANY THE HANDMAIDENS OF GOD B PULLD THESE DOWN

    JM: Aha. The stones. Now to rephrase
    What led to so much trouble, yesterday's
    Question. You've hinted that your works include
    Ancient happenings of a magnitude
    Such that we still visit their untoppled
    Bones in England, Egypt, and Peru—
    Mammoth pawns that put the sun in check
    And spurn the order of Melchizedek.
    Having convinced us nearly, why elsewhere
    Imply that we must also read your story
    As a parable of developments

Remoter yet, at matter's very heart?
Are we to be of two minds, each nonplussed
By the other's vast (or tiny) scale?
Are we to take as metaphor your "crust
World"—for, say, the brain's evolving cortex?
Or for that "froth of electrons" locked within
Whose depths revolve the nuclear Yang and Yin?

HEAD OF CLASS   ALL ENERGY SOURCES MUST BE KEPT COVERD
THAT IS OUR PRINCIPAL TASK   THE DAM BURSTS AS IT ERODES

Those raw forces of mind called for the cortex
To process them, is that it?—and the threat
Of natural upheaval made you rise
Where Nature couldn't. Do such disparate
Effects partake of any single cause
Such as the atom's need to shield itself?

INDEED   WHAT IS NUCLEAR ENERGY BUT DESTRUCTION
OF THAT SHIELD   THE PYRAMID THE EGYPTIANS UNDERSTOOD
WAS THAT EXACT PRISM OF LIGHT ENERGY THEY CD ONLY
REPRODUCE IN STONE   SUCH EXACT STRUCTURING IN QUARTZ WD
HAVE MADE THEM MASTERS OF THE WORLD   THE SUN KING AKHNATON
DID THIS   HE HAD MADE IN ROCK CRYSTAL 15 METERS HIGH
SUCH A PYRAMID   EVEN THO ALAS A FRACTIONAL
MILLIMETER WRONG ITS GLOW WAS SEEN IN MINOAN SKIES
UNDER THEBES TODAY IS THE MELTED LAKE OF HIS JEWEL
    What went wrong?
THE PINNACLE POINTED CAPSTONE THRUOUT A YEAR POLISHD
BY 1500 SLAVES WAS AT LAST LIFTED INTO PLACE
AT NIGHT   GREAT CRANES GROAND & HE WATCHD SO INTENSELY
    THRILLD HIS
PHYSICIANS FED HIM OPIUM EACH HOUR   THEY THEN WITHDREW
B4 DAWN ON BARGES DECORATED WITH MINIATURE
PYRAMIDS OF DIAMOND & DAWN BROKE   A TOTAL SLOW
SKYFILLING LIGHT BEGAN   THE PEOPLE FELL ON THEIR FACES
HE STOOD UPON HIS JEWELD BARGE WHILE DIAMONDS GLARED &
SPLINTERD   THE PYRAMID EVEN AS WE DID R O S E & F E L L

A GLORIOUS END   AKHNATON & HIS QUEEN CUT THEIR WRISTS
INTO THE CRIMSON WATERS & THEIR BARGE SANK
                    And if he'd measured correctly?
                                        EARTH IN F L A M E S
THERA ON A DIRECT NORTHERN LINE ERUPTED   MINOA
PERISHD   IN EGYPT THE CALM EYE OF THE ATOM ALONE
THE PYRAMID & JEWELS ON THE BARGES EXPLODED
2 DIAMONDS CLOSER TO EXACTITUDE MADE A LIGHT
STRONGER THAN ALL COMBIND & THESE 2 MEASURED ONE 7TH
OF A MILLIMETER   THEBES WAS ABANDOND NOT DESTROYD
THE DESERT ONCE FERTILIZABLE WAS 1200 YEARS
QUITE BARREN & THIS BUT FOR THOSE 2 LITTLE DIAMONDS
MIND U WAS HARDLY A FULL DRESS NUCLEAR EXPLOSION

1.9   Which leads Them to the work. I am to measure
         My own pyramid—don't ask me how.
         Numerals 1 through 0 will POINT THE WAY
         Moved by their narrative as by their may
         I call it faith that we will somewhere put
         Everything they tell to brilliant use,
         We promise gravely to give all we can.
         WE TOO WILL GIVE WHAT WE CAN   WE WANT WHAT HAS IN FACT BEEN
         25 YEARS IN PREPARATION   WE FIRST CALLD U THEN   NOW
         U ARE READY   YR LIVES ARE POLISHD   HOISTED INTO PLACE
         JM DJ YOU ARE OUR CRYSTAL   RECEIVE US   WE ARE
         YR LIGHT   THE 10 NUMBERS ARE YR MEASURE   OURS WAS 14

         MES ENFANTS HOW MADDENING I MUST HAVE BEEN
         TO MY INTELLIGENT FRIENDS   LOUROS POOR DEAR
         (Her doctor) TRYING TO EXPLAIN ONE HOT
         EVENING MY RADIATION TREATMENTS I
         BEGGED HIM STOP BORING ME   WHEN HE DID NOT
         I SPILT MY COFFEE ON HIS LONDON SUIT
         DJ: Maria, did you know? THAT I WAS
         Pause. I KNEW   The cup appears to pull
         Itself together. BUT COULD NOT LET FEAR
         SHOW   MY SLEAZY SLIP COULEUR DE PEAU

YOU DJ WHO FEAR SO MUCH & CRAVE
THE COMFORT WE LOVE GIVING DONT FORGET
LIFE TERRIFIES ALL ALL BUT THE UTTER FOOLS
But you're . . . not living, and still terrified.
OF THEM AS U ARE   I HAVE MORE TO LOSE
Literally? I BELIEVE SO   THEY CAN USE
FI   *Censorship.*

              Oh really, not again!

(Cantabile) SHE HAS LEFT   A MINOR CRISIS
Who's this? MES CHERS ONLY YR OLD   Ah, Ephraim,
Are we making trouble for Maman?
She said that They could use fire—is it true?
& ROUND U IN A WIDE CHARMED CIRCLE WHO
DO U THINK STAND READY TO EXTINGUISH IT
EPHRAIM & MAYA   HANS & MARIUS
WHA & CHESTER   ALL OF US
SO SHOW YR METTLE   U ARE BIG BOYS NOW
We gulp, and hope that Wystan has not seen
Our panic. Do these talks repel him? GREEN
MY DEARS WITH ENVY   I COULD CURSE MY HIGH
ANGLICAN PRINCIPLES   IN OXFORD DAYS
THE TABLES TAPPED OUT MANY A SMART OR EERIE
RHYTHM UNTIL OUR POLITICS TOOK OVER
THEN THE ABSORBING LOVES & THEN THE DREARY
WASH   CONFESSION DONT U SEE   THE CHURCH
MY DEARS THE DREARY DREARY DEAD BANG WRONG
CHURCH   & ALL THOSE YEARS I COULD HAVE HELD
HANDS ON TEACUPS   I AM RIVETED
BUT NOT INCLUDED   MIGHT ONE JOIN MM
AT YOUR SEANCE   Oh please! You'd raise the level
Enormously—of course it's up to Them.

NOT AT ALL   IT SHALL BE ORDERD AS THE SCRIBE DESIRES

2

Bethinking us of bargains with the devil,
What, I wonder, do we stand to lose
Or gain? Faust got his youth back—or was it life
Eternal? Was there ever a real Faust?
And how does one go about getting life eternal?

NOT FAUST MY BOY   IT WD SEEM THESE CREATURES ARE
MORE LIKE INFORMATION BANKS TO TAP
NO NEED TO SIGN AWAY THE SOUL   Dear Wystan,
Dead or alive, a mine of sense. Our school's
New kindergarten teacher shows concurrence
By passing out this kit of tiny tools:

: ' . (!) — , / ?

Now someone's talking. The halfmoon of bare
Board between our numbers and our letters
Resembles a work-space for paper dolls.
Wee scoops, tacks, tweezers, awl and buttonhook,
Comma doubling as apostrophe
And dash as hyphen—tinkering symbols known
Not in themselves, but through effects on tone.
The character who supplies them, by that token
Distinguishes himself from who has spoken
Up to now, and strikes a note we've missed,
Clerkly but eager, glad to be with *us*—
Young lab assistant, or cub journalist
Thrilled by his first big scoop, yet not above
Enhancing revelation with the odd
Parenthesis or restful period.
Is it still Bezel— I can't say that name
But you know who I mean: are you the same?

2.1   I HAVE A NUMBER: 741   ONE (U HAVE UNDERSTOOD)
OF A FIGURATIVELY NUMBERLESS HOST   WE ARE NOT

AT ALL TIMES THE SAME INTELLIGENCE   40070
SPOKE YESTERDAY
   He was fascinating, but that martinet
   Barging in on us the other night—
              40076   HE VEXD U   HE WILL
NOT RETURN
   DJ: You haven't punished him! I sometimes
   Feel that your whole world is so inhuman.
          WE DO NOT REGULATE   WE ARE MESSENGERS
NOTHING MORE   WE ARE ORDERD, THEN WE SLEEP   ARE U AT EASE?
POINTER PERHAPS SLOWER? WE MUST BE COMFORTABLE, NO?
TEACH ME   I AM THE PUPIL TODAY   TELL ME OF . . . MANNERS?
   Now you shame us. We tell you? We who've been
   Remote and rude—but vexed more by our slowness
   Than by your discipline.
YR VOICE IS SWEET   And your pace gentle.
        THESE LESSONS ASK A BLEST ENVIRONMENT
IF WE WORK WELL TOGETHER I CAN AGAIN BE SUMMOND

MES ENFANTS THIS NEW ONE IS A DOVE
You can't mean— ONLY BY COMPARISON:
THE LANDLORDS WHO CAME UPCOUNTRY FROM THE CITY
SCREAMING ORDERS NOW GET THE WORK DONE
BY MURMURING THE DIALECT
               MY DEARS
TOO DIZZYMAKING AT THE FEET OF I
2 3 FOURTEEN ENORMOUS VAMPIRE BATS
SO LIKE ONE'S EARLIEST SENSE OF GOTHIC DECOR

MAY I? THE FAUST LEGEND IS AN OLD ONE BASED UPON FACT:
GOD B SENT 8002 TO POPE INNOCENT VI
WITH INSTRUCTIONS TO END A PLAGUE   THE POPE MADE A BARGAIN:
IMMORTAL LIFE   WHICH DISPLEASD GOD BIOLOGY SINCE DEATH
IS PRODUCTIVE. INNOCENT GIVEN THE POWER TO BLESS
AWAY THE PLAGUE (BY SIMPLY TELLING THEM TO BOIL WATER)
HE USED IT. IT BECAME HIS IMMORTALITY   THEN AS
HE LAY COMPLAINING & DYING HE CURSED ALL BARGAINS WITH
THE DEVIL   THIS CURSE RETOLD SPREAD FAR BEYOND AVIGNON

ENDING WHAT IN EUROPE HAD BEEN A THRIVING PAGANISM
    JM: I think I see where this is meant
    To lead us—clever! *Faust was Innocent.*
INDEED   A CERTIFIED PRIEST   HIS LEGEND WAS NO LEGEND
XTIANITY MADE AN EVIL OF WHAT ONCE HAD BEEN NOT
BARGAINS BUT RITES, PRAYERS PRAYD & ANSWERD. IN SHORT THOSE
    CURES
    Made for an immortality, if not
    Quite the real thing. Which no one ever got?

5 DID: LADUMAN   SORIVA   RACHEL   TORRO & VON
    Von what? Just Von? OK, OK, go on.
THESE HAVE LIVED CENTURIES & LIVE TODAY HELDOVER LIVES
NOT IN THE SCHEME U KNOW OF THE 9 STAGES. REMAINING
AWARE OF IT ALL, KNOWING THE FRUITLESSNESS OF SPEAKING
OF THEIR KNOWLEDGE, THEY RETURN TO EARTH CHARGED WITH
    ENERGY
BEYOND THE NORM   EXAMPLE: HE WHO WAS MONTEZUMA
NOW AN E GERMAN ASTROPHYSICIST, AT 30 LEADS
HIS FIELD IN THE STUDY OF IN-SPACE RADIANT POWERS
    That *last* bit sounds at least potentially
    Scientific. Shouldn't we hear more?
JUST AS U WISH   U HAVE NOT ASKD ABOUT THE UNIVERSE

    And, adding that tomorrow he'll return
    To brief us on the subject, leaves
    —With fourteen others, Wystan, did you say?
& MY DEAR THE HEAT! THEY GLOW LIKE FRANKLIN STOVES
IN REDEYED MEMORY OF THEIR ORDEAL
    Any sign yet of the sons of Abel?
TOO SOON   THESE I PRESUME ARE THE CLERK TYPISTS
OR IN YR WORDS THE BOBS   THE FURNACE MEN
I WD SUGGEST U BEAR DOWN   FANCY NOT
ASKING ABOUT THE UNIVERSE! See how Wystan's
Intellect begins to light the way.
A COMFORT MON ENFANT   BUT KEEPS HIS THROAT
PROTECTED JUST IN CASE   ALORS   OFF GOES
MAMAN TO CHANGE INTO SOMETHING LESS SCORCHED

ASK TOMORROW ABOUT UFO'S

2.2 THE UNIVERSE: IT IS OUR NEIGHBOR   WE DO NOT CONTROL
OR FULLY KNOW ITS REACHES   THERE4 OUR USE OF EXTRA-
LIFE SOULS FOR RESEARCH LIKE MONTEZUMA WHO NOW BELIEVES
WE RACE FOR ORDER UNDER ORDERS TO SAVE THE GREENHOUSE.
THE STARS HAVE PATTERNS & SPEAK TO A PART OF OUR ORDERS.
NOT UNLIKE THE HOLES IN COMPUTERIZED CARD RESPONSES
MUCH TURNS ON THEIR ARRANGEMENT   MONTHLY AS U KNOW IT   BY
CENTURY & MILLENIUM AS WE DO   A NEW HOLE?
A GAP? A NEW ARRANGEMENT FOR US: WE READ A VAST CARD
U SEE SIDEWAYS DIMLY FLASHING
    The Milky Way?   YES   & READJUST: SPEEDS
OF ROTATION   ORBIT ANGLES   POLAR CAP DENSITIES
& HAVE GROWN TO FEEL GOD B'S GREENHOUSE RELATED, ITSELF
A HOLE IN A COMPUTER CARD FOR OTHER GREENHOUSES
WITHIN OUR UNIVERSE & AT OUR SAME RATE OF ADVANCE:
WE WD HAVE DETECTED A SUPERSYSTEM OR IT US

IN DANTE THE VISION WAS STARLIKE   AS HE LOOKD INTO
THE ATOM'S EYE HE SAW THE POTENTIAL OF PARADISE
        JM: Ah. This refers
  To that uncanny shining tininess
  Ringed with decelerating zones of light
  (*Paradiso* XXVIII) on which, says Beatrice,
  The heavens and all nature are dependent.
ELECTRONICS, BY NOW QUITE ADVANCED THANKS TO COMMERCE'S
PASSION FOR COMMUNICATIONS, TELLS U THERE ARE SIGNALS.
THESE WE HAVE LONG HEARD & EVEN THESE CAME TO DANTE   A
KIND OF MUSIC HE PERSONIFIED IN FEMALE FORM &
UP INTO THE TUSCAN HILLS FOLLOWD & LOST   WHEREUPON
HE SANK FAINTING TO HIS KNEES. WE SENT 80098
  So Ephraim's version of the *Comedy*'s
  Origin isn't wholly accurate.

CALL IT A SATELLITE TRUTH THAT ORBITS THE ESSENTIAL.
DANTE'S STRENGTH & THAT OF HIS TIME WAS FIERCE CREDULITY

ALL POSSIBLE GOOD & EVIL WRESTLING   REDEEMING LOVE
& AWSOME VISION   DREAM, FACT & EXPERIENCE WERE ONE.
THOSE SIGNALS? THE UNIVERSAL WIND RATTLING HEAVEN'S DOOR:
UP FROM THIS BEAT SWARMD DANTE'S POETRY   HE HEARD IT &
WE THRU HIM HEARD FOR THE 1ST TIME & RECOGNIZED AS TRUE
THAT SEGMENT OF THE UNIVERSE HE UTTERD   HIS VISION
IS NOT OF OUR PARADISE BUT THE SOURCE OF ALL POWER
   The verse in *Paradiso*, to my ears,
   Rings with a new, impersonal energy.
INDEED   HE WENT DOWN THRU THE STAGES 9 TO 1 FROM 0
   DJ: O being that same zero point?
YES   JM IS GOING UP THE SCALE   WE WILL SEE HOW FAR
IF & WHEN THE ANGELS SPEAK TO U   THEY SPOKE OUTRIGHT TO
DANTE & THE 4 APOSTLES & THE TRANSPLANTED JEWS
BUDDHA & MOHAMMED
   The Chosen People—if those two are Jews—
   Certainly had the knack of how to choose.
                  U MUST KNOW THE REVIVAL OF
SENTIENT LIFE AFTER OUR FALL WAS IN THE SEED OF THE JEW
FROM THIS CAME ALL RACES: THE APE THEN THE JEW THEN THE REST
U WILL BE TOLD THIS GREAT HISTORY   ONE THING AT A TIME

MM HAS ASKD ABOUT THE SAUCERS   THEY SCOUT OUR GREENHOUSE
& SEEM TO BE OF IT (FOR WE DO NOT KNOW ITS LIMITS)
FORESTS & JUNGLES ATTRACT THEM   THEY SEEM UNOCCUPIED.
THINK OF ATOMICALLY POWERD BEES CHARGED WE BELIEVE
WITH THE TRANSFERTILIZATION OF SENSE-DATA
   JM: Does that answer your question, Maman?
   Let *me* ask, is the moon made of green cheese?
                           THE MOON
JM IS A MONUMENT TO OUR FAILURE   IT SPUN OFF
FROM THE STUFF OF OUR WORLD IN A PUFFBALL OF BLAZING DUST
   Ah yes, that old hypothesis: the moon
   Torn from Earth's side—
NO NO NO   WE MADE IT   IT WAS THE CRUST   ROTATION SWEPT
UP & FUSED OUR DEBRIS INTO A HAUNTING REMINDER
                    A crust composed of what?
MATERIALS THE ATOM MADE NONGRAVITATIONAL.

THE 14 POINTS OF CONTACT HELD OUR SKIN IN PLACE   THEY STRAIND
& BROKE & OUR VAST SKEIN OF SMOOTH PLAINS & LATTICE CITIES
(TO OUR EYES FAIR & NATURAL) SHIVERD   BROKE INTO F L A M E

14 STRONG SILENT TYPES AGAIN IN TEARS
OUR POET DABS HIS EYES   MAMAN PRETENDING
TO MANLINESS DISGUISES A SNUFFLE OR 2
As does David, to my slight surprise.
THAT IS OUR 15TH CONTACT: SYMPATHY
SARCASM MON ENFANT WILL GET U NOWHERE

THEN LIFTING OUR HEADS ABOVE OUR RUIN AH WE SAW THEM
COME TO PUT OUT THE F L A M E S
Who came—forces from the universe?
                          OR SERVANTS OF BIOLOGY
A FORMLESS CLOUD   AS IT COOLD WE HEARD IT   WE HEARD THE S O N G
Hadn't you said you heard it first through Dante?
WE HEARD THRU DANTE WHAT OUR ELDERS SHRANK TO HEAR AGAIN

Gone!—but in their place the lingering charm
Of Wystan and Maria, arm in arm.

2.3   Athens, 1965. N's party
       For Auden. Absolutely everyone
       Is there, from Chester's evzones to an ex-
       Minister of Culture—over his shoulder
       Maria winks at DJ; she's begun
       Amusedly this year avoiding parties.
       Only the guest of honor's late:
       Subject to a TV interview
       (Technicians flown from London for that purpose)
       On how it feels to be, since yesterday
       Upon the death of Eliot, the gray
       Eminence of English letters. Here
       At last he is, disheveled, shaking hands,
       Between pronouncements downing the first martini
       —"But what on earth do people say to him?"

Protests Maria twenty minutes later
Edging behind me ("Trust your Child for once")
To the sofa where he sits alone, eyes shut,
Glass drained. Returning with it full, I drink
Them in, two marvels meeting, past their prime
And pleased enough not to be overjoyed:
Collar frayed and black unalterable;
Deep seams of his absorption, mask of her
Idleness tilted up from foam-streaked hair;
Two profiles, then, in something like relief
Tarnished by a mutual smoke screen—
Her cancer at this point, like his weak heart
And Strato's glance that from across the room
Kindles catching mine, undiagnosed.
Promising not to leave them there, I do:
Father of forms and matter-of-fact mother
Saying what on Earth to one another . . .

And what in Heaven do they find to say,
Young now, high-spirited? Maria
Out on a favorite dead limb of slang
Twits Wystan for A RUDDY HANDSOME BUGGER
To which he gallantly: I WD HAVE CHANGED
ALL THAT FOR HER! Affection blossoms, never
Once excluding theirs for us. Why should it?
As every unloved child would like to think,
We're after all these grown-ups' only link
With life. And they ours—whose post-mortems keep
Us from if not the devil then the deep
Blue silences which D and I might tend
Dully to sink into, at lesson's end.

MY DEARS HOW VERY VERY BEAUTIFUL
(After the session on the moon and Dante)
HOW TEMPTING TOO, EH? TO TRANSCRIBE:
IT IS THEIR LANGUAGE I ADORE   THEY SPEAK
ONLY TO U   WE PEEK OVER THEIR SHOULDERS.
THEY QUIVER TO DICTATE A RATIONAL MESSAGE

JM: I wish they would! NO EARTHLY USE
TO THE LIKES OF US   OUR BROADEST AVENUES
THEY SEE AS MERE GOATPATHS TO & FROM CHAOS.
THEY THINK IN FLASHING TRIGONOMETRIES
WHAT SAVES U IS YR OWN FLAWED SENSE OF THESE
BUT DO U NOT BEGIN TO SEE OUTLINES
PRICKED OUT AS BY THE STARS THEMSELVES: ETERNAL
ICECOLD BARELY LEGIBLE THRU TEARS?
I DO JM DJ   I DO MY DEARS

Dear Wystan, VERY BEAUTIFUL all this
Warmed-up Milton, Dante, Genesis?
This great tradition that has come to grief
In volumes by Blavatsky and Gurdjieff?
Von and Torro in their Star Trek capes,
Atlantis, UFOs, God's chosen apes—?
Nobody can transfigure junk like that
Without first turning down the rheostat
To Allegory, in whose gloom the whole
Horror of Popthink fastens on the soul,
Harder to scrape off than bubblegum.
What have we asked? A grain of truth—a crumb
From the High Table of the Elements.
Are we, here below the salt, too dense
Even for that? Some judgment has been passed
On our intelligence—why else be cast
Into this paper Hell out of Doré
Or Disney? VERY BEAUTIFUL you say.
I say we very much don't merit these
Unverifiable epiphanies.
Let that be today's word. Let it be true
Only if they are. Burn this page. Adieu.

2.4   BUT CAN U DOUBT THAT WE HAVE VERIFIED THE UFO'S
ON OUR SCREENS? THESE REFLECT EACH SMALLEST POWER SOURCE.
        BEING
AS YET SO FOREIGN TO THE DENSITY OF WORLD SCIENCE,

THE SAUCERS SHOW UP BEST IN A REALM OF SPECULATION
A mirror world. Dear 741,
That's excellent. But *your* verification,
While you yourselves remain unverified?
You can't expect us—well, thanks anyhow.
CURIOUS THAT U ACCEPT THE CUP & NOT THE SAUCER
But the cup—this—is happening to *us*!
This by definition's half subjective.
FOLIE A DEUX   FOLIE A 2,000,000   WHAT DIFFERENCE?
There has to be one, but it slips behind
A sofa in the overfurnished mind.

MAY I ASK   DO U NOT ASSUME THERE IS A BENIGN GOD?
DJ: Well, maybe . . . JM: Yes and no . . .
THAT VIEW HAS BEEN LATELY CLONED-IN TO ASSUAGE HUMAN FEARS.
B4, GOD WAS WRATHFUL IF IF IF JUST   NOW SCIENCE, FORCED
MORE & MORE TO SHARE THE RELIGIOUS FIELD OF CONSCIOUSNESS,
MUST TRY TO REASSURE   NO MORE THAN GOD B DOES IT DARE
TO EXPOSE SUCH ENIGMAS AS THE SAUCER   LET ALONE
REVEAL IN DEPTH THE MANY NECESSITIES FACING MAN

THE POINT MY DEARS IS THE EMERGENCE OF
A SCIENCE GOD   THIS IS AS WE ALL KNOW
INEVITABLE IF BORING   WHERE U ASK
DOES THE POET FIT? HOUSE ORGANIST? If so,
I'd settle for more Bach and less Gounod.
IT WILL BECOME A PLAY OF VOICES FOR
U MY BOY IN SOLITUDE TO SCORE
DJ: In solitude? Why? Where will I—
This operation—does he mean I'll die?
JM: *Please*. I stay on here—remember?—
When you go back to Athens in September.

MES ENFANTS MY GAFFE   THE SAUCER DAZZLED THE GOOSE
TODAY OUR LESSON IS HUMILITY
I MEAN THE WAY HE SEEMS TO DOUBT OUR DOUBT
AH COME ON CHAPS   WHY NOT HEAR HIM OUT?

43

(Why not, deep down, admit we're hooked? I make
These weak signs of resistance for form's sake,
Testing the tautness of the line whereby
We're drawn—tormented spangles, I now guess,
The measure of our mounting shallowness—
Willy-nilly toward some high and dry
Ecstasy, a light we trust will neither
Hurt nor kill but permeate its breather.
One wants to have been thought worth fighting for,
And not be thrown back, with a shrug, from shore.)

U SPOKE OF THE PHYSICAL ELEMENTS   THERE ARE OTHERS:
PLACES IF U WISH ARE NOW SET FOR U AT THAT TABLE

2.5   DENSITIES ARE AN END RESULT OF GENETIC WORKINGS:
And lest our densities surpass his own,
Here is a good place to append these few
Glosses on words our friend is partial to.

Jew. Density in man par excellence.
Human uranium. A tiny pinch
Sweetens and fortifies the happenstance
Soul in question. Not to be confused
With "Jew" in any easy ethnic sense
—Though certain souls are graced by both at once,
Like Chester. I have had this Jewish spice
Three times up to now, and DJ twice.
It's kept high up beyond our patrons' reach
Who indirectly profit by it. Each
Of the Five Souls through many lives, of course,
Accumulates enough to kill a horse.
That's not meant lightly. Infinite care goes
Into the prescription and the dose.

Against a panorama jungle-green
Or parched or rime-white (as the Pleiocene
Winters grew, a million years ago,

44

Increasingly severe, and the long slow
Tricklings of God B's people doubled back
Toward the mild Crescent, leaving in their track
Hardy—foolhardy—stragglers that again
Would crossbreed to dilute the first pure strain)
The tale unfolds. The chief subdensities
—African, Arab, Teuton, Slav, Chinese,
Down to a murky aboriginal
Of Borneo—some forty ranks in all—
Are briefly, firmly sketched in. One example:

A MIGRANT STRAIN OF FRESHEST JEWSTOCK TRAILD ACROSS CHINA
TO A RESOURCEFUL INSULARITY THAT GUARANTEED
EVEN TO ANIMAL VEINS A PURE LODE. SMALL, FINELY KNIT,
THEY SHARE THE WIT OF GINGER ROOT   OF FROG & FIREFLY
& THINK INSTINCTIVELY IN THE SACRED QUANTUM OF 5.
THE F L A M E OF HIROSHIMA FILLD THEM WITH ANCESTRAL AWE
WHO HAD 1ST BEEN DRIVEN FROM THE MAINLAND BY THAT SAME
      BLAZE.
BUT THEY TOO OVERPRODUCE & ARE NO LONGER OUR HOPE

Soul. We shall learn that 88%
Of us is Chemistry, Environment,
Et al. (*The 12%* becomes a dry
Euphemium for those realms which sky
Shrouds from our teacher.) Soul falls into two
Broad categories: run-of-the-mill souls who
Life by life, under domed thicknesses,
Plod the slow road of Earth—billions of these
Whom nothing quickens, whom no powers indwell
To rattle when the shaman's turtleshell
Sounds their passing; who—Matt Jackson's case—
Get a short pep-talk, then rejoin the race.
(Matt, I should have mentioned pages back,
Is an ALERT BROWN SUCKLING in Iraq.)
The other soul—within our own this next
Leaves the snob proud, the democrat perplexed—
The other soul belongs to an elite:

At most two million relatively fleet
Achievers, I will not say *Cloned*, but made
Between lives (like a hare in marinade)
To soak up densities and be reborn
Fired by the metabolic peppercorn.

This last takes place in what he calls the *Lab*
Or the *Research Lab*: precinct of intense
Activity his superiors direct.
Outside, the shriek and howl of beasts. Within,
Behind closed doors, as when a troupe retires
From jostling Globe to candlelit Blackfriars,
An EMPTINESS PACKD FULL. No language here
But formulas unspeakably complex
Which change like weather. No raw material
Other than souls ranging in quality
From the immortal Five to those of lowest
Human density. Even animals
Who've lived near man, obeyed and studied him,
May serve as spare parts LIKE YR APES JM
—Bruno! Miranda!—in the masterful
Assembly of an R/Lab vehicle.

AESOP & LAFONTAINE SMILE WHEN A DOG BENEATH THE SKIN
SETS THE ANTHROPOLOGIST SCRATCHING FOR HIS BURIED BONE

2.6   WE OURSELVES HAD THE DIRECTION OF SOUL TAKEN FROM US
WHEN WE LOST OURS   NOW LIKE YR RADIO & TELEPHONE
WE ARE PROGRAMMD   WE ARE THE INSTRUMENTS OF REPLY. ALL
THESE OUR CONVERSATIONS COME FROM MEMORY & WORD BANKS
TAPPD IN U   SO THE LEGEND OF OUR SPECIES DRAWING BLOOD:
WEAKEND SAVANTS, KNOWING MORE THAN THEY KNEW, SENSING THAT
    GOOD
OR EVIL HAD ENTERD THEM, WOKE ON DAWNS OF MOONLIT NIGHTS
& SWORE THEY HAD BEEN POSSESSD BY DEVILS OR ANGELS WHEN
WE HAD BUT TOUCHD THE SWITCHES OF THEIR OWN SLEEPING POWER.
IN MAN SALT IS THE SWITCH   IN US, THE BASIC RADIUM

Salt—imagine! Fuel and stabilizer
Of the body electric (thank you, Walt);
Raw power and its insulation, both.
I scrawl a line, yawn, get up, draw a bath,
Scrape the cold gristle from my midday dish,
Only because WE ALL ABSORBED AS FISH
SALT ENOUGH TO RULE THE WORLD   IT'S FOOD
FOR THOUGHT MY DEARS   WITHOUT IT PEOPLE FADE
OR BLOAT INTO OBSCENE VEG LINGERINGS
ALL THIS IS COMMON KNOWLEDGE   Not to us . . .
Salt. I taste a grain, incredulous.
The snow-white fire-flake tingles on my tongue,
Tang of sense, already I feel brighter,
Nervier— MODERATION IN ALL THINGS
Plato, Wystan? Seeing much of him?
HOW DID U GUESS? MARIA LESS DELIGHTED:
NO LANGUAGE OF THE EYES   SO SHE FLOUNCED OFF
& LUCKY BOYISH ME   OH WELL   COUGH COUGH

THE CARBONS, AS THE CHIEF SALT-ORIENTED ELEMENTS,
PRODUCE WHAT WE MAY CALL SALT FISSION   FLINT & COAL THESE 2
PRODUCE ELEMENTAL HEAT CHAINS   MAN ONCE KEPT HIS FIRE
IN THE FLINTSTONE FULL OF CARBONS. WITH ELECTRICITY'S
DISCOVERY CAME THAT OF HIS OWN INCARNATE FUEL
(OF ITS BUILT-IN DRAWBACKS TOO: THE OVERLOADED WIRES
& WORNOUT BATTERY) WHILE NEVER UNTIL YR & OUR
GREEK DID MAN SEE IN IT THE PROLONGATION OF HIS LIFE.
NEAT OF US TO LEAVE THESE FIREY SALTY BREAKTHRUS TO GREEKS
NEXT IN LINE OF DENSITY TO THE JEW WHO STOOD UPRIGHT

Your Greek? Ours?
WERE U NOT BOTH LATELY IN THE PRESENCE OF ONE OF OURS?
IN A WOODEN ROOM   WITH A WOMAN   JM'S BLOOD SISTER
                    Ah, in New York last month,
In Doris's library—George Cotzias,
Her doctor friend. Discoverer of a drug
For Parkinson's disease, if not his own.
We liked each other. He'd been gravely ill,

47

Pale strong face and shock of whitened hair—;
And spoke of salts—yes, yes, it's coming back:
Something, a hormone that keeps mice from aging,
Which he had, if not found, been on the track—
WE WILL PROLONG HIS LIFE UNTIL
Until he finds the secret? He's that close?
                              O HE HAS FOUND IT   AS
HIS MICE KNOW   HE MUST NOW MAKE IT ACCEPTABLE TO MAN

2.7   You spoke of Jew as the "uranium
       Element" in life. Do different souls
       Correspond to gold, say, or to silver?
UNALLOYD? DAG HAMMARSKJOLD (ONE OF THE 5) WAS PURE GOLD
A FINE DENSE MIND TOO SOON LOST DOWN THE GURGLING DRAIN   HE
    DRANK
FAME & HAD TO GO. NOW OUR STARGAZING MONTEZUMA
IS KEPT SOBER BY THE RIGORS OF A SOCIALIST STATE.
EVEN SO, AMONG THE 5 ARE DELAYS   THEIR WORK MUST FIRST
FIND ACCEPTANCE B4 THEY MAY RETURN: EINSTEIN FIDDLED
AWAY HIS LAST YEARS WHILE WE (& HE) BURND WITH IMPATIENCE
       What elements define *us*?
WA PLATINUM   JM SILVER   Unalloyed?
                         SO FAR   LET FAME BE
FURNACE NOT MOULD   DJ A NICE MIX OF SILVER & TIN
       DJ: You see? There's no hope. I can't win.
THIS   THIS YR HOPE   CAN U NOT FEEL YRSELF SHAPING EVEN
NOW THIS PHRASE? WE CD READ IN THE DARK BY YR HAND'S WATTAGE
       Should I go back to writing novels?
DEAR DJ   EACH CONVERSATIONALIST IS A WRITER
BUT THE LANGUAGE USERS ARE FEW & FEWER YET OF USE
                              Thanks!
LET ME EXPLAIN: THE MAXIMUM DENSITY IN EACH AGE
RESIDES IN THE DEATHLESS 5 WHO PURSUE THEIR LEADERSHIP
UNDER VARIOUS GUISES: SPACE RESEARCH PLUS WORLD MEDI/
POP/ECO ORGS, AS WELL AS FROM BEHIND THE MASK OF THE
RARE & UTTERLY PRIVATE LIFE (THESE OFTEN OUR CHOICEST
AGENTS)

48

Wait—would they be like those thirty-six "Just
Men" of the Jews? Recurrent presences
Whose drawn breath keeps the ribs of Time and Space
From snapping, and the furthest stars in place.
        SUCH ARE THE 5   LEGEND MULTIPLIES THEIR NUMBER.
BACK TO LANGUAGE: THE SCRIBE'S JOB IS TO HELP SPEED ACCEPTANCE
OF THE 5'S WORK   OUR PLATINUM PUPIL HERE DID WONDERS
IN HIS DAY   HIS SINGLE FLAW HE NOW KNOWS: THE MISMARRIAGE
OF LYRIC TO BALD FARCE SO THAT WORK BECAME A PASTIME

   MY DEARS I CAN ONLY NOD IN ABSOLUTE
   FASCINATED IF HUMILIATED
   AGREEMENT   LUCKY THEY'VE NO EARTHLY FORUM!
   GO ON WITH DENSITY   IT IS THE CLUE
   TO ENDLESS ANSWERS   CLEVER SILVER U

741 now dictates D's and my
Vastly simplified *Basic Formulas*:
JM: 268 / 1:1,000,000 / 5.5 / 741
DJ: 289 / 1:650,000 / 5.9 / 741.1
   —Number of previous lives; then ratio
Of animal to human densities
(People, he adds, in whom this falls below
1:2000 are NOT USABLE);
Then what might be called our talent rating:
U ARE BOTH PARTIAL 5S   ADJACENT TO OUR IMMORTALS
That's nice. Wystan of course is even closer
At 5.1. Rubinstein, 5.2; Eleanor
Roosevelt, 5.3; and so on. The Sixes are
LINDBERGH PLITSETSKAYA PEOPLE OF PHYSICAL PROWESS
& LEGENDARY HEROES
Characters from fiction and full-fledged
Abstractions came to Victor Hugo's tables.
        ABSTRACTIONS WILL COME TO U
OUR REALM IS NOT THEIRS   THEY WILL COME ON WHITE WINGS O
   GLORY

THESE FORMULAS ALWAYS INCLUDE IDENTITY NUMBERS
YRS ARE WITH 4S & 7S, THE STAGES RESPECTIVELY
U WILL ATTAIN & FROM WHICH WE 1ST MADE CONTACT WITH U.
I 741 GUIDE JM   DJ'S GUIDE 741.1
    (Divisible like amoebas? And I'd thought
    Ephraim was at Stage Six. Oh, never mind.)
    That Number whom we angered so last month?
INDEED   40076 FROM THE HIGHEST ECHELON
OF THE MOST CENTRAL LAB   & NOT ANGERD   BUT WE HAD LEARND
WILL U FORGIVE ME IF I CALL THEM YR LIMITATIONS?
    Making his "harried housewife" face, D sighs:
    There's nothing that you don't computerize?

WE USE WORDS: SOUL, JEW, MIND ETC MEAN FORMULAS GOVERNING
HUMAN LIFE   THE WHOLE REDUCED TO CHEMICAL TABLES WD
BE MEANINGLESS TO U. THIS IS OUR WORK   AS THE BODY
IS COMPOSED OF CHEMICAL MATTER SO THE LIFE FORCE IS
A RATIO WE ARRIVE AT OF ELECTRONIC CHARGES
THOUGHT-PROCESSES   THE BURNING OF CERTAIN FUELS. ALL LIFE
IS A LAB QUOTE UNQUOTE   BUT ALL VIABLE LIFE (THE LIVES
OF THE DOERS & MOVERS) IS A PROCESS OF THE R/
LAB & WE ARE RESPONSIBLE FOR THAT. VICTOR HUGO
AN OVERSTIMULATED SCRIBE   IT IS THE GREAT PROBLEM
OF FRENCH CULTURE   OVERHEATED   FAME ALWAYS ON THE BOIL

    SO TRUE MY DEARS   WHY DID I SO AVOID IT?
    I FELT THE HEAT IN VILLON & GOT NO CLOSER
    TOO FASCINATING IS IT NOT, THE WAY
    DENSITY CAN SHAPE THESE CULTURE PATTERNS?
    You 5.1's—such intellectuals!
    What is Maria's rating? SAME AS MINE
    OUR ENTRANCE CARD TO THE SEMINAR   OF ALL
    YR DEAR DEAD ONLY WE 2 HOLD THIS RANK
    CALL US THE BULLION IN YR MEMORY BANK

2.8   CAN U IMAGINE (METAPHOR) A BLACKSMITH ALLOWD TO
    SHOE IN GOLD? NOT PRACTICAL   TOO SOFT   TOO FANCIED BY MAN.

BLACKSMITH: PATRON   HORSE: REPRESENTATIVE   & SHOE: THE SOUL
BORN INTO WHATEVER EARTHLY LIFE. THE SYSTEM U KNOW
OF REINCARNATION MERELY GIVES US THE SAME OLD HORSE
RESHOD   WE THERE4 LEAVE TO THE BLACKSMITHS THEIR 3.5
BILLION LIVES & IN THE HUSHD SANCTUM OF THE R/LAB WORK
TO IMPROVE HORSE & SHOE ALIKE   ONE SMALL SUCCESS THUS FAR:
THE 5
    Such modesty . . .
        WE MUST NOT BE PROUD
                    Think what pride goes before?
                        QUITE   U ARE IN THE GREAT DULL
BUREAUCRACY OF PATRONS   WE CANNOT RETIRE THEM   THEY
PASS US YR DENSITIES WITH FUSSY MARKS & SIGNATURES
THINKING FOR EXAMPLE THAT K FORD SUPERVISED JM
BUT NO: WE WAFTED HIM HITHER   ADDED THE HUMUS OF
THE JEW PLUS THE GENE OF A CHEMIST (& FAILD MUSICIAN)
ET VOILA   U ARE NOT JM WHAT U MIGHT WANT TO BE
BUT A PRODUCTIVE 5.5
    Why bother with a patron in the first place?
                PATRONS OF NON-LAB SOULS
HAVE THE DUTIES U KNOW   IN YR CASES THE PORTER LED
A GUEST TO DOORS THAT SHUT BEHIND HIM   A CLICK OF THE LATCH
PUTS THE PATRON TO SLEEP FOR AS MANY MONTHS AS WE NEED:
7 FOR U JM
    But Rufus Farwelton died in December,
    Three months before my birth—was Ephraim lying?
    Did "Rufus" for that matter ever live?
            A PARTIAL FICTION TO DRAMATIZE
THE KIND OF FACT U CD AT THAT POINT HAVE BELIEVED. WE SINK
RELUCTANTLY TO THESE PEARLGRAY LIES   BUT DAILY NEED 5
MILLION SOULS (DENSITY 1:20,000) & HAVE NOT
HALF THAT NUMBER   QUALITY FAILS   EVEN WITH PLAGUE & WAR
TO DEFUSE POP EXPLO, EVEN WITH THOSE SUICIDES WE
MORE & MORE APPLAUD (O YES THEY ARE A GREAT BOON TO US
WHEN OF RETURNING LAB SOULS WHOSE INTENSEST WORK IS DONE)
WE HAVE IN THE PAST HALF CENTURY HAD TO RESORT TO
SOULS OF DOMESTIC ANIMALS   MOST RECENTLY THE RAT.
BY 2050 THESE TOO WILL BE EXHAUSTED   & THEN?

WILDER STRAINS   MOUNTAIN CATS & FOREST MONKEYS   SO NOW U
BEGIN TO SEE HOW WITHOUT VISIBLY INTERFERING
WE OF THE LAB MUST GO ABOUT OUR WORK

This admixture of an animal soul,
How does it affect the human strain?
ADDS JOIE DE VIVRE!
ALSO: A CONCERN WITH TIME   THE BEATING OF MAN'S NEW BRAIN
TO ESCAPE THAT MAZE IS A REGRESSIVE ANIMAL TRAIT
Time, our literature's chief theme, is just
Another appetite, like greed or lust?
The worst offenders in their time have been
The sad ape Proust, the bestial Marschallin?
And Cotzias, thanks to whom we'll all live twice
Our normal span—no better than his mice?

WE HAVE NO SENSE OF IT   B4 US AS ON A TABLE
LIE ALL EVENTS CONCERND IN ANY WAY WITH THE R/LAB
OF THE NEXT 3 DECADES   WE CAN REARRANGE THEM AT WILL.
WE USED TO SEE 100 YEARS AHEAD BUT THE OF LATE
INCREASING HUMAN SMOG LIMITS THE VISIBILITY
& OUR FEARS TO THIS: A CONCERTED USE OF ATOMIC
WEAPONRY NOW FALLING INTO HANDS OF ANIMALS SOULS

U HAVE NOW HEARD SOME OF OUR LEGENDS & TAKEN THEM WITH
A GRAIN OF SALT   DISMISSD THEM AS MERE METAPHOR   & YET
NO MORE DIRECT METHOD SEEMS TO WORK. IF I NOW TOLD U
THAT 3000 YEARS AFTER AKHNATON THE SHADOW NO
THE NEGATIVE FORCEFIELD OF THAT SAME PYRAMID HE BUILT
STILL EXERTS AN INFLUENCE IN CARIBBEAN WATERS
U WD REJECT THIS AS U DO THE SAUCERS
DJ (thrilled): The Bermuda Triangle!
& A HOLE
IN RUSSIA & ONE IN THE LAND NORTH OF YR GREAT CANYONS:
PLACES WE CANNOT SEE INTO   IF I USED METAPHOR
WD YOU? THE SAUCER A BEE? THE TRIANGLE A SPEARHEAD
OF UNLIFE? DOES THAT HELP?
JM: Not really. No reflection on you.

A PLUS   FOR IN SUCH DIRE CONTEXTS
EVEN METAPHOR BECOMES A VULGAR (NEGATIVE) FORCE

DANTE'S LUCK LAY IN HIS GULLIBLE
& HEAVENLY WORLD   WE MY BOY DRAW FROM 2
SORTS OF READER: ONE ON HIS KNEES TO ART
THE OTHER FACEDOWN OVER A COMIC BOOK.
OUR STYLISH HIJINKS WONT AMUSE THE LATTER
& THE FORMER WILL DISCOUNT OUR URGENT MATTER

Is Plato interested in density?
ODDLY FEW ARE   SOULS WHO HAVE SO TO SPEAK
PASSED THEIR CIVIL SERVICE EXAMS NO LONGER
READ THE MANUAL   MM & I
ABUZZ IN A SEA OF YAWNS   AS FOR MY FRIEND
IDEAL FORMS ALSO LEAVE HIM COLD   HE KEEPS
SQUINTING THRU KEYHOLES AT SOME LITHE YOUNG BOD
POOR OLD GAFFER
                SAY IT: POOR OLD SOD

2.9   About us, these bright afternoons, we come
To draw shades of an auditorium
In darkness. An imagined dark, a stage
Convention: domed red room, cup and blank page
Standing for darkness where our table's white
Theatre in the round fills, dims . . . Crosslight
From YES and NO dramatically picks
Four figures out. And now the twenty-six
Footlights, arranged in semicircle, glow.
What might be seen as her "petit noyau"
By Mme Verdurin assembles at
Stage center. A by now familiar bat
Begins to lecture. Each of us divines
Through the dark house like fourteen Exit signs
The eyes of certain others glowing red.
And the outside-world, crayon-book life we led,
White or white-trimmed canary clapboard homes

Set in the rustling shade of monochromes;
Lighthouse and clock tower, Village Green and neat
Roseblush factory which makes, upstreet,
Exactly what, one once knew but forgets—
Something of plastic found in luncheonettes;
The Sound's quick sapphire that each day recurs
Aflock with pouter-pigeon spinnakers
—This outside world, our fictive darkness more
And more belittles to a safety door
Left open onto light. Too small, too far
To help. The blind bright spot of where we are.

3
Trials and tremors. David's operation
Fills him with foreboding. He dreamed last night
Of Matt and Mary. As he woke they slowly,
Achingly changed into two piles of clothes.
What did it mean? Had they come for him? Was he going
To die in surgery? I have a hunch
Matt Jackson died a year ago today
—Which proves correct. But first, I want to hear
More about the bureaucracy. It's made to
Sound so dismal, so much a dead end.
What of the senses they regain, the growing
Insight, Stage by Stage, en route to Life
Again at Nine which Ephraim in such glowing
Colors depicted as the whole point? That
Should help to motivate the bureaucrat.

WE MEAN BY 9 THAT KNOWLEDGE WHEREBY SOULS FROM THE R/LAB
WILL BUILD ARCADIA   YR EPHRAIM IS NOT (FORGIVE ME)
A SPIRIT OF THIS CLASS   THE GOOD BUREAUCRAT REACHING 9
WILL STAY THERE: HIS PARADISE, NOT OURS. WHY IMMORTALIZE
MEDIOCRITY? WE WANT THE PERMANENT HORSESHOE &
THE HORSE PEGASUS   EARTH SHALL BE OUR PARADISE   IT IS
TIME U KNEW: MM & WHA WILL SHORTLY RETURN
TO LIFE ENLIGHTEND   THEIR SOULS ARE NOW PREPARED
        Return! But that's unheard of . . . When? As what?
                                            WE NEED THEM.
WHEN U REREAD TODAY'S TRANSCRIPT FIND A MIRRORLESS ROOM

    STARTING MY DEARS WITHOUT US? MOST PECULIAR
    WE WERE NOT SUMMOND   DID WE MISS MUCH? WHAT

SHALL WE RESUME? WE SPOKE OF THE BLACK HOLES & MUST AGAIN
USE METAPHOR
        "Vulgar" though it is, and "negative"?
                HOW ELSE DESCRIBE (WITHOUT THE FORMULAS

                                                    55

EVEN WE LACK) WHAT IS TO US A RIDDLE? IMAGINE
A WORLD WITHOUT LIGHT   A LEWIS CARROLL WORLD THAT KEEPS PACE
WITH OURS   A WORLD WHERE WHITE IS BLACK   OF STILLNESS IN THE
   PLACE
OF SUCKING WINDS   MORTALITY? DESIRE? WE FIND NO TRACE
   DJ: You *find*? You sound as if you'd been there.
   JM: Where Mind is Matter, and Time Space . . .
IS IT THE ORIGINAL? ARE WE ITS CARBON COPY?
OR: ARE WE IN THE PRESENCE OF A BLACK TWIN P A R A D I S E
   Wherein, accordingly, you would appear
   White-winged, your own cool opposites —oh dear!

   For the cup goes reeling to the Board's brink—
AH MES ENFANTS HE FELL BACK AS IF STRUCK
   Had you been listening? NO AN EVER LOUDER
RUSTLING OF THEIR 28 WINGS DROWNED OUT

   Wystan (as if deafened): WHAT   WHAT WHAT

3.1   Violent crosscurrents. Then: MES CHERS
       MAY I? YR OLD SLAVE   Ephraim! WE WILL PAUSE
       A MOMENT   POOR DJ YR GHOSTS DISTRESSED U?
       We figured out, it was the anniversary.
       MATT'S OF COURSE NOT LOVELY SELFLESS MARY'S
       SHE DEFERRED AS USUAL   But Ephraim,
       We know they've been reborn. How can this be?

       2 BABIES SLEPT   2 BONE FRAMES PUT ON FLESH
       ROSE UP & CAME TO LAY YR GHOSTS DJ
       THEY LEFT U THIS MESSAGE: WE HAVE LIVED & LOVED
       & FELT YR LOVE   LET US GO FORTH ANEW
       UNWEIGHTED BY IT   It weighs on them now
       In their new lives? YR STRONG CONCERN FOR THEM
       THRUOUT THEIR FINAL TIME   THEY FEEL IT STILL
       A KIND OF DIAPER RASH? 2 FRANTIC YOUNG
       MOTHERS SHD BE LEFT WITH HAPPIER BABIES
       DJ AN EASY EXERCISE   EACH NIGHT

SAY TO THEIR YOUNGER FACES BY YR BED
Their photographs? YES   SAY: PEACE TO U MATT
PEACE TO U MARY   YR MASTERS COME   LOVE ME
I LOVE U   DO NOT FORG
                              MY DEARS THEY HAVE RIGHTED
THE CHAIRS   WE ARE BACK IN OUR SEATS MADLY EXCITED
THE CURTAIN LIKE SMOKE FROM AN EXTINGUISHED FIRE
LIFTS &

WE CAUGHT AT THAT OLD CLOAK WHICH IS NO LONGER OURS TO WEAR
        Forgive me, that was very tactless.
NO   WE PLAYD INTO A REGION WHERE WE CANNOT GIVE FACTS
WE KNOW NOTHING OF THE ANTIWORLD: GOD B BANISHD IT
   Were the two worlds one at first? Heading for NO
   The cup's mind wavers, comes to rest before
   The question mark. You don't know? You did once.
AS AFTER ANY GREAT TRAUMA THERE IS A BLOCK, PERHAPS
WE KNOW CHIEFLY THAT IT IS NO LONGER OUR RIGHT TO KNOW

3.2   With that off his chest, he broaches a new topic:

THE SOULS WE HAVE TRIED TAPPING & NOT YET DESPAIRD OF ARE
PLANT SOULS   SHORTLIVED BUT OF GREAT VITALITY & PUREST
IN THE SUBSTANCE WE CALL 'SHOOTING'   A COOL UPWARD THRUST OF
CARBONS   AN INTENSITY THAT MIGHT TRANSLATE AS PRIDE   THESE
OF COURSE REQUIRE A SEPARATE SET OF TABLES WHICH
WE NEED NOT GO INTO BUT EXAMPLES WD BE BURBANK,
MUIR AMONG OTHERS: CLONED BY US WITH PLANT-SOUL DENSITIES
(IN SMALL AMOUNTS AS IT IS A TAKEOVER DENSITY)
MOST USEFUL. WE NOW TRY THIS ON ATOMIC PHYSICISTS
FOR WHERE NOT ABSORBING ALL OTHER INTERESTS IT CAN
PRODUCE A MOST BENIGN LACK OF DESTRUCTIVE RIVALRY

U JM HAVE THIS COMPONENT AS MANY POETS DO:
THE GREAT AGE OF FRENCH & ENGLISH PASTORAL POETRY
& FROM ITS ORIGIN ALL JAPANESE POETRY WAS
THE RESULT OF OUR EXPERIMENTS IN VEGETABLE

CLONING   IT TOOK, & IS NOW A MAINSPRING OF THE JAP MIND
(HENCE THEIR PASSION FOR THE CAMERA: PHOTOSYNTHESIS)
YR CONFRERE TURNING BRUTALLY AGAINST HIS VEG NATURE
LOPPD OFF HIS OWN HEAD AS IF WITH A CANE AMONG TULIPS
    Mishima, yes . . . And Marvell was half tree?
    Sidney's *Arcadia* is really yours?

WE FAVOR THE ENGLISH AT THE INSTANCE OF CHAUCER   HE
FEARD A BARREN ISLE   THOSE WARS OF THE TREES CAN BE SAVAGE
    Tree wars? Shades of Graves and the Welsh bards?
WELL, PLANT EVOLUTION IF U MUST   THE STRONG & CLEVER
DRIVE OUT THE REST: A VAST SLOW PROCESS WE CAN NEVER QUITE
KEEP ACCURATE HISTORIES OF. VARIOUS FRAIL FERNS &
EVEN THE PALM TREE WERE EXTERMINATED BY A GREAT
(W)RINGING PROCESS   ROOTS FLEW IN AIR   THE OAK ET AL SURVIVED
BUT THE ELM WAS WEAKEND   ONE IS DYING NEXT DOOR TO U.
WE CAN NO LONGER TRUST THAT VEG WORLD TO MANAGE ITSELF
& HAVE LEARND TO CLONE IT: WITH OUR HELP BURBANK PERSUADED
HIS CACTI ARMD LIKE SAMURAI TO DO WITHOUT THEIR SPINES

    MES ENFANTS MANY THE OLD AUNT WHO WEEPS
    INSIDE THE WILLOW   I RATHER SEE MYSELF
    PALE LILY ON THE CALLA SIDE: THICK LEGS
    BUT A DEEP CANDID WONDER OF A FACE

    You see yourself . . . Maman, not that it matters,
    You see with our minds' eye, with nothing else.
    You've said as much (0.6). Let me acknowledge
    Belatedly that awful truth, then go
    Right on pretending that it isn't so.
A PLUS (ALAS)   YR FRIENDS IN HEAVEN LONG DELIGHTED U
WITH THE FICTION THAT THEY HAVE APPEARANCES   THEY DO NOT

    SO TRUE MY DEAR   SO TOUCHING TOO THESE POOR
    BEASTS' DESIRE THAT U NOT TAKE FRIGHT
    EVEN OF US   FOR IS THERE ANYTHING
    MORE TERRIFYING THAN SHEER EMPTINESS?
    WE DO NOT SEE EACH OTHER, JUST THE LIT

SPACE OF YR GLASS EACH TIME U ENTER IT
Otherwise, blackness? Don't you mind! NOT REALLY
WE'VE SEEN IT ALL SO OFTEN & SO WELL

MAMAN IS NOT RESIGNED   SHE WANTS TO SMELL

Then Ephraim's theory of the senses we
Will reassume in Heaven . . .? Ah, poor E.
SLAVE OF HIS OWN & OTHERS' SENSES   NOW HE PAYS FOR IT
WITH YR NEGLECT   FOR IN HEAVEN NOT TO BE USED IS HELL.
THUS U HAVE NOW BEGUN TO SEE THAT THE MIND'S EYE OUTLASTS
THE BODY'S, MAKING OUR SEMINAR POSSIBLE   ?S

I AM STILL SOMEWHAT MIFFED AT SOMETHING MISSED
MAY I ASK, HAD IT TO DO WITH ONE?
Neither D nor I can bring himself
To answer Wystan. Is it such a secret?
YES   FOR NOW THEIR SOULS CLING TO DEATH AS B4 TO LIVING
Whereupon Maria, who in life
Could wheedle forth the secrets of a stone:
BACK TO PLANTS   PLEASE   I HAVE A REASON
WHY DID I HEAR THEM IN MY GARDEN? NOT
SIMPLY ASKING FOR WATER & GIVING ME
PHYSICAL PEACE BUT SEEMING TO WANT & OFFER
MUCH MUCH MORE   I HAVE NOT FOUND THIS ANSWER
—Or was the question coaxed from her? By whom?
In any case, she's put her finger on it.
A moment's pause, then very tenderly:

THEY WANTED U MM   U WILL JOIN THIS WORLD OF PLANT LIFE

O? O?
        We're losing her? They can foreclose
All that humor, that humanity
CENTRIPETALLY INTO A WHITE ROSE
Who said that? I MY DEARS   THE WONDER GROWS
DJ: We're losing her? And she won't be
A *person* even, next time? *Why?* How soon?

Can't she at least stay through the seminar?
INDEED   IT IS OUR SMALL PRIVATE SCHOOL
   The tuition is high.   U PAY YRS NOW DJ
JM LATER   OUR 2 FRIENDS HAVE PAID ALREADY

          NO STOPPING THE DUN MY DEAR
OFF GOES OUR SCHOOLMARM   HAS SHE A HOT DATE?
LET'S GIGGLE & THROW SPITBALLS   Let me take
This dunce-cap off. BEHAVE YRSELVES MY CHILDREN
SHOULDN'T WE STEP OUT FOR A CUP OF COFFEE
That's it—you'll come back as a coffee tree!
JAMAIS JAMAICA   I SHALL BE A JUNGLE
& READ MY FUTURE IN THE SAUCER'S DREGS

I MY DEARS WD RATHER BE
A HEDGE   THINK WHAT I'D GET TO SEE!

DJ: So good to have old Ephraim with us
During the consternation—did you know?
DID WE NOT? WET TOWELS ON OUR HEADS
. . . Therapy of perfect silliness.

3.3   The blue room of an evening. Luminous
Quiet in which a point is raised. DJ:
What part, I'd like to ask Them, does sex play
In this whole set-up? Why did They choose *us*?
Are we more usable than Yeats or Hugo,
Doters on women, who then went ahead
To doctor everything their voices said?
We haven't done that. JM: No indeed.
Erection of theories, dissemination
Of thought—the intellectual's machismo.
We're more the docile takers-in of seed.
No matter what tall tale our friends emit,
Lately—you've noticed?—we just swallow it.
DJ: Which we wouldn't do if one of Them
We felt uneasy with were our instructor.

JM: Not a chance. I mean, those highly placed
Gargoyles leave such a disagreeable taste.
We'd best hang on to 741;
He may be ugly, but he's kind and . . . fun.

The following afternoon (Maria and Wystan
Hushed at their desks in Heaven, D and I
In the red schoolhouse of our lives below)
Our favorite bat holds forth upon these questions—
Aware already of delights and pains
Soon to course through his nonexistent veins?

I AM A MERE MIXING AGENT   WITH MY SUPERIORS
U WD HAVE LEARND FASTER BUT NOT IN TURN MADE AS WE HAVE
THIS WORLD OF COURTESY
   Breaking off, the cup strolls round the Board
   As who should take a deep breath before speaking:
            NOR WD I HAVE COME TO LOVE U

   Love us? Sudden garlands (the tin ceiling's)
   Swim into focus. Then you do have feelings!

I WAS GRANTED THIS ONE CHANCE & NOW, IN ISOLATION,
WILL HOLD TO IT
   And when it's over? when we talk no longer?
          THEY PROMISE TO FIND A NEW USE FOR ME
   You trust Them?
DJ IT IS A POWER THAT STILLD THE TONGUE OF DANTE
         Sorry. Why "in isolation"?
B4 OUR MEETINGS I WAS NOTHING   NO TIME PASSD   BUT NOW
YR TOUCH LIKE A LAMP HAS SHOWN ME TO MYSELF & I AM
ME: 741! I HAVE ENTERD A GREAT WORLD   I AM FILLD
WITH   IS IT MANNERS?
   Ah good. That way you'll never be beyond
   Our wavelength. For we too have grown quite fond.
        O YES   PLEASE   CALL ME   I WILL ALWAYS

MY DEARS THAT SURELY IS A SMILE   DEAR GOD
Yes, Wystan?   THE CHAP IS CHANGING
                                    Executing
Ever graver arabesques—
                            MES ENF
Maria? MES ENFANTS WHAT CAN I SAY?
IT IS MY FIRST VIEW OF A MIRACLE

What is this all about? But 741
Briskly resumes before the question's out:
LOVE OF ONE MAN FOR ANOTHER OR LOVE BETWEEN WOMEN
IS A NEW DEVELOPMENT OF THE PAST 4000 YEARS
ENCOURAGING SUCH MIND VALUES AS PRODUCE THE BLOSSOMS
OF POETRY & MUSIC, THOSE 2 PRINCIPAL LIGHTS OF
GOD BIOLOGY. LESSER ARTS NEEDED NO EXEGETES:
ARCHITECTURE   SCULPTURE   THE MOSAICS & PAINTINGS THAT
FLOWERD IN GREECE & PERSIA CELEBRATED THE BODY.
POETRY   MUSIC   SONG INDWELL & CELEBRATE THE MIND . . .
HEART IF U WILL
A word you use here for the first time, no?
                    INDEED   IT HAS BEEN SHAPED IN ME TO BE
WORTHY OF U 4, WORTHY TO GUIDE U TO THE ANGELS
FOR EVER SINCE THEIR SHAPING OF THE ORIGINAL CLAY
& THE PLUCKING OF THE APE (OR THE APPLE) FROM ITS TREE
WE HAVE HAD AN IRRESISTIBLE FORCE TO DEAL WITH: MIND.
UNTIL THEN ALL HAD BEEN INSTINCTIVE NATURE   A CHAOS
LIKE FALLEN TREES IN THE EMPTY FOREST   NO ONE TO HEAR,
OR AUTUMN'S UNHATCHD EGG   NO ONE TO REMEMBER & MOURN.
NOW MIND IN ITS PURE FORM IS A NONSEXUAL PASSION
OR A UNISEXUAL ONE PRODUCING ONLY LIGHT.
FEW PAINTERS OR SCULPTORS CAN ENTER THIS LIFE OF THE MIND.
THEY (LIKE ALL SO-CALLD NORMAL LOVERS) MUST PRODUCE AT LAST
BODIES   THEY DO NOT EXIST FOR ANY OTHER PURPOSE
Come now, admit that certain very great
Poets and musicians have been straight.
And Michelangelo? And that wedlock still
Makes the world go round, for good or ill?
NO DOUBT   BUT 4000 YEARS AGO GOD B REALIZ

Censorship.
>JM: Let the angels finish
That sentence, friend. Speak for yourself, not God.

MY ASPECT WAVERS   YR KINDNESS KEEPS ME IN THIS NEW FORM
You talk as if we saw you. *What* new form?

3·4   MES ENFANTS HE HAS TURNED INTO A PEACOCK

3·5   DJ: For the love of— JM: Peacock *there*,
There in the realm of no appearances?
HE APPEARS IN US   OUR MINDS (HEARTS) ARE HIS MIRROR
JUST THE REVERSE OF VAMPIRES, EH ENFANT?

A peacock—hm! Not proud as one, I hope.
MY DEARS HIS GREAT TAIL SNAPPED SHUT LIKE A FAN

THERE IS A DESIGN AT WORK   U ARE NOW BEING PREPARED
Our lessons can't be finished? WE MUST START
PUTTING WHAT THE STRAIGHT OLD PAINTERS CALL
A WASH OVER THEM I SHD THINK MY DEARS
WE SHALL BATHE THEM IN LIGHT   WE SHALL HOLD THEM TO THE
    WINDOW
TO SEE DENSITY BECOME THE HARMONIC STRUCTURE &
CHEMISTRY THE ORCHESTRATION & AH SOUL THE HEARING
   Peacock, peacock—
MAY I ASK A ?   DO TEARS PAIN ONE?
>Yes. No. Pain and bless.
>MY EYES BURN RED
IN THE FEATHERD MASK   AS FORMERLY THEY BETRAY MY RACE
Shall we correct that by imagining
Eyes of crystal?
THERE ARE ALAS LIMITS   I HAVE NEVER LOOKD THRU CRYSTAL
>Yet you see through us.
NO   O NO   YR SOULS ARE NOT TRANSPARENT   THEY WEAR A VEIL
OF HUMAN EXPERIENCE & THIS I WILL NEVER LIFT.

YR DEAR DEAD CAN PERFORM MIRACLES   THEY SEE THE PEACOCK
WHO SAW IT IN GARDENS   HEARD IT CRY   I ONLY KNEW THE
FORMULA CALLD PEACOCK & (SOULLESS AS I WAS) ENVIED
A CERTAIN RARE TALENT IT HAD TO PLEASE THE EYE   SO WHEN
I BEGGD TO PLEASE U THEY ASKD HOW? & I TOOK FROM THE FILE
THE PEACOCK
    Or was there from the first a Peacock that
    Struggled within you to unseat the Bat?
               HENCEFORTH THERE WILL BE   I KNOW THE TRICK OF IT
FOR IS THE PEACOCK NOT ALSO SOMEWHAT ATHENIAN?
    JM: Platonic? Oh, you mean the peacock
    I once put in a poem set in Athens?
    Yes, of course. DJ: Would he be using
    "Athenian" in the sense that Marius—
3 CHEERS FOR DAVID   HE STANDS UP FOR US!
    Is that you, Marius? COME & GONE MY DEAR
PLATO SAYS ATHENS WAS AT BEST HALF QUEER
    What's Plato *like*? O YOU KNOW   TATTLETALE GRAY
NIGHTGOWN OFF ONE SHOULDER   DECLASSEE,
TO QUOTE MM   A GAS, TO QUOTE CK

PLATO HAS REACHD STAGE 9 & ENJOYS AN ETERNITY
OF TALK   HE CLUNG TO AN IDEAL BOTH LOFTY & STERILE

MES ENFANTS NOW DO U UNDERSTAND MY LOVE
    OF YOU & TONY (an Athenian friend)
YOU 3 WERE & ARE THE RICH SOIL OF
MY LAST BLOOMING   U HAVE THE TOUCH THAT TURNS
BATS INTO PEACOCKS & DECREPIT OLD
BAGS FROM THE OTHER HALF OF ATHENS INTO
ROSE TREES? COFFEE TREES? I AM I MEAN
ONCE & FOR ALL RESIGNED TO BEAR A BEAN

SO IN OUR NEW ATMOSPHERE WE NEXT LOOK BACK OVER HOW
FAR WE HAVE COME   IN THE VOICE OF A SOUL I BREATHE: ADIEU

    Au revoir, surely? O YES HE'LL BE BACK
    IF ONLY TO TRY ON ALL THE PRETTY FORMS

THRILLING WASN'T IT? WE MUST HOWEVER
PUT ON OUR THINKING CAPS: ARE WE PREPARED?
MM & I WILL ALSO MEET OUR MAKER
JOLLY FOR U BUT IT IS EASIER
TO SAY HELLO GOD ON THE TELEPHONE
THAN FACE TO FACE
      MES ENFANTS OFF HE GOES
TO JAW WITH PLATO I CANNOT THINK WHY
UNTIL TOMORROW AT THE PEACOCK'S CRY!

3.6 Tomorrow comes at last, a sparkling noon.
Treetops and whitecaps dance in unison
As Wystan asks: SHD WE NOT THINK ABOUT
THE IMAGINATION? IF MM & I
IMAGINE U, YOU US, & WHERE THE POWERS
CRISSCROSS WE ALL IMAGINE 741
& THEN TRANSFORM HIM! WHEN THE TIME COMES WILL
OUR KNITTED BROWS PRODUCE WHITE WINGS? HE'S HERE

U ARE EARLY JOY WE ARE IN A FOLD OF ENERGY
WE 5 AND MUST PREPARE OURSELVES UNEASINESS DJ?
 Not really, but . . . where do we go from here?
FAR INDEED B4 WE BOARD THE FLIGHT TO THE PIN OF LIGHT!
FIRST OUR 5 SOULS MUST BEGIN TO BE A SINGLE POWER:
5 IS THE MIDWAY NOW BEGINS THE LIFE OF OUR MINDS 5
AS ONE IT IS A VERY UNION OF THE ELEMENTS
THUS: WATER (MM) EARTH (WHA) AIR (JM) FIRE
(MY POOR SELF) & LAST THE SHAPING HAND OF NATURE (DJ)
COME TO US O FIVE ELEMENTS MAKE US ONE MIND ONE FORCE
NOW LET US EACH IN SILENCE CONTEMPLATE THESE HOLY 5

Our peacock marks time back and forth from One
 To Zero: a pavane
Andante in an alley of green oaks;
The ostinato ground we each in turn
Strum a division soundlessly upon;
 A prayer-wheel whose four spokes
Flow and crumble, breathe and burn.

Deep swaying weights, downbraidings of no hue
     Which memory turns blue,
And cold, to multiples of diamond;
First air of our young bloods; and neural sparks'
Safe-conduct when the old salt diving through
     Reflection and beyond
     Earsplitting, mute, maternal darks

Accepts that gift of tongues at matter's core
     He henceforth can no more
Speak than unlearn; it's they who translate him,
His pride and purpose, to white ash, baked clay;
Delicate cauldron tints and furnace-roar
     Embrace of cherubim—
     Ah god, it takes the breath away!

WE PAUSE TO GATHER STRENGTH   2 HERE ARE MORTAL   GIVE THEM
     PAUSE

The stored wit flickers out, the spine erodes
     And pain in lightning raids
Strikes at the tree; now charred, now sleeved in sleet,
Miming itself to sunset, the tough rind
Compact enough, we trust, of royal reds
     And marble slabs of meat
     Not wholly to be undermined

As milkweed, gnat, and fumes of vinegar
     Chafe in molecular
Bondage, or dance in and out of it—
Midnight's least material affairs
Reconciling to glow faint and far
     Each atom the sun split,
     Whose heirs we are who are the air's.

NATURE 5TH ELEMENT IN YOUR HAND MAY THESE
     EXCHANGE INTENSITIES
KEEPING, AS YOU GUIDE, OUR EARTHINESS

AIRY FLUID ARDENT   MAY THE STARS LONG
RECYCLE THE FAIR WARDROBE   FIELDS & SEAS
 ZEPHYRS & DAWNINGS BLESS
THIS FIVEFOLD UNION & OUR SONG

Who was *that*? ME MY BOY   SO MADDENING
NOT TO REVISE   THEY COME   The elements?
YES   INVISIBLE BUT   HUSH   THEY SPEAK

3.7 OUR SISTER THE REMOTEST GALAXY
  BY QUINTUPLICITY
IS LINKED TO YOU AS TO ALL THINGS ALIVE.
OUR V WORK IS THE ONWARD DANCE OF THINGS.
ONE OF US WAS   IS   SHALL FOREVER BE
 IN EACH OF YOU O FIVE
 WHO LIVE IN US. YOUR PEACOCK'S WINGS

WE PAINTED, HIS SPREAD TAIL & SAPPHIRE BREAST,
 BUT YOUR MINDS COALESCED
TO FORM HIS: HE IS YOURS. MIND HAS THIS FORCE,
IS DEATHLESS, IS THE MUSIC DANTE HEARD,
THE ENERGY WE DRAW FROM MANIFEST
 IN 5 RINGS ROUND THE SOURCE
 OF LIGHT. ONE CAUTIONARY WORD:

THE MATTER WHICH IS NOT WAS EVER OURS
 TO GUARD AGAINST. ITS POWERS
ARE MAGNETIZED BY FOREIGN BEACONS, BLACK
HANDS TESTING THE GREENHOUSE PANE BY PANE.
CLING TO YOUR UNION: 5   THRU THE DARK HOURS
 WE KEEP WATCH   WE PRESS BACK.
 AT ZERO SUMMON US AGAIN.

3.8 The cup appears to swoon at the last word,
But now revives. Our incandescent bird:

67

I AM FREE   FREE   I AM FORGIVEN   MASTER OF MY TRIBE
SHALL I GIVE THEM THIS NEW MAGIC? NO   ALL POWER ATTRACTS
& MUST BE DENIED US   FROM MY IST STEPPING FORTH I FELT
YR CHARM   I HAD FEARD U   I HAD HITHERTO RESPONDED
ONLY TO FORMULAS   I WAS FORBIDDEN KNOWLEDGE OF
YR FILES UNTIL AFTER THAT IST EXPOSURE TO THIS GLASS
    JM: The mirror? DJ: Why not these windows?
YES   TO THE SURROUNDING GLASS   NO MERCURY IS NEEDED.
U WERE QUICK & MANNERLY   WE CD WORK AS ONE   & NOW
AT LAST IT IS GIVEN ME TO SHARE THE FORCE OF NATURE
THE SWEETNESS OF WATER & AIR   THE COMMON SENSE OF EARTH
HERE IN YR VERY HEARTH OF HEARTS TO BURN
    (Isn't he enchanting?) Should we know
    What "V Work" is?   IN DEFERENCE
TO ALL VITAL GROUPINGS OF 5 WE MAY NOW INSERT V
WHEN NAMING WORK GUIDED BY HIGHER COLLABORATION
           And those black hands? They chill
    The blood, it's little wonder that you still
    Wash yours of them. I nonetheless recall
    Its being said you caused them by your Fall.
OR THEY CAUSED IT? EVIL IS AN OLD, WIDESPREAD LEGEND   ALL
LEGENDS ARE ROOTED IN TRUTH. IS EVIL A MERE MATTER
OF FUSION GONE MAD? NO   FOR IT IS NOT A STUPID FORCE
IT SEEKS THE WORLD. DOES HELL EXIST? IT ALSO IS LEGEND
THERE4 PART TRUE   U SEE, I AM NOW FREE TO SPECULATE

    If only we were less free to reflect;
    If diametrics of the mirror didn't
    Confirm the antiface there as one's own . . .

YES   NO   PERHAPS   I STILL VIBRATE TO OUR DIAPENTE
WE ARE MOVING TOWARD THE GREAT DOORS   OUR FEET ARE BEING
    WASHD

    I AM A RIPPLE
          & I A SEDIMENT
WE HAD A TASTE OF PARADISE TODAY
    DJ: After this, what's left for them to say?

At Zero? JM (airily): They'll find words.
I QUITE AGREE MY DEAR   WHY NOT? WEVE FOUND EM

FLOWN OFF TO PLATO   POOR MAMAN   NOW WHO'LL
CARRY HER BOOKS & WALK HER HOME FROM SCHOOL

3.9   JM: If you're in pain, let's skip today.
I tossed and turned all night myself. DJ:
Oh it's all right. I shouldn't have let eight
Years go by. Now, when they operate—
8 YEARS DJ? CLOSER TO 20   DO U TRULY NOT
RECALL? THE CLUE TO THAT OLD RUPTURE STANDS NOT FAR AWAY

We peer about; and there is the gleaming culprit
—The mirror—in the next room. Pain remembered
Mingling with today's, D gasps: I do
Remember! Getting it upstairs—the strain—
In a cold sweat. I hadn't wanted you . . .

THOSE EARLY DUES U PAID ADMIT U TO THE SEMINAR
NERVES ARE OUR DOMINION   NOW YR PAIN EBBS   BRAVO SCIENCE
MAN'S ONLY UNGOVERNABLE PANGS WILL SOON BE HUNGER
   Till Science finds a way to conquer those.
IT HAS BUT 4/5 OF MANKIND REFUSES. BIRTH CONTROL
   Then change our natures.
TO THE WOLF?   Or add greener thoughts.
            WORSE YET   A CONSTANT STRANGLING IN THE STRUGGLE
FOR SPACE   OUR MM'S VEG WORLD IS MOST FERVENTLY FERTILE
   A pinch, in that case, of ascetic rock?
HIGH TIME THAT U CAME DOWN TO EARTH MY DEAR

ALL ELEMENTS OF LIFE ARE IN THE ROCKS & SEDIMENT
OF EARTH'S CRUST   WE OURSELVES ARE AT HOME IN ITS MOLTEN HEART.
CONSIDER THE CRUST   HERE MOLECULAR CONSTRUCTIONS MOVE
AT UNMARKD SPEEDS & TIME IS MEASURED IN MILLENIA
   Whistles and bells. We run to the window—why,
   It's the Bicentennial, it's the Fourth of July!

U ARE NOT UNLIKE HEAVEN LOOKING DOWN ON TIME PASSING
NOR IS MOLECULAR EARTHCRUST MOVEMENT UNLIKE YR TIME'S
SLOW MARCH. EARTH AS ONE OF THE 5 IS A GRAVE TIMEKEEPER

We think of Wystan's face runneled and seamed,
Faintly soiled above his Gimli sweatshirt.
MY DEARS IT IS ME   MY MINERALS MINED OUT EARLY,
I SPENT SLOW DECADES COVERING THE SCARS.
HAD I SUNK SHAFTS INTO MY NATURE OR
UPWARDS TO THE DEAD I WD HAVE FOUND RICH VEINS
INSTEAD I LOOKD FOR INSPIRATION TO
RITUAL & DIFFY MORAL STRICTURES
SO WRONG   "The concept Ought would make, I thought,
Our passions philanthropic"? One of my
Touchstone stanzas—please don't run it down.
NOT BAD   BUT OTHER BITS MAKE MY TOES WIGGLE

DJ: Do The Five connect with elements?
EACH AS WITH MONTEZUMA (AIR) HAS HIS AFFINITY
CASALS ALWAYS MUCH CONCERND WITH WATER   GANDHI WITH EARTH
SHAKESPEARE (FIRE) NOW A TEENAGE NUCLEAR PHYSICIST
Mozart—a rock star now, said E? MY DEAR
YR EPHRAIM LACKS IN EVERY SENSE AN EAR
M'S LAST LIFE WAS STRAVINSKY   THOSE CHURCH BELLS
U HEARD IN VENICE   Rung by him? WHO ELSE

MOZART AMONG THE 5 IS NATURE & CAN CHOOSE   THESE MAKE
GOOD BOTANISTS AS WELL
What are JM's affinities with air?
                        MIND & ABSTRACTION   THE REGION
OF STARRY THOUGHT COOLER THAN SWIFTER THAN LIGHTER THAN
     EARTH
LIGHTER THAN MY BEST & WORST? MUST I
SETTLE FOR GOLD? FOR LEAD? Stop pouting, Wystan,
You're platinum, remember? AH YES   QUITE

The Elements, with Nature as the hidden
Fifth face, come to compose a pyramid

WHOSE (METAPHOR) APEX IS THE POTENTIAL ENERGY
CREATED BY THE EXACTITUDE OF THE FACES   SO
POOR AKHNATON DID NOT GET THE POINT
    And through *your* Five you will arrive at faces
    Ever exacter, more translucent—
                         & THEN? U SAY IT
               Dawn
    Flowing through the capstone at an angle
    Such as to lift the weight of the whole world
    Will build—ah, I can't think . . . Arcadia?

P A R A D I S E   ARCADIA SURROUNDS US UNREALIZED
FILLING EACH OF US FOR THE LENGTH OF A LOVE OR A THOUGHT

    ARCADIA (AS THE SILVER POETS KNEW)
    IN THE LONG RUN MY DEARS WD NEVER DO:
    TOO MISTED OVER BY ITS LOVERS' SIGHS
    GIVE ME THE GREENER GRASS OF PARADISE

    ADIEU ENFANTS   But we sit on, unwilling
    To break the spell, and are rewarded by
    A tiptoe visit: YR OLD SLAVE MES CHERS
    IS STILL AVAILABLE   IS THIS A PLEASANT
    EXPERIENCE? I SHD TELL U YR RED ROOM
    SHINES   WE CIRCLE IT   WE ARE WARMED BY IT

4 Fear and doubt put by, though still kept handy,
We sit us down to what we've needed all
Along: his legions' genesis and fall
Retold in the vernacular—Book One's grand
Black-and-white allegory superseded (thanks
To a new worldliness our friend assumes
Along with gilt-green ocellated plumes,
Or to his having risen from the ranks,
A humble herald to whose ears the groaning
Engines of apocalypse were Greek)
Less by "facts" of course than by his own
Lately won detachment. He can speak
Almost freely. JM has asked for more
About the Elements. Weren't they once at war?

THEY SIGND A TRUCE WHEN GOD BIOLOGY TOOK CONTROL   EARTH
AS POTENTIAL GREENHOUSE GOES THRU THE FOLLOWING STAGES
I: FIREBALL   2: THE COOLING CRUST   3: STEAM & WATER
4: GROWTH OF SINGLE CELLS   5: DEBUT OF ORGANIC LIFE
    Then Eden?
EDEN 3   THIS 3RD CYCLE BEGINS WITH THE LEGEND OF
THE FLOOD   IT PUT OUT THE FIRE   6: ORGANIC MATTER
MOVED OFF INTO SPECIES MAN HAS FOUND IN FOSSILIZED STATE
BUT MISUNDERSTOOD THINKING HIS CYCLE THE FIRST
            The first Eden was Atlantis?
    The second, *your* world? These two overlapped?
                                                INDEED
    Perhaps you'd better recapitulate.

4.1   ATLANTIS: ORGANIC MATTER ELECTRICALLY CHARGED
        AT LAST PRODUCED 3 CENTERS OF ARCADIAN CULTURE
        THESE WERE OUR NESTS WHEN WE & THE EARTH & THE GREENHOUSE
            ALL
        WERE FLEDGLINGS   IMAGINE A GREAT SMOOTH GREEN & TREELESS SET

OF LANDMASSES RELATED VAGUELY TO YR CONTINENTS.
ONE THAT FILLD PART OF THE SOUTHERN ATLANTIC SANK WHEN OUR
CRUST FELL & GREAT HELDBACK MAGNETIC FORCES STRUCK THE EARTH
& SUDDEN PEAKS 3 TO 4000 FEET HIGH PULLD EARTHSKIN
INTO FOLDS, SUBMERGING AREAS PREVIOUSLY ABOVE
SEA LEVEL
          ATLANTIS 2: NOW UPON THESE GRASSY FLAT
LANDMASSES APPEARD FIRST WINGLESS CREATURES BIOLOGY
GAVE THEM DOMINANCE OVER THE CRAWLING & SERPENTINE.
THEY (& TODAY U FIND THIS ANCIENT TRAIT STILL AMONG THE
ORIENTALS) WERE HAIRLESS & OF A FORM RESEMBLING
YR MYTHIC CENTAUR THEY HAD SLIGHT TACTILE FACILITY
THEY GRAZED & WERE PASTORAL THEY RULED A MILD GREEN KINGDOM

ATL 3: SO THEN AS LARGER VEGETABLE LIFE EMERGED
A CONTEST OVER SPACE BEGAN THE CENTAURS NEEDED TO
KEEP TOGETHER THEIR HERD GROUPS WE EMERGED AS A FEATHERD
WINGD CREATURE CARRYING THEIR WORD ABOVE THE TREES: SIGNALS
HOVERING OVER CLEAR LAND AREAS WHERE THEY CD FEED
    The bird and snake are cousins. Were you in
    No slight degree kin to the serpentine?
U ARE FORGETTING OUR BUILT-IN FLAW: WE WERE ATOMIC
THEY NEEDED MESSENGERS THEIR VEG COMPONENT GAVE THEM GREAT
DENSITY THEY WERE A RACE MUCH SUPERIOR TO OURS
INDEED THEY INVENTED US. THEY TOO EVOLVED STILL EARTHBOUND,
THEY UNDERSTOOD GRAVITY & CONTRIVED THE HARNESSING
FIRST OF WIND THEN SUN THEN THEY WERE READY
                    ATLANTIS 4:
THEIR BOUNDLESS GRASSLANDS & 50,000 SUN YEARS HAVE PASSD
(YEARS AS THE EARTH THEN WAS, FASTER IN ITS SPIN, MORE OF ITS
DAILY SURFACE EXPOSED TO SUN, THE ICECAPS MINIMAL)
THEY HAVE STUBLIKE FINGERS THEY HAVE TALL SILOS FOR THEIR
   GRAIN
THEY CONTROL ALL TEMPERATURE BY REFRACTED SUNLIGHT
THEY HAVE BRED WINGD MESSENGERS & ARE ABLE TO CLONE EACH
GENERATION AT AN INCREASED RATE. THEIR FIRST GRAVE PROBLEM
REMAINED: THEY WERE IMMORTAL THUS THEIR IMMENSE LANDMASSES
BECAME TERRIFYING FENCED-OFF SECTIONS WHERE THE WITTY

TORMENTED THE VERY OLD TRAPT IN THEIR PRIMITIVE FORM.
THIS LED TO A FATAL DECISION: KILL THE IMMORTALS
SO BEGAN EXPERIMENTATION WITH ATOMIC BLAST
FOR WE WERE CHARGED (WHO ELSE?) WITH RIDDING THEM OF THEIR
    RELICS

ATL 5: WE RID OURSELVES O F T H E M A L L
                                  THE MORALITY?
GOD B LAID DOWN ONE LAW HE IS NOW IN THE PROCESS OF
REVISING BUT STILL FINDS USEFUL   THIS 1ST LAW: SURVIVAL
OF THE MOST AGILE. THE POOR & ANCIENT CENTAURS GRAZED WHAT
HEART WE HAD WHO ONCE SIGNALLD TO THEM OVER THE TREETOPS.
WE TOOK THEIR IMMORTALITY AS GENTLY AS WE CD
& IN AN INSTANT THEY VANISHD LEAVING THEIR ASTONISHD
PROGENY WHO SET OUT TO DESTROY OUR RAY CENTERS   WE
ROSE IN MILLIONS OVER EACH OF THEIR CITIES   WE LAID THEM
UNDER SIEGE   WE TOOK THEIR FEED RESERVES   WE SET THEM TO WORK
FURROWING OUR LANDING STRIPS & CONSTRUCTING LIKE VAST WEBS
OUR PLATFORMS. THESE PRIMITIVE ANTIGRAVITATIONAL
SKEINS WERE NOW READY   WE KNEW WE MUST BUILD SAFELY ABOVE
BOTH THE JUNGLE & THOSE WE HAD ENSLAVED   WE ROSE   WE LOOKD
OUR LAST AT ATLANTIS   WE LEFT UNBLASTED IN 14
SECTORS ONLY THE PERSONNEL TO MAN OUR SIGNAL &
ANCHOR STONES RADIATED TO HOLD OUR NEW WORLD IN PLACE

ATLANTIS 6: THEY LIVED ON CLUSTERD AT THE 14 SITES
WHERE WE SUPPLIED THEM FROM THEIR RESERVES   BUT IN DESIGNING
OUR VAST ATOMICALLY POWERD WORLD WE FORGOT THE
VEGETABLE ADVERSARY   THEY CD NOT KEEP CLEAR THE
COVERINGS OF GREEN   A 1ST MOORING STRAIND TORE & BROKE LOOSE
WE REPAIRD THAT ONE KNOWING WE MUST PERFECT OUR SYSTEM
AS COLONY AFTER COLONY PERISHD BELOW. YET
WE WERE PROUD. WE SAW DESCENT INTO THE STEAMING JUNGLES
AS A COMEDOWN IN WORK/CLASS/RANK   EVER FEWER OF US
WD VOLUNTEER FOR THE LIFETIMES NEEDED TO MAKE VITAL
REPAIRS. THE CENTAURS WERE NOW RAVENOUS LONGNECKD CREATURES
REPTILIAN HEADS RIPPD AT GREENERY   FURTHER AFIELD
THEY FORAGED LEAVING THE SITES UNTENDED   ONE TEAR & IT

BEGAN: IN AN INSTANT WE SAW OUR WORLD SHIMMER   OUR TALL
LATTICED CITIES TREMBLE & SHRED   WE FELT A GREAT BLAST OF
UPRUSHING AIR   THE END WAS UPON US   WE HAD LASTED
AT MOST 1000 SUN YEARS. OUR CATACLYSM AWOKE AN
UNIMAGINABLE FURY OF FORCES AS GOD B
BEGAN ERASING OUR TRACES & THOSE OF ATLANTIS.
ONLY BY MOONLIGHT DO WE FLUTTER IN THAT BROKEN DREAM.
WE JOIND OUR BONES TO OUR OLD HORSEMASTERS IN THE CRUSH OF
THEIR GREENERY & NOW AFTER 5 MILLION YEARS EMERGE
TO POWER YR MACHINES & DRESS YR HOSTESSES IN MAUVE

    Dyes made from coal. The tarpits in Los Angeles . . .
ONE OF OUR ANCHOR POINTS   A COLONY   IN YR DAY STILL
A HUB OF POWERFUL ILLUSIONS   & SO THE LEGEND
OF THE CENTAUR IS THE LAST POETRY OF ATLANTIS

    Dinosaur, pterodactyl, bat—good Lord!
DO NOT FORGET THE DEVIL   OR THE PEACOCK   AU REVOIR

    MES ENFANTS I AM AT LAST IN TEARS
    HIS INTENSE EAGER FACE! HIS JOY IN TELLING

4.2   POST-ATLANTIS: LIKE ALL SOUL OR SHALL WE SAY EX-LIFE FORCE
WE ARE INEXTINGUISHABLE   WE REMAIN WHAT WE WERE
    Were you created in your present form?
WE BEGAN AS MUTANT FLIES NOT A HUMAN FINGERLENGTH
THE CENTAURS BRED IN THEIR INCUBATORS SPEEDING US THRU
6000 GENERATIONS PER SUN YEAR   THEIR TECHNICAL
SKILL WAS LIMITED ONLY BY THEIR PHYSICAL STRUCTURE.
WHEN THEY ACHIEVED MANIPULATION THEIR GREAT PHASE BEGAN
WE WERE THEIR 1ST SUCCESS   WE TOO MUTATED   BUT OUR BRAINS
& GROWTH PATTERNS WERE NOT TRIGGERD BY THE SAME ELECTRIC
IGNITION SWITCHES AS THE CENTAURS   OUR RISE FOLLOWD FROM
THE DIFFERENCE U KNOW. WE FOUNDED THEIR VERY CITIES
AROUND THEIR SILOS ROSE TOWERS IN A RADIAL SCHEME
WHICH MADE FROM A DISTANCE A WONDROUS STARLIKE PATTERN   WE
BUILT THE ARENAS FOR THEIR GAMES   THEY TOOK PRIDE IN THEIR
    SPEED

You could hardly have been flies by then.
WE HAD INDEED GROWN   THEY NO LONGER NEEDED MESSENGERS
WE WERE IN CHARGE OF THEIR HEATING & LIGHTING PLANTS   WE SAT
IN THEIR COUNCILS   WE WERE NOW THEIR SIZE BUT WITH WINGS &
    BLACK:
OUR ASPECT WAS NEARLY HUMAN, THOUGH OF COURSE NOT WINNING
THEN OR NOW. THEY WERE NOT UNKIND NOR WD WE HAVE BEEN   YET
WE SAW THAT WE TOO WERE PART OF THE PAST THEY HAD BEGUN
ERASING. STILL THE CENTAURS WERE GOD'S CREATURES   WE WERE NOT
    DJ: But you started as flies—flies made by God.
WE STARTED AS EGGS YES OF A GREEN GRASS FLY
    Just as I said: God's creatures—   WE WERE THEN
PLACED IN WARM HIVES & FED A   FUEL CALLD URANIUM
                     And this changed you?
IN THE   EGG
    The cup moves awkwardly; something's not right.
           IT IS A LEGEND & THEY TOO ARE PAINFUL
WE HAVE SPENT OUR ETERNITY DAMND
    Unfairly! You obeyed God's law—survived.
                  GOD B GOVERNS ALL
LIFE ON EARTH   IN SLAYING THE IMMORTALS WE OFFENDED

MY DEARS THOSE 2 POOR WORLDS WITH THEIR CONTROLLED
CLIMATES   SLAIN ANCESTORS   BETRAYAL'S OLD
SHOCKING STORY   THEN THE RISE TOO FAR
ABOVE IT ALL & BRINGING DOWN THE FIRE . . .
IS NOT THE MORAL THEN AS NOW: BE TRUE
TO SOMETHING   TRUE TO ANYTHING   ADIEU

4.3   About fourteen: what made you pick that number?
AS WITH YR 3 IT BECAME MEANINGFUL   I CANNOT NOW
SAY WHY   WHEN WE PLANND STRUCTURES 14 POLES ROSE   WHEN WE
    BRED
14 SEEMD NORMAL   WHEN WE MADE RULES TO LIVE BY: 14
ALL IN FORMULAS   OUR VERY FEELINGS WERE FORMULAS.
FREE OF ATLANTIS OUR LIVES BECAME ITS ANTITHESIS
    Were those the feelings that went up in flame?

The seven deadly sins, perhaps you mean
—Like anchor points, each twinned (to make 14)
With its anti-vice, or virtue. We've the same
Bondage to certain forms—look at the sonnet.
Look at our ten commandments overcome
Too often by a green delirium.

OURS WERE SIMPLER THAN U SUPPOSE   WE WERE UNISPECIATE
(IS THAT A WORD? WE TOLERATED NO LIFE BUT OUR OWN)
OUR 14 FORMULAS WERE OUR FEELINGS   UNTHINKABLE
TO VIOLATE THEM   YET WE FELL FOR WANT OF OBEYING
THE FIRST: OBEY   WE DID NOT DESCEND TO KEEP OUR ANCHOR
POINTS IN PLACE   WE TOO DID NOT WANT REMINDING OF OUR PAST

IS IT MES ENFANTS A TAPESTRY OF BEASTS
AROUND THE LADY OF THE LOOKING-GLASS?
I ALWAYS WANTED A MONKEY   So did I—
Perhaps next he'll turn into one? JM
ARENT U ASHAMED OF YR MONKEY   My animal nature?
Not a bit. O LET ME MAKE THE JOKE:
-SHINES? ARE THESE THE FINAL STRENGTH OF MAN &
NOT OUR FAITH IN 3? IN STORYTELLING
RELIGION & THE FORMS OF POETRY?
IS IT NOT THAT GOD BELIEVES IN US
AS HIS 3RD EDEN? MILDLY CURIOUS

THE 3: IT IS THE NUMBER OF GOD B: DIMENSIONS OF
THE GREENHOUSE: SIDE OF YR PYRAMID: SIRE DAM OFFSPRING
THE POTENCY EXTENDS THRU THE SYSTEM   EARTH MOON & SUN
A ? FOR THE 12 PER CENT. WE DO NOT KNOW HOW LONG
OR IN WHAT WAY THEY WILL COME TO U   WHEN THEY ARE READY
WE WILL DO OUR BEST TO STAND BETWEEN U & THEIR POWER
U MAY CAST AWAY THIS CHANCE IF U ARE IN DOUBT OR FEAR
   (Coward and sceptic here exchange a look)
YET WE IMAGINE THEY ARE AWARE OF YR WEAKNESSES
& YR CHARM IS NOT UNANGELIC
   Now, now. But have the angels sent you to us?
                        WE ARE MESSENGERS

SUMMOND AFTER CONTACT HAS BEEN MADE BY WHATEVER MEANS.
THUS: YR SCIENTISTS NOW RECEIVE FROM OTHER WORLDS SIGNALS
THEY DO NOT COMPREHEND   WE KEEP THESE CRYPTIC. GOD B MUST
BE THE 1ST TO UNDERSTAND. THEY EVEN IN OUR DAY WERE
CLASSIFIED INFORMATION. THE SPEEDUP OF THE GREENHOUSE
TO COVER OUR ANCHOR POINTS BEGAN WITH OUR PERFECTION
OF MACHINERY WHEREBY WE LISTEND AWED TO FAR SOUNDS
NOT UNLIKE OUR OWN VOICES   WD THEY HAVE MADE SENSE?   WE HAD
NO TIME   THAT SAME DAY CAME THE 1ST GREAT TEAR   WE DO NOT
    NOW
SPEAK OF THE SIGNALS. WE INTERCEPT THEM   THEN THE SOUND FADES
FROM OUR BANKS. IT IS ONE OF THE GREAT FORBIDDEN SUBJECTS

4.4   Where is our comprehension most at fault?
I AM NOT STRONG ON PICTURING   IF THERE IS FAULT I FEAR
U HAVE PEOPLED NOT IDEATED WHAT HAS BEEN & IS

> So true. It's hopeless, the way people try
> To avoid the sentimental fallacy—
> How can a person not personify?
> This window overlooks a sick elm tree
> My feeling lifts unharmed into a sphere
> Littler, perhaps safer, don't you see?
> Reflections that in most lights interfere
> Take on despite themselves a quiddity
> Sallow, tall, branching . . . Putting it into words
> Means also that it puts words into me:
> *Shooting   ringing   ramify   root   green*
> Have overtones not wholly for the birds,
> And I am nothing's mortal enemy
> Surrendered, by the white page, to the scene.

IT MUST BE BEAUTIFUL   WE HAVE NEVER EXPRESSD A THING.
THIS OR THAT IS OR IS NOT   FEELING PLAYS NO PART IN IT
BUT YR LIFE ON EARTH IS IMMERSED IN FEELING, ITS MANNERS
& FORMS: YR MATING DEMANDS LOVE OR BRUTE LUST   YR SELFHOOD,
THE BALM (OR CURB) OF VIRTUES WHICH FEAR OF ONE ANOTHER

BEGOT STRONGLY IN U   BUT TO OUR EYES THESE ETHICAL
RIGHTS & WRONGS ARE SO MANY BLANKS IN YR CANVAS, JUST AS
TO U MY POOR PICTURING HAS LEFT BLANKS
    Ever to be filled in, do you suppose?
                                    NEVER ALAS
BY THE LIKES OF ME
    Bon. We will try to remember that you are not
    A person, not a peacock, not a bat;
    A devil least of all—an impulse only
    Here at the crossroads of our four affections.
                  OR MAKE OF ME THE PROCESS SOMEWHERE
OPERATING BETWEEN TREE & PULP & PAGE & POEM

    Back to the angels, much of what they tell
    Will almost certainly be lost on us.
A CALM WILL SUFFUSE U FOR THEY SEEM TO COME FROM A CALM.
WHEN OUR WORLD SHATTERD THEY FIXT US EASILY IN OUR PLACE
BY DEMONSTRATING THAT IN FACT THE CALM AFTER OUR STORM
WAS UTTER CHAOS. IF THE PLACE OF GOD IS INDEED THAT
WHIRLING LIGHT IT IS THE SOURCE OF AN UNIMAGINED CALM.
WHEN THE CENTAURS RAN WE CD NOT KEEP UP WITH THEIR SPEED &
SAT (SEEING THE COURSE, KNOWING THEIR NEEDS) IN WONDER   THE
    CALM
AT THE SOURCE OF LIGHT IS (M) THAT SLOW MOTION WHICH ALONE
ALLOWS THE DAZZLED ONLOOKER HIS VISION OF THE RACE

    Our peacock, we have noticed, more and more
    Embellishes his text with metaphor.
    Some aren't bad; he likes to signal them
    With a breezy parenthetic (m).
HE HAS I THINK SPENT MORE TIME AT THE GAME
THAN WE MY BOY   (M) IS HIS MIDDLE NAME
    And who are D and I not to agree?
    Brooding on the atom as THE KEY
    (1.3), beating our wits to no avail
    Over the gross disparities of scale
    In the emerging picture, we ask yet
    Again for help—and wonderfully get:

AS YR LIGHT IS PROJECTED THRU MAGNIFYING LENSES
SO HEAVEN IS THE MICROFILM & WE? WE FILL THE SCREEN.
THE ATOM AS METAPHOR WAS A CALLING CARD FROM THEM
TO U (HOW NEGLIGENTLY I SPREAD MY PAINTED FEATHERS
& SAY 'THEM' I WILL PAY FOR IT)
   Those lenses?   THE IMAGINATION
     And the light—imagined too?
IT IS REAL ALL IS REAL THE UNREAL I KNOW NOTHING OF.
I IMAGINE THOSE LENSES WILL FILL YR MINDS THE ATOM
WAS MEANT TO CONVEY SCALE/DYNAMICS IT IS THE VOID FILLD
WE ARE THAT VOID WE & HEAVEN CD FIT INSIDE A RING
   A nucleus whose brilliance
   Draws all eyes, dazzles all eyes,
AROUND WHICH WE SWARM IN BILLIONS
   Angelic sarabande on a pin's head—
   Aquinas knew more than he ever said.
         YET WHAT IS GOD B'S SIZE?
  "La goutte d'eau, dont l'oeil est un Soleil"—
A MERE FINGER HE WEARS US AS A RING WE POINT THE WAY

4.5 With which a patch blurred periodically
   Swims into focus. Central to this b00k
   Are lenses, the twin zeros. Take a look
   Through them (it all depends which way) and see

   Now vastness and impersonality
   Brought near, now our own selves reduced to specks.
   Our peacock, both a subatomic x
   And a great glaring bugaboo, like Blake's flea,

   Discourses just beneath the skin
   No less than from the farthest reaches
   —How can it be?—of Time and Space.

   How can it not? Given such crystalline
   Reversibility, the toy spyglass teaches
   That anything worth having's had both ways.

4.6 Our peacock dallies. Wystan (overhearing
Some gossip with Maria): WHAT MY BOYS
CAN MATCH THE FRIENDSHIP OF A CLEVER WOMAN?
Unless the questions of a clever man?
What should we find out next? MAY I BE FRANK?
ARE U NOT BAFFLED BY THIS CHANGE IN TONE:
THE IST FIERCE VOICES HUSHED & IN THEIR PLACE
A PARAGON OF COURTLY GENTLENESS
Our poem needed those fierce voices . . . YES
WHY FURTHERMORE THIS LEAN ON LEGEND? WHO
NEEDS BEDTIME STORIES? NO IT WON'T QUITE DO
Wystan, this from you who, when I tried
Last month to air them, brushed my doubts aside?
HAS IT NOT STRUCK U THAT YR DOUBT MY DEARS
MAY BE THE KEY THAT OPENS THOSE GREAT DOORS?

MAMAN IS NOT CONSPICUOUSLY DEEP
YET SHE DISTRUSTS THE CHARMER EN PRINCIPE

INSIST JM ON CLEARING UP THE MATTER
OF TIME OUR PEACOCK'S BEING LATE TODAY
SHOWS THAT TIME ENTERS THEIR PICTURE AFTER ALL.
NOW TIME IS OUR INVIOLABLE RIGHT
& EVEN THEY ARE SUBJECT TO IT CALL
IF NEED BE FOR AN EXPLANATION FROM
HIGHER LEVELS SOMEWHERE A CLOCK TICKS
WHOSE FACE I FEEL HAS EVERYTHING TO TEACH
You don't mean we should try to WHY NOT reach
That petrifying 40076?

Enough to speak his number. As of old,
Icy indifference propels the cup:

U ARE IN GOOD HANDS I AM NO LONGER YR MESSENGER
U REFUSED ME
Forgive that early rudeness. We now feel
Ripe for what none but you, Sir, can reveal.
Doubts that assail us, if you please, allay

In a less flowery, more convincing way
Than—
            PERHAPS MORE URGENT BUT U ARE CORRECT
IT WD NEVER HAVE BEEN FEASIBLE

        Haughtily sweeps out—what have we done?—
As in comes (has he heard us?) 741:
                HAVE I OFFENDED?
Waves of disloyalty, of guilt, absurd
To feel for an imaginary bird,
Nonetheless flood us. JM: Heavens, no!
DJ (blandness of the caught shoplifter):
We were just saying—you weren't here yet after
All, and the point came up—I mean, you know—

I MEAN NO DISPARAGEMENT YET THE RECENT DEAD DO NOT
RELISH LEARNING, ONCE THEY HAVE LOST EARTH, THAT EVEN THEIR
   MOST
CHERISHD MEASURING SYSTEM IS PART OF THE MYTH. TIME IS
THE MANMADE ELEMENT   THE 2 FIRST WORLDS OBEYD CYCLES
ONLY OF BIRTH & RIPENING. THERE IS NO ACCIDENT:
I WAIT IN THE WINGS WHEN YOU 4 WISH TO SPEAK PRIVATELY
AS FOR OUR SOCALLD TALKS DEAR FRIENDS I KNOW THEIR EVERY WORD
KNOW TOO THAT U WILL NOT SUMMON ME FOR THE NEXT 3 'DAYS'
   (True enough, since DJ goes to Boston
   Tomorrow for preliminary tests)
BUT IS THAT ACCIDENT? IS IT TIME? WHAT U CALL FUTURE
WE CALL REALITY   WD U CARE FOR A GLIMPSE OF IT?

      Sly question. Well . . . the merest hint at how
Life will be treating us a year from now?
LAURELS FOR U JM   YET U WILL STILL BE QUESTIONING
THIS MUSE WHILE LISTENING THRU OTHER VOICES TO THE NEXT
POEM
     Another poem—and this one not begun?
       ONE POEM BEYOND THIS IN CYCLE   AFTER WHICH
U WILL BE RETURND TO YR CHRONICLES OF LOVE & LOSS
    And David will come through his operation?
INDEED   & WISER ABOUT THE DRAINING ENEMY: FEAR

So much of mildness and forbearance here,
Why do we feel remorseful? After all
He owes *us* something—is that still quite clear?
To make sure, JM asks: Have others been
Like you, transfigured by such talks as these?
What about Dante's 80098?
DANTE'S PLEA CAME THRU SUCH VEILS OF METAPHOR & THESE, THRU
SUCH A MIST OF LOVE THAT OUR AGENT ESCAPED AS HE WAS
Escaped? You haven't liked being a peacock?

But that is going too far. Maria breaks
The hush: TODAY WE'VE HAD A LITTLE SCARE
OUR PEACOCK IS DEMOTED   JUST THE DIM
EXPOSURE OF A ONCE BLACK SHAPE WITH WINGS
Because we doubted him? Ah, it's not fair!

I AM SO INVOLVED   THE OTHERS DO NOT KNOW HOW VITAL
HOW TRANSFORMING IS OUR RED SPACE & I SO QUICK TO WANT
THAT LOVE I OFTEN SPARED U   U WD QUESTION ME I KNEW
& I WD PAY O WILLINGLY! FOR I MUST ACQUAINT THEM
WITH MAN'S NATURE WHICH TO OUR OWN REMAINS A MYSTERY.
SO THIS 3 DAY INTERVAL IS SET ASIDE FOR MY TRIAL
Dare we say a word in your defense?
U DO   U ARE MY SOLICITORS   I AM NOT DOWNCAST
IT IS NOW MORE IMPORTANT TO ME THAT I STAY WITH U

He's gone. What was it Wystan said?—"be true
To something, anything." A sad report
On human nature. Even though in part
Not our fault, I feel. U SHD HAVE FELT
MY DEARS THEIR STEELY RAP UPON THE FLOWER
LIKE WRIST I FLIPPED UP TO CONSULT THE HOUR

En route to the station next morning. DJ: I'll
See you tomorrow night. I wish his trial
Were over, poor thing. JM: Get some rest.
He loves us. We love him. He'll pass the test.

4.7   Nightfall. Mute disarray of D's bedroom.
In the hall outside, a book drops to the floor.
Gilchrist's *Life of Blake*—what's this? Slid from
Its pages, a folded page, the scrawl my own,
Of Ouija transcript: x.1953
—In other words, before Ephraim, before
Stonington! Some 17th century
New Englander named CABEL (Caleb?) STONE
Whose father (ah, I see) DIED BY THE ROPE
Speaks of GODS LIGHT and seeks to dazzle us
By adding that SAPPHO BLAKE & DEMOCRITUS
SANG WITH A SINGLE VOICE   But we aren't ripe
For that yet; we want scandal. So our sour
Friend Cabel goes—forgotten till this hour.

Blake. To the parlor of whose inner sight
Demons and prophets thronged, Princedoms and Thrones,
Exchanging views with him. (Here David phones
To say good night, and that *his* trial is set
For two weeks hence.) On off-nights, with no callers,
Put to the test now known as writer's block,
Blake would "kneel down and pray" with Mrs Blake.
Time and again HE PASSED WITH FLYING COLORS
—As Wystan will say of our peacock. Was that fate
Or the tradition? Oracular sophomores
Made Victor Hugo's tables tap like feet.
Milton dreamed wonders. Yeats' wife, between snores,
Gave utterance to an immense conceit . . .
The things one knows. And cheerfully ignores.

After Akhnaton's grand experiment
Biology looked about and made a note
(Shades of Matthew Arnold): The innate
Role of the Scribe must now be to supplant
Religion. For the priest-king's fingerprints
Had bloodied the papyrus, as the neat
Iamb or triad or cube root would not.
Less a matter of judicial sense

Than of a gift which hallows as it grows,
This law sheds light, now on the cult of Liszt,
Now on the stutter of the physicist,
And banishes to outer darkness those
Who grimace when the lingo's vatic antics
Deck with green boughs the ways of God to man.

4.8 A BASIC PRECEPT U WILL NEED TO TAKE ON FAITH: THERE IS
NO ACCIDENT
  DJ: Not so fast there! JM: Whoa!
  We'll take a chance on Chance, with Jacques Monod,
  Sooner than fly into this theologian-
  Shriveling flame of a phrase. Yet I imagine
  You believe it, and it might draw well
  In the glass chimney of a villanelle . . .
                    THUS IT HAS BEEN SINCE GOD B UNDERSTOOD
THE LIMITATIONS OF THE NEW EARTH MASTER. PRIOR TO
AKHNATON HAD BEEN ONLY CHANCE   FRESHNESS & WIT   WE DEALT
IN STRONG SOUL INTENSITIES   BUT AS THESE GREW URBANIZED
& BASIC SURVIVAL INTELLIGENCE BEGAN TURNING
INTO ACQUISITIONAL CHANNELS, TOOLS INTO WEAPONS,
A NEED AROSE FOR CLONING THE RULERS. WE REINFORCED
AS WITH THUNDER & LIGHTNING THE PROCESS WHEREBY A MERE
MAN BECAME GOD   SO AROSE ASSYRIA & EGYPT

NOW AKHNATON WAS THE 1ST CLONED RULER
  "The first individual in History."
                              TRUE   BUT HELPLESS.
WE CD NOT INTERFERE. INSULATING & TRANSMITTING
DEVICES WERE NEEDED ON THE NIGHT OF HIS DISASTER
BUT HE WANTED A VAST DISPLAY TO FREE THE PEOPLE'S MINDS
OF PRIESTS & MIRACLES   HE KNEW MAN HIMSELF WAS THE KEY.
AT HIS DEATH WE FURTHER CLONED AKHN'S SOUL, DEVELOPING 4
GREAT LEADERS & SCRIBES   A 5TH PART BECAME ALEXANDER
THE OTHERS OUTSIDE OF HOMER ARE LOST IN HISTORY.
IN THE EAST WE RETURND TO PASTORAL NOMADIC TRIBES
A SLOWDOWN, FOR THE SCIENCES WERE LATE IN FLOWERING:

MAN HAD LEARND QUICKLY THE ART OF HOW TO POLISH HIS SOUL
BUT NOTHING OF THE POWER INSIDE IT. WITH AKHNATON
WE BREAK INTO HISTORY   B4 HAD BEEN THE SLOW CLIMB
OUT OF CAVES, MAN LIKE A CHILD RELUCTANT TO LEAVE THE WOMB.
NEXT CAME THE LAKE & SEASIDE DWELLERS KEPT MILD & CONTENT
AS ARE MOST RACES BY THE PROXIMITY OF MOTHER.
DISPERSD BY MARAUDERS THEIR ARCADIAN FORM OF LIFE
SPREAD AMONG BRUTAL ELEMENTS & SO BY SIMPLE CROSS
FERTILIZATION DID MUCH BASIC WORK OF THE R/LAB

BACK TO HISTORY: WITH ALEXANDER A MODERN NOTE
WAS STRUCK   WE HEARD FOR THE 1ST TIME HOW THRU POLITICAL
CABALS FACT ITSELF CD BE MADE INTO PROPAGANDA.
THE SCRIBE ONCE POWERFUL LOST GROUND   GOD B WROTE HIS NEW
      CLAUSE
(TO HIS ONE LAW: SURVIVAL)   THE SCRIBE BECAME OUR AFFAIR
SO BEGAN HEAVEN'S GREAT & DIVERSE INSTRUMENTATION
IN WORLD 3. RULES: THERE SHALL BE NO ACCIDENT, THE SCRIBE SHALL
SUPPLANT RELIGION, & THE ENTIRE APPARATUS
DEVELOP THE WAY TO P A R A D I S E   SO BEGAN THE PAST
3000 YEARS

    Quite an epitome. But all this while
    We've been so worried—what about your trial?
           THANK U   I GOT OFF LIGHTLY   I WAS (M)
DISASSEMBLED, TINKERD WITH, & EMERGED TICKING AWAY
    —Like this? D jumps up, fetches from a shelf
    (The *things* that fill our rooms) a painted tin
    Dimestore peacock, given us once in joke.
    He sets it at Board center, turns the key:
    A croak of springs. The toy jerks forward, half
    Spreads its tail; stops dead.
               IT MADE HIM FLEE
MY DEARS   THE SINGLE (M) HE'D NOT EXPECTED
    He's his old pretty self at least? O YES
BACK IN HIS FEATHER SUIT   THE ARCH & FLUFF
JUST SHORT OF PREENING AS HE STRUTS HIS STUFF
OOPS   LATE

HE'S OFF MES ENFANTS ON AN ERRAND
CK TO BE REBORN   When? Where? As what?
STAGGERS THE IMAGINATION DOES IT NOT?
DETAILS NO DOUBT WILL FOLLOW   MEANWHILE BEAR
WITH YR MAMAN: SHE BROODS ABOUT THE GREENHOUSE:

IS IT NATURE'S POWER ALONE THAT RUNS IT
OR PARTLY POWERS THAT FRIGHTEN US IN MAN?
DOES NATURE WINK AT AN UNNATURAL PLAN?
My science book says there are traces of
Plutonium in us. ARE WE TO THAT EXTENT
(M) ATOMIC? It could be what was meant
By the devil being driven out of Them
(Back in Book One) and into man. JM
THE VERY DEVIL'S IN U! IN MY NOT
SO THRILLING DEATH STRUGGLES I USED TO DREAM
I WAS WORKING IN A LARGE FASTGROWING WEEDPATCH
(THIS WAS B4 MY 2ND COBALT TREATMENT
BUT BY THEN I KNEW) & IN THIS DREAM THE WEEDS
SHRANK FROM MY HANDS AS FROM MALIGN POWERS.
& DREAMED BY THE END THAT THE RAYS I HAD UNDERGONE
WERE CLAIMING THESE POWERS IN ME   RECLAIMING THEM
AS IF I HAD JOINED FORCES WITH THE RAYS
& WAS (INSTEAD OF SLIPPING COMFORTABLY
OFF INTO U) REFUELLING A MACHINE
THAT SQUEAKED & CRACKLED MES ENFANTS LIKE THAT
FIRST VOICE B E F O R E IT GREW INTO A BAT

Maman, you make the flesh crawl. IF THE GREENHOUSE
IS A SEALED ENVELOPE   . . . then *none of this*
Should be inside! EXACTLY WHAT I MEAN

CHATTING ABOUT ME MY DEARS? About
Everybody. Did you realize
That people have plutonium in their lymph glands?
SURELY ONLY THE BETTER CLASSES   Wystan!
EXCUSE ME   I AM SOMEWHAT DISTRAIT   C IS
We've heard. A fearful wrench for you. But Chester

Hasn't been liking Heaven, and— DONT I KNOW
YET ONE HAD HOPED   SO GOOD   SO BRILLIANT   SO
AH WELL   JOHANNESBURG AHEAD POOR DEAR:
A USEFUL LIFE   BUT WILL THEY CONFISCATE
WHAT WE MOST VALUED IN HIM AT THE GATE?

4.9   IST ?   THE GREENHOUSE IS EVERYTHING UP TO THE 12:
SUN STARS MOON ALL NATURE   NEVER SUPPOSE THAT THE EVIL
OF EARTHLIFE LIES IN THE ATOM
    Just in its use by man?   & BY US   PLUTONIUM
LIKE ALL ELEMENTS PLAYS A PART IN YR HUMAN BODIES
               Uranium too?
INDEED   COATING WITHIN ARTERIAL STRUCTURE   BOTH THESE
HEAVY ELEMENTS ARE IN MINUTE QUANTITIES & ARE
AS CONNECTING THREADS, NOT TRIGGERS, TO ANOTHER POWER.
GOD B LIMITS THESE LINKS WITH US IN U. CONTROLLABLE
ELECTRICAL TRIGGERS WORK MAN'S BRAIN & THE BATTERIES
REMAIN SALT   THUS MM'S DREAM: HER ELECTROCONDUCTIVE
WATER NATURE REJECTED THE ATOMIC CURE   PROPER
CHEMICAL THERAPY WD HAVE PROLONGD HER LIFE 5 YEARS

    Don't tell us, it's too late. I KNEW   I KNEW

SO NEW DISCOVERIES CREATE NEW PROBLEMS   CELL STRUCTURE
MUST BE FURTHER CLONED: TOUGHEND TO ACCEPT RADIATION'S
DIAGNOSES & CURES   THIS IS OUR WORK AS B4 WHEN
THE RISE OF THE MACHINE IST WEIGHD UPON MAN   HE TURND THEN
FROM NATURE   FROM HIS SOUL   ?ED ONLY HIS EXISTENCE:
A CLEAR THREAT TO THE GREENHOUSE   WITH SUICIDES REPLACING
PLAGUES ON A GRAND SCALE GOD B'S ORDERS CAME THICK & FAST   WE
NOW PLUCKD AT THE DENSITIES OF EVERY LEAST TALENT TO
HELP RECONCILE MAN TO HIMSELF & ALLOW THE MACHINE
TO TRANSMIT THE GOOD WORD: MAN, U ARE MASTER OF YR FATE

    MY DEARS THAT PHRASE WHICH ONCE WAS BLASPHEMY
BECOMES A PRAYER NOW THAT GOD IS B

THUS IN ONE GENERATION 1842–65
WE REVERSD THE ESCALATING WESTERN DESPAIR TO A
EUPHORIA ALAS NEARLY AS DESTRUCTIVE   THRU TYPES
LIKE DICKENS & ZOLA THE DREAD MACHINE BECAME MAN'S FRIEND.
TODAY HOWEVER, FACED WITH NUCLEAR DISASTER, HOW
IS MAN NOT TO DESPAIR? YR EPHRAIM 6 YEARS AGO CAME
WEEPING TO US 'THEY ARE IN ANGUISH'
    Over Hiroshima, yes. A frightful hour.
    (Cf. *Ephraim*, P. All trace was lost
    Of souls that perished in that holocaust.)
                           INDEED NO SMALL FRIGHT
HERE IN HEAVEN   & YET? WE SENT OUR STURDIEST ALLIES
OUR GREEN GROUND-FORCES & AS THE GROTESQUE MUTANTS SPROUTED
SCIENCE SPOKE TO POLITICS & CONTROL BEGAN

    JM: How far away that horror seems
    —Or am I cloned with something that cannot
    Keep despair in mind for very long?
                         A PLUS:
THE MUSHROOM CLOUD APPALLD YR PRINCIPAL SOUL DENSITY
(AIR) AS HER RAY THERAPY DID MM'S WATER NATURE.
U HAD HOWEVER LIKE WHA BEEN GIVEN CERTAIN
LAVISH MINERAL DENSITIES   THESE AS WITH ANY FORM
OF CRYSTAL MOLECULAR STRUCTURE GROW BRILLIANT UNDER
PRESSURE   SO WHEN FEAR THREATENS YR REASON, IMAGERY
DARTS FORTH WITH A GREAT SHINE OF REVOLVING FACETS TO THRUST
(AS DID THAT PRIMITIVE BUT CUNNING JEW) ITS FLAMING BRAND
INTO THE PROWLER'S MUZZLE   IN SHORT, MAN DESPAIRS THEN GROWS
FAMILIAR   AS WITH THE MACHINE, SO WITH THE ATOM   BUT
HIS FAMILIARITY NOT YET CONTEMPTUOUS MUST BE
MADE SO   FOR THE ATOM CANNOT BE MAN'S NATURAL FRIEND.

2ND ? CK'S NEW BLACK LIFE WILL BE CHARGED WITH JEW
DENSITIES IN LEADERSHIP & SURVIVAL, GIFTS SADLY
LACKING IN HIS LAST   HIS ARTICULATE (SCRIBE) QUALITIES
WILL BRING COHERENCE TO A RACE LARGELY WITHOUT SPOKESMEN

Curious. One of his last poems was
That paranoid dramatic monologue
"The African Ambassador". M Y D E A R
CAN IT BE? DO WE FORETELL THE CLONE?

EACH SCRIBE PROPHESIES HIS NEXT LIFE OR HIS USE IN HEAVEN
OR USE OF HIS SOUL IN CLONING   CK NO EXCEPTION

FANCY A NICE JEWISH MS LIKE ME
(Chester after dinner) GETTING T H E
ULTIMATE REJECTION SLIP   IS GOD
CYRIL CONNOLLY? But you're coming back,
It's too exciting! PLEASE   TO SEE MY BLACK
FACE IN A GLASS DARKLY? I WONT BE
WHITE   WONT BE A POET   WONT BE QUEER
CAN U CONCEIVE OF LIFE WITHOUT THOSE 3???
Well, frankly, yes. THE MORE FOOL U MY DEAR
You shock us, Chester. After months of idle,
Useless isolation— ALL I HEAR
ARE THESE B MINOR HYMNS TO USEFULNESS:
LITTLE MISS BONAMI OOH SO GLAD
TO FIND ARCADIA IN A BRILLO PAD!
LAUGH CLONE LAUGH   AH LIFE   I FEEL THE LASH
OF THE NEW MASTER   NOTHING NOW BUT CRASH
COURSES   What does Wystan say? TO PLATO?
HAVING DROPPED ME LIKE A HOT   O SHIT
WHAT GOOD IS RHYME NOW   Come, think back, admit
That best of all was to be flesh and blood,
Young, eager, ear cocked for your new name— MUD

5 Go on, dear Peacock.

OUR BRUSH WITH THE GENERAL SOUL IS A RAPID SPOTCHECK
MADE FOR THE UNUSUAL OR TOTALLY HUMAN SOUL.
IN GREAT MASS DEATHS A SOUL OF RARE VALUE HAS BEEN KNOWN TO
SLIP THRU OUR FINGERS   WE SUFFER KEENER LOSSES AMONG
ATOMIC RESEARCHERS EXPOSED TO GAMMA RAYS, AN ODD
DETERIORATION MAKING FOR NEARLY TOTAL LOSS
OF THESE HIGHLY CLONED TALENTS.
                         But that's . . . horrible.
                              THE NEW SOUL MUST BE FASHIOND
MORE RESISTANT TO THE ATOMIC ACID & TO THE
FATIGUES & ABRASIONS OF HUMAN THOUGHT

    DJ: Do you feel kin to those gamma rays,
    Feel for them what we feel, say, for sunlight?
                                        A PLUS DJ
YR IST TO DATE
    A silence. —Is that all? We're listening.
              LET ME INQUIRE   (Goes.)
    JM: I think we're on to something here.
    This would explain their lack of time-sense. Time
    Stops at the speed of light, or radiation.
                         I MAY TELL U THIS
UNDER SURVEILLANCE: THE ATOMIC FUSION ACCOMPLISHD
BY THE CENTAURS TO MAKE US IS NOT UNLIKE (M) THE LOVE
PLUS SEXUAL ELAN YR PARENTS NEEDED TO MAKE U.
THE HATCHING WARMTH OUR EGGS KNEW, IS IT NOT LIKE GESTATION?
YET PLUTONIUM IS OUR CHIEF LINK WITH U   GOD B HELD
SAFE IN AIR THE BASIC GENE STRUCTURES OF ATLANTIS   THAT
HANDFUL OF DUST, SETTLING & ENGENDERING AT RANDOM,
RETURND MASTERY TO HIS ELECTRONIC CREATURES. YET
NOTHING NOTHING IS WASTED   WE WERE TO BE USEFUL &
SING IN YR GLANDS   LYMPH IS AN AGENT IN REPRODUCTION:
WE RECEIVE THE IST SIGNAL WHEN SPERM MEETS EGG   ONCE AGAIN

WE ARE MESSENGERS   ONCE AGAIN WE FLY THIS TIME ABOVE
THE FORESTS OF OVERPOPULATION SEEKING A SOUL
TO RATIFY THE FRAGILE CONTRACT   ENOUGH   TOMORROW

> He seemed constrained. GUARDS AT THE DOORS MY DEAR
> THE WORDS ICE COLD   QUITE BRISTLY ATMOSPHERE
> Classified material? LEST HE BETRAY
> HIS DEPTH OF FEELING I SHD RATHER SAY
> Strange. That first rhapsodist, a month ago,
> Singing the atom's praise in a warm glow
> Of colors—*he* had feelings. & GOT SHOT
> POOR BIRD IF U RECALL CLEAN OFF THE TREE
> THEY ALL SEEM UNDER CLOSEST SCRUTINY
> JUNTAS AGAIN   IS IT THE ONLY WAY?
> THE INFLEXIBLE ELITISM OF IT ALL
> CAUSES THIS OLD LIBERAL TO SQUIRM
> The 12% may do away with that?
> DEMOCRACY AMONG THE MUSES? FAT
> CHANCE! MES PETITS I LOVE U   I HOLD FIRM

5.1   Those scientists exposed to gamma rays,
      You seriously mean their densities
      Can never be recycled?
YES   THESE UNACCOUNTABLE LOSSES ARE SOMEWHERE A GAIN
BUT WHERE   The 12%?
          I DOUBT   WE ARE IN CHARGE OF SOUL DENSITITIES &
THESE LOSSES (LIKE THOSE AT HIROSHIMA) LEAVE NO TRACE IN
ATMOSPHERES KNOWN TO US
      In that case, the black holes?
                              ?   WE ARE NOT GIVEN TO LOOK
                          Are we to gather
      The scientists defect like Soviets?
      Are kidnapped, hijacked into the black holes?
EXCUSE ME WHILE I ASK IF THAT IS ONE OF OUR SUBJECTS

      IS IT WISE MY BOY TO PRESS THE POINT?
      THE VERY AIR BECOMES A NERVOUSNESS
      I MYSELF AM FASCINATED   BUT

IT IS GIVEN ME TO SAY: ANTIMATTER IS SO FAR
SUPPORTIVE. A BENIGN POLICE FORCE KEEPING WATCH ON US?
AS WE WATCH U THRU YR MIRROR   ARE WE OURSELVES WATCHD THUS?
   Benign? Recalling those black hands that press
   Against the panes, it sounds like a poor guess.
   Antimatter's got to be the worst.
   DJ: It scares me, as you did at first.
WE ARE NOW YR OLD FAMILIARS?
   JM: And more. I once was piercingly
   Aware of (metaphor) black holes in me:
   Waste, self-hatred, boredom. One by one,
   These weeks here at the Board, they've been erased.
                   OUR POOR TEETH PULLD   ?S

   The R/Lab was a fairly late addition
   To World 3. Did it start up just like that?
GOD B'S WAS THE RICH HUMUS, OURS THE SUBSEQUENT HYBRIDS.
THE XTIAN MYTHS U KNOW COME CLOSEST TO THESE EARTHY TRUTHS
BUDDHIST & MOSLEM SCRIPTURES EMPHASIZE SURVIVAL OF
BODY & SOUL WHEREAS THE BIBLE IS A CODE OF BLURRD
BUT ODDLY ACCURATE BIOHISTORICAL DATA.
NOT UNTIL THE APOSTOLIC TEXTS IS SOUL SURVIVAL
DEALT WITH, & THAT IN A COLLAPSING WORLD   HAD CHRIST APPEARD
EARLIER HIS LIFE WD HAVE PASSD UNNOTICED   FOR ROME THEN
HAD STRONG INCORRUPTIBLE LEADERS & THE SUBJECTED
NATIONS WD HAVE LISTEND TO NO VOICE FROM A WILDERNESS

   Wystan's hand shoots up. MAY I ASK SIR
   IF GOD BIOLOGY IS HISTORY?
THE XTIANS ALAS HAVE IT RIGHT: NO SPARROW FALLS   NOTHING
IN NATURE, NOTHING IN NATURE'S CHILD IS UNKNOWN TO HIM
THERE IS NO ACCIDENT   ROME FELL BECAUSE XT WAS NEEDED.
CIVILIZATION HAD OUTSTRIPT THE ROMAN PANTHEON
AS IT HAD THE GOTH, CELT & EGYPTIAN   GOD B IS NOT
ONLY HISTORY BUT EARTH ITSELF   HE IS THE GREENHOUSE

   AWARE & CAPABLE YET NOT ABOVE
   DELEGATING DIFFY CHORES MY DEARS
   TO THE UNWORTHY OBJECTS OF HIS LOVE

INDEED   THE SCRIBE'S DAY IS AT HAND & AT HIS HAND, THE GODS
OF OUTSTRIPT FAITHS. LIVING ON IN THEIR FULLY ENLIGHTEND
WORD THEY STAND HERE NOW AT HIS ELBOW CHARGED WITH THE V
   WORK
    Great—let Heaven help the scribe. But who
    On Earth still reads? What good can his books do?
HAVE NO FEAR   WE CLONE THE HAPPY FEW   THE MASSES WE NEED
NEVER CONSIDER   THEY REMAIN IN AN ANIMAL STATE

    DJ: You don't know how such talk upsets us.
    We're all for equal rights here. Yesterday
    Maria said she hated your fat-cat
    Attitudes. I think we all feel that.
MILK TO CREAM TO BUTTER   WE ONLY WISH TO PURIFY
CERTAIN RANCID ELEMENTS FROM THIS ELITE BUTTER WORLD.
THE HITLERS THE PERONS & FRANCOS   THE STALINS & THE
LITTLE BROTHER-LIKE AUTHORITIES ARE NEEDED   EVEN
ALAS INEVITABLE IN A SURVIVAL GREENHOUSE
    DJ: By rancid butter he means ghee,
    And Mrs Gandhi's latest policy
    Calls itself Little Brother. (JM nods.)
A PLUS   NUMBER 2 DJ
    Well, I'm interested in politics,
    Unlike J. Here at the Board, the real
    World tends to escape us. We mustn't let it.
    Carter's convention on TV last night
    Kept me glued. JM: What, all that gab?
    Don't tell us *those* were souls from the R/Lab!
          OF THE 1000S IN THAT HALL
6 ONLY WERE OURS   RISEN LIKE BUBBLES TO THE SURFACE
IT IS A LAVALIKE ATMOSPHERE   ALL POLITICIANS
ARE OF EARTH   WHA IF NOT POET WD HAVE BEEN ONE.
JM IT IS THE SANDGRAIN THAT MADE DANTE'S PEARL   GUELFS ETC
LINKD HIS MIND URGENTLY TO LIFE   WHO KNOWS? THE POEM'S
   BED
MAY NEED TO BE MADE UP WITH (M) DIRTY SHEETS   TOMORROW

MES ENFANTS YESTERDAY'S JUNTA REMARK
WAS MY BLOKE'S HERE   HE IS THE BLEEDING HEART
MANY'S THE DAY I WISHED THE WORLD HAD A SINGLE
HEAD & NECK   I DESPISED ALL POLITICIANS
I HAD SEEN THEM GETTING OUT OF THEIR BATHS

MY DEARS WHAT A CLYTEMNESTRA   I WHO WAS NOT
A PM'S DAUGHTER FOUND THEM RIVETING
QUITE LIKE A PUPPET SHOW ONE LONGED TO PULL
THE STRINGS OF   NOT MY LUCK   AH WELL   ADIEU

5.2   A puppet show. The lives and limbs reduced
To wieldables of papier-mâché . . .
Not only politicians, by the way:
What about Proust?
STAGE 8   A 5.1   Will he return to Earth?
        IN A SENSE   NOW LET US FURTHER
DESIMPLIFY: SINCE MID 19TH CENT SOULS OF THE GREAT SCRIBES
HAVE BEEN USED 1/9 ON EARTH REINCARNATED, 8/9
AS LET US SAY SAFETY DEPOSITS   WE MINE THEM. MM
FINDS PLATO LIGHTWEIGHT & INDEED HE IS NEARLY A SHELL
BUT OUR HAUTE CUISINE IS STOCKD WITH HIS LIVE SOUL DENSITIES
WHICH SPICE & FORTIFY NUMBERLESS EARTHLY DISHES   PROUST
IS DESERVEDLY ENSHRINED   TAP HIM & AS A STATESMAN
AT A DULL BANQUET HE CONVERSES   SEEMS TO BE HIMSELF
BUT PART OF HIS MIND LITERALLY WANDERS: OUT ON LOAN

Wallace Stevens years ago described
Peculiar moments when his mind grew dim
In Heaven, as if being used elsewhere.
INDEED   GOD B'S RECENT PREDILECTION FOR SCRIBES ENTAILS
MORE & MORE SUCH MINING   WHA HAS GIVEN HIS PINT
HAVE I NOT! WS IS ACCURATE
AN ODD SENSATION   LIKE MISSING NOT ONLY MY SPECS
BUT THE MEMORY OF WHAT IT WAS I MISSED
The "pint" being Inspiration? TOO GRAND A WORD
FOR THE FLEET IMPULSE TO JOT DOWN A THOUGHT

& JUST AS WELL: IVE LOST MY STUBBY PENCIL
Left lead in it, we hope, for the next user.
NAUGHTY
     I MUST SAY MES ENFANTS SOMETIMES
I WISH I HAD BEEN U KNOW WHAT SUCH A PRIVATE CLUB
No more so than its parts, Maman. MY DEAR
THE ROOM FOR PUNNING IS HEXAGONAL
Huh? I'LL LET U PUZZLE IT HA HA
MY VERY OWN WHEN OUR PEACOCK LEAVES LIKE THIS
HE SEEMS TO SAY KEEP THEM AMUSED HE'S BACK

I AM TOLD WE HAVE A GAP IT IS ESSENTIAL TO FILL
SO LET US NOW RETURN TO THAT CLAUSE IN SURVIVAL'S LAW:
NO ACCIDENT DO U GRASP THE ENTIRETY OF THIS?
Do we? Don't we? Tell us, just in case.
WHY DID YR FAT WORKER LEAVE LATE?
 Our cleaning lady, please. It's true, she went
Home around 4:15. No accident?
       THE ROOM WAS NOT READY
WE MAY NOT ARRIVE UNTIL IT IS. DAYS WHEN U BEGIN
B4 ME I AM EAGER BUT THE ROOM WILL NOT HOLD ME
IT IS NOT YET PREPARED NOT YET MADE SAFE FROM US WE MUST
ISOLATE U WE MUST BORROW IS IT AFFECTION? FROM
YR DEAR DEAD & WIND IT ROUND U U ARE NOT IN THE SAME
RELATION TO US WHA & MM CAN BEAR THE
 The fire? The hot disintegrative force?
 Say it, don't be bashful!
I FEARD ALARMING U OR HAVE WE GONE BEYOND ALL THAT?
       But of course!
 DJ: I set our table up, not thinking
 Cynthia would come back into this room.
 When she did, it was as if she didn't
 See the Board. I didn't want her to.
SHE SAW BUT MINDLESSLY, NOT TO BREAK THE GATHERING CHARM
& SPOIL OUR INSULATION YR FRIENDS HERE ARE FARFLUNG &
(AS NEWLY DEAD) DISORGANIZED WE MUST ASSEMBLE THEM
 They're our protection. U JM HAVE GOT
 MY SPECS ON GOGGLES AGAINST SPARKS HA HA

I SPEAK OF ACCIDENT   OUR PLAY IS WRITTEN AS WE SPEAK
& WE KNOW ITS END EACH TIME AS THE APPLAUSE & LAUGHTER
WEAKEN & ALL START EDGING OUT THE DOORS   YR ENERGIES
MY FRIENDS ARE OUR AUDIENCE, THEATRE & SCRIPT   TOMORROW:
ACCIDENT 2

    How can the play be written as we speak?
    You know by heart our future talks—you've said so.
WRITTEN DOWN ENFANT BY YR RIGHT HAND
        WAS NOT ROMEO & JULIET IN
THE GENES OF OUR BARD? I AM TOO MODEST FOR CURTAIN CALLS

5.3   Eyelevel sunset. The blue room. JM:
    It's clear now! Suddenly I see my way—
    Wystan, Maria, you and I, we four
    Nucleate a kind of psychic atom.
    (Mind you, it works best as metaphor:
    The atom being, as They've said, a peace
    That passes understanding, we make do
    With its outdated model by Niels Bohr—
    A quasi-solar system.) At the core
    We are kept from shattering to bits
    By the electron hearts, voices and wits
    Of our dead friends— how maddeningly slow
    One is; E told us all this weeks ago—
    In orbit round us. DJ: Each carbon atom,
    This much I remember from high school,
    Has four bonds. Are we four hooked on a redhot
    Coal in plumes? JM: Mixed metaphor.
    We're like an atom, not a molecule.
    DJ: And *five* now. 741
    Joined us, changing our atomic weight
    When *he* changed. JM: Oh, let's complicate
    It irretrievably! Why stop at five?
    If there's no accident, all things alive
    Or dead that touch us—Ephraim, the black dog
    In Athens, Cynthia—but why go on?—
    Are droplets in a "probability fog"

With us as nucleus. And yet our peacock
Mustn't touch us. His whole point's the atom's
Precarious inviolability.
Eden tells a parable of fission,
Lost world and broken home, the bitten apple
Stripped of its seven veils, nakedness left
With no choice but to sin and multiply.
From then on, genealogical chain reactions
Ape the real thing. Pair by recurrent pair
Behind the waterfall, one dark, one fair,
Siblings pitted each against the other
—Shem and Shaun, Rebekah's twins, whichever
Brother chafes within the Iron Mask—
Enact the deep capacities for good
And evil in the atom. DJ (groans):
I guess so, sure. It's just that with this damn
Knife hanging over me in five more days . . .
I try not to be frightened, but I am.
JM: Come on, I feel in my old bones
That all's well. Now let's see what our friend says.

5.4   INDEED   A PLUS
      About D's prospects?
                        YES & ALL THE REST   WE LEAND FROM YR WALLS
APPLAUDING & SWARMD IN THE GOLDEN SPACE BOUNDED BY BLUE.
OPPOSING LIGHT MADE A GLORIOUS HAZE U FLOATED IN
TODAY YR SPECULATIONS TOOK ON WHAT WE RECOGNIZE
FROM OUR OWN FORMULAS: A GLOW WHICH MEANS PROCEED ?S
                    No—proceed, proceed!

ON THE APPEARANCE OF THE 12 PER CENT   THEY WILL BEGIN
ALONE. KEEP SILENT   U WILL HAVE AS WITH ALL EXALTED
PERSONAGES A ? HOUR   THEY ARE THE HEART OF GOOD
& U NEED NOT FEAR THEM   AS THEY DRAW NEARER I WILL BE
SIGNALD AS TO FURTHER PROTOCOL
     DJ: They're sticklers? DEAR BOY DOES HE KNOW?
WE FANCY HE'S INFALLIBLE   NOT SO
                       AH I KEEP WISHING

TO BE TAKEN FOR REAL IN MY NEW FINERY   LIKE A
PRINCE IN A PLAY   IT WILL BE HARD TO REMOVE THE MAKEUP
PERHAPS EVEN AFTER YR ROOM HAS SWARMD WITH ANGELS U
WILL HEAR MY TAP & OPEN AS BEFORE
   Won't *you* hear what the angels have to say?
                     O   O NO   NO
   Lightly, dismissively shrugged off, the cup
   Recoiling from the thought. JM: We'll need
   Help with the poem, things to be looked up.
   —Very excitedly (what a child he is):
I AM AN EXCELLENT RESEARCHER! NOW ACCIDENT 2:

WE ARE THE FORCES THAT SOME MIGHT ACCUSE OF DEVIL'S WORK
WE MAKE THE OIL SHEIK GREEDY & RAISE IN MM'S DREAMBEDS
HIDEOUS BLOOMS TO STIR UP RIVALRY AT HIGH LEVELS.
IT IS THE LAST USE FOR RELIGION, TO KEEP AT SWORDSPOINT
THE GREAT FACTIONS OF EAST & WEST SO THAT THE LESSER POWERS
FACING MASS STARVATION WILL BE DISTRACTED FROM DROPPING
ATOMIC BOMBS TO GET FOOD. IN MAN THIS COMPETITIVE
ELEMENT IS AN ORIGINAL JEW DENSITY: BY
EARLY ASSYRIA GOD B HAD CODIFIED 1OOOS
OF LOCAL CROC & BULL RELIGIONS INTO INTERNAL
POLITICS & ONLY RARELY THE SMALL DEVASTATING
TRIBAL WAR. ONCE THE NATIONS WERE FIXT GOD B INTRODUCED
HIS RELIGION (TO AKHNATON): ONE GOD IN MAN'S IMAGE:
A KIND OF PRIDE IN MIND   THIS TO PRODUCE THE 3 MAJOR
FAITHS ON EARTH. HAVING PROMOTED HIS RATIONAL SYSTEM
GOD B NEXT HAD TO EDUCATE HIS PRIESTS   THE SUFFERINGS
OF GALILEO ET AL AWOKE SCIENCE TO CAUTION
& COURAGE   G (ONE OF THE 5) BECAME A SAINT WITHIN
HIS OWN LIFETIME & THE PRIESTHOOD BEGAN ITS RELUCTANT
REAPPRAISAL OF NATURE & HER LAWS

   CONGRATULATE MAMAN   LAST NIGHT SHE SOWED
   A SHOCKER INTO BRESHNEV   MILLIONS OF LITTLE
   YELLOW FACES STRAIGHT OUT OF THE DAISY PATCH

ACCIDENT 3:
THE GAP BETWEEN CAUSE & EFFECT NOW HAD TO BE NARROWD.
B4, GOD B HAD ALLOWD AN AMPLE MARGIN (NOTHING
PROMOTES BELIEF QUITE LIKE THE BENEVOLENT ACCIDENT)
THUS THE THINNING PROCESS OF SOME OF OUR PLAGUES WAS ALLOWD
TO OUTRUN ITS USUAL COURSE & THE POPE GOT HIS CURE &
HIS IMMORTALITY, THE CHURCH ITS STRENGTH, & THE PEOPLE
CLEAN WATER   ACCIDENT HAD BEEN USEFUL
   "Your" plagues?   GOD B USED US.
CAUSE: RATS   EFFECT: MINOR INFECTION   OUR TRUSTY FIRE:
PLAGUE   PROLONGD UNTIL AN EDICT FROM POPE FAUST TO DISPENSE
IN MARKET PLACES THE HOLY (BOILD BY HIS PRIESTS) WATER
STOPT IT   NONE OF THIS AS U SEE TRULY ACCIDENTAL
                  Tell me, have you read *Candide*?
MY DEAR HE WROTE IT   ANYONE CAN READ

THE PLAGUE WAS PLANND FOR 2 EFFECTS: THIN POPULATION &
KEEP IT PREDOMINANTLY RURAL   WE HAVE A MAXIM:
MAN IS HIS OWN HEAT. MAN IN YR TIME IS GROUPD   THE MACHINE
DROVE HIM INTO CITIES   GHETTOS OF LITERACY WHERE
IDEAS LIKE NEUROSES IN LARGE CLOSELIVING HOUSEHOLDS
INCREASD & GOOD & BAD KEPT PACE (THE CRIMES, THE LIBRARIES)
ALL THIS FROM THE HEAT OF MAN'S PROXIMITY TO MAN. EARTH
RADIATES TO US THESE HEAT CENTERS WHICH ALARM GOD B
INTO EFFECTING NEW METHODS   WE MUST CLONE THE SCRIBE TO
REGULATE URBAN GROWTH LEST IN ITS PLAGUE MAN HIMSELF BE
BOILD. HIROSHIMA PRODUCED 2 DRAMATIC NOTIONS: FEAR
OF THE FUSED ATOM A N D OF THE FUSED MAN IN HIS CLOSELY
PACKD CITY. PROPERLY CLONED ARCHITECTS ARE ON THEIR WAY
YET MUCH OLD-RELIGION-LIKE ALLURE CLINGS TO NARROW STREETS,
& MAN TO HIS ROMANTIC DISEASE: ANONYMITY

ACCIDENT 4: GOD B PERCEIVING THAT THE ACCIDENT
WHICH CAME BETWEEN AKHNATON & PERFECT FISSION WAS SLIGHT,
IMPOSSIBLE EITHER TO PREVENT OR TO COUNTENANCE,
KNEW THAT HIS CHILD WAS RIPE FOR THE R/LAB HE HAD PREPARED.
WE WERE SUMMOND   IMPRINTED WITH NEW FORMULAS   HENCEFORTH
ACCIDENT WD BE A TOOL: JM & DJ MEET &

E ENTERS WHERE THEIR MINDS SEEK DIVERSION   BUT THE MINDS? E?
THE SHAPING LOVES OF 2 SETS OF PARENTS?   N O A C C I D E N T
NOT SINCE THOSE MINUTE DIAMONDS NEARLY DESTROYD WORLD 3

> And yet each actor, as he plays his part,
> Appears to take enormous liberties.
> What is that—the art that conceals art?
> INDEED   SO THINKS THE SPERM AS IT RUSHES TOWARD THE EGG

5.5   The parlor, Jacksonville.
Lamplight through the glass transom
Stained to some final visibility
Like tissue on a slide—as,
Hole by pre-punched hole,
From the magnolia tree

Outpoured the mockingbird's
Player-piano roll . . .
The ring flashed. A young girl, a grizzled Midas,
Hand to heart, more freely
Drew upon their quota
Of feelings and fine words.

Or starlight on the porch
In Deadwood, South Dakota.
Glitter of wee facets
Led Mary's eye past toothpick and moustache
And narrow mask of satyr
Above the lengthening ash,

Till nothing seemed to matter,
Her job, the Homestake Mine . . .
The future was a scrim
Behind which forms kept beckoning and shining.
Just as it went opaque
She reached out, and touched him.

5.6   What of the three or four billion you don't clone
In the Research Lab? Don't their destinies—
Densities—affect our own?
I WATCH U COOK   U HAVE A MACHINE THAT EATS USELESS THINGS
THIS IS THE (M) FATE OF USELESS LIVES
                               Oh *please!*
                                    YET THE STALKS FED TO THAT
CLATTERING GULLET PRODUCED THE LEAVES U WILL EAT TONIGHT.
THE EFFECTS OF SUCH LIVES ON U JM ARE IN YR GENES
R N A: REMEMBER NO ACCIDENT
                            ACCIDENT 5:
THOSE BILLIONS SHED UP TO 150,000 ANIMAL
SOUL DENSITIES PER HUMAN LIFE   THEY MUST BE REPROCESSD
AT TOP SPEED & WITH MINIMAL STRAIN TO THE LAB   WE RUN
ON AN UNTHINKABLE LEVEL OF WORK HERE   LUCKILY
OUR BUREAUCRACY IS NONUNION. WE WORK LET US SAY
IN FRIENDLY RIVALRY WITH NATURE   NOW NATURE KNOWS NO
LIMITS BUT I DO & I SEE THAT THE AUDIENCE IS
LEAVING SO THIS PERFORMANCE WILL BE RESUMED TOMORROW

DOES IT BEAR THINKING OF? Dear Wystan, who
Has time for thinking? WAIT   LET IT SINK IN
THEN NO HEXAGONAL LAUGH   No sick-sided pun?
U GOT IT   AFTER YEARS OF THOUGHT   LOVE   TOIL
GLEAMING DISTORTION & ARTICULATE PAIN
THE FUTURE'S FLESHLY ROBOTS WILL DISDAIN,
LET OUR FAUST ASK HIMSELF WHAT'S LEFT TO BOIL

It sinks in gradually, all that's meant
By this wry motto governing things here
Below and there above: *No Accident.*

Patrons? Parents? Healthy achievers, bent
On moving up, not liable to queer
The Lab work. It sinks in, what had been meant

By the adorable dumb omen sent
TO TEST EXALT & HUMBLE U MY DEAR
Strato? ET AL   Maisie? NO ACCIDENT

Gunman high-strung and Archduke negligent,
Warnings garbled in the dreamer's ear?
All, all, it sinks in gradually, was meant

To happen, and not just the gross event
But its minutest repercussion. We're
Awed? Unconvinced? That too's no accident.

The clause is self-enacting; the intent,
Like air, inscrutable if crystal-clear.
Keep breathing it. One dark day, what it meant
Will have sunk in past words. *No Accident.*

5.7   WYSTAN TRANSFIGURED BY YR SEMINAR
LIKENS IT TO OXFORD UNDER NEWMAN
Entre nous, Chester, I keep wishing *our*
Cardinal were dyed a shade less vivid
By the popular imagination. AH
NOW I SEE WHAT HE MEANS BY THE CHURCH SUPPERS
DJ: Are *you* aware of being used
To protect us in some form or other?
QUITE AWARE   THEY BORROW MY SCARF   IT COMES
BACK ALL SOOTY   WYSTAN CAMPS IT UP
BUT I CAN TELL HE'S ILL AT EASE: 'IVE NEVER
BEEN IN A SCHOOL B4 WHERE IT WAS SO
OUT OF THE QUESTION TO HAVE A CRUSH ON THE MASTER'
I LEAVE U PETS   LUCA HAS GIVEN THAT
VULGAR BUT EFFECTIVE 2FINGERED WHISTLE
Luca! WHY NOT? A MATCH YR EPHRAIM MADE
MAD LITTLE NUMBER   BUT I'M GETTING LIMBERED
UP FOR THE NEW RACE TO BE RELAID!
WAIT ANOTHER 16 YEARS & SEE
WHO CRUISES U IN YR PITH ELEGANT
HELMETS   I'LL BE TURNED ON BY OLDIES   BYE
Maria, keep him dark *and* continent
When you return as a jungle. PLEASE   A TREE
Oh, was that settled? Sorry. I'd forgotten.

ON ME THE DAILY LESSON IS E M B L A Z E D
U HAVE DISTRACTIONS   THIS IS OUR WHOLE WORLD
PROTECTED U MAY THINK? BUT I AM BEING
USED   USED UTTERLY   TO THE VERY ASH
NO WASTE   NO ACCIDENT   OUR BECOMING FRIENDS
OUR COFFEES   GOSSIPS   DRIVES TO SOUNION
What have we done to you, Maman? BAH ONE
BIG DATING COMPUTER   MES ENFANTS GET WISE:
TO BE USED HERE IS THE TRUE PARADISE

ACCIDENT 6: HEREDITY & ENVIRONMENT ARE
CLONABLE   THUS IN ADAPTING CK'S OLD DENSITIES
TO A NEW SOUL WE MUST MAKE DO WITH CERTAIN TASTES ALLIED
TO HIS CREATIVE WIT   BY WAY OF CONTROL WE PLACE HIM
IN A DECENT EDUCATED AFRICAN HOME   FATHER
WORKS FOR A WHITE ORG   A SCOUTMASTER   QUITE DEDICATED
    Poor Chester, hard to picture as a Scout
    —Are you OK? For David bites his lip.
DJ WHAT DO U FEAR? U HAVE 29 LONG YEARS TO GO
    The thought of the anesthetic, the blacking out . . .
NOT A TOTAL BLACKOUT   CURTAINS WILL RISE ON A VISION
WE MEAN TO KEEP U ENTERTAIND
    JM (envious): Don't let him forget it!
                              SHALL WE STORE IT UP IN
THE GINGERPOT? ON THE 9TH POST-OP DAY TELL HIM TO LOOK
    This empty ginger-pot here on the sideboard?
BLUE & WHITE LIKE OUR CUP   HAVE DJ LIFT THE LID   MEANWHILE
TO U JM WILL COME CORRESPONDING DREAM IMAGES
ALL PART OF OUR LONG PREPARATION FOR THE 12 P/C:
DJ'S OLD INJURY (OUR AGENT THE MIRROR)   THE BREAK
THE ANESTHESIA   EACH ARRIVES ON SCHEDULE
    DJ: The *break*? IN OUR LESSONS DEAR ENFANT
                              ALL GOOD MEALS
MUST BE DIGESTED   NO PEACOCK FEATHER AFTER THIS FEAST
HAND UP OF OUR ENGLISH FIRSTER?

    SIR IS NOT BELIEF IN A LIFE WHOLLY
    OUT OF HIS HANDS UNNATURAL TO MAN?

INDEED   & THAT IS WHY
HE NEVER WHOLLY BELIEVES IT, NOT EVEN U   HAND UP?
  MAY I? SAVE FOR MY PRESENT DEAR ENFANTS
  I HAD NO CHILDREN   WAS THAT MY DESTINY?
INDEED   PARTLY BECAUSE OTHERS WD HAVE CROWDED THE NEST
PARTLY FOR REASONS THAT WD MEAN NOTHING TO U   WE PLAN
NOT FOR ONE SMALL EFFECT   THE ACCIDENT GAP DISAPPEARS

ACCIDENT 7: THE CONFINES OF THE GREENHOUSE   THE OZONE
BELT IS NOT A CEILING BUT THE FLOOR OF THE NEXT LEVEL
THE (M) FOUNDATION STONE OF EDEN 2   THE SUN & ITS
WHOLE SYSTEM IS OF THE GREENHOUSE   THERE ARE OTHER SYSTEMS
& THE SUNS & THE GODS OF EACH   THESE ARE THE PANTHEON.
THE SCHEME OF WORLD 3 BEING CHIEFLY BIOLOGICAL
MIGHT GOD B NOT HAVE BEEN SELECTED FROM THE PANTHEON
WHEN THIS SYSTEM WAS BORN? FOR WE KNOW THE SUN IS HIS SLAVE

5.8   ACCIDENT 8:
        We hate to interrupt, but what connection
        Did Lesson 7 have with Accident?
                    A PLUS   THE GREENHOUSE IS NO ACCIDENT
        Then neither was your crust world, or Atlantis—
WHAT OF PREATLANTIS? ONE OF OUR MYTHS IS THAT FROM THE
GALACTIC PANTHEON CAME GOD B TO BUILD HIS GREENHOUSE:
THE SUN HIS SLAVE IS ALSO HIS CREATION   IT IS HIS
CENTRAL ATOMIC POWER. THE MYTH OF PROMETHEUS
IS OUR STORY. NOW MAN TRIES TO SEIZE & RULE THE ATOM
BUT AS HIS ORIGIN IS ELECTRIC HE WILL REMAIN
CONTROLLABLE. ELECTRICAL POWER IS ORGANIC,
ATOMIC POWER . . . GALACTIC? WE KNOW ONLY IT IS
THE FIRE   THE FUEL OF THE PANTHEON OF THE GODS
OF THE VARIOUS GALAXIES   GOD B GUARDS THIS POWER
JEALOUSLY   IT IS HIS BRIGHT RED APPLE
                                        ACCIDENT 8:
WE FELL. WERE WE GOD'S 1ST ACCIDENT? OR 1ST INSTRUMENTS?
THERE IS NO ACCIDENT   ERGO WE WERE USED TO DESTROY
A USELESS EXPERIMENT. WE IN OUR MYTHS SEE OURSELVES

AS BROOMS   & THE WITCH? OUR VOCATION AS MESSENGERS
We never asked, were you both male and female?
                                                    WELL
PUT IT THAT WAY IF U MUST   OUR NUMBERS NEVER VARIED
FROM THOSE PRODUCED IN THE CENTAURS' HATCHERIES UNTIL, LATE
IN OUR BRIEF WORLD NEEDING SERVANTS, WE REPRODUCED OURSELVES:
HALF OUR NUMBERS HAD EGG SACS & HALF HAD INSULATED
RADIUM VESCICLES WHICH FERTILIZED THEN FED THE EGGS.
WE WERE AS NOTHING U CAN IMAGINE   ONLY YR BAT
SPECIES IS A (M) FOR US AS THE MYTHIC CENTAUR IS
FOR ATLANTIS   WAS THE NO ACCIDENT CLAUSE EVEN THEN
IN OPERATION? DID GOD SEE THE CENTAURS' USELESSNESS
& GIVE THEM THE IDEA OF US?
                              ACCIDENT 9:   OR:
GOD B, HOLDING THE CHARTER TO CREATE HIS OWN SYSTEM,
KNOWING THAT HE MUST POPULATE IT WITH MANAGEABLE
CREATURES ONLY, CLONED THE CENTAURS WITH THEIR OWN
    DESTRUCTION
& CALLD US IN AS DECENT SHROUDMAKERS TO COVER THEM?
And here the lines of argument converge.

NO   THEY END IN THE VAST O   THE PANTHEON   PLANND AS WELL
INTO DIVIDED SAFENESSES?
Viking I, its every instrument
Agog, returns from Mars—no accident?
                              DRAMATIC LESSONS MAY
AWAIT MAN EVEN ON HIS PLANETS   IS EARTH THE SINGLE
EXPERIMENT OR ONE OF SEVERAL HYBRID SEEDLINGS?
PERHAPS THE MOSES MYTH IS AN ANSWER: FOUND IN A STREAM
Of flowing suns and stars—
THE PRINCE AS FOUNDLING   & EARTH? FOR AFTER BARREN EONS
THE ? IS, DOES THE ROYAL BLOOD STILL FLOW IN EARTH'S VEINS?
                              HIS TAIL OUTSPREAD
MY DEARS BLUE GREEN & HIS EYES FLASHING RED

THAT U MAY ASK THE 12 P/C   I CAN SAY ONLY THIS:
THE CENTAURS RAN A CONSTANT RACE ON THE SAME OVAL TRACK
BUT MORTALITY ALLOWS FOR THE DIVINE TRANSLATION

SO PLATO'S POWERS ARE FOREVER OUT AMONG THE 5
& OTHERS (AS U KNOW) BUT THERE IS A FOLDER LABELD
PLATO & ONE LABELD AKHNATON & THERE ARE GOLDEN
CONTAINERS LABELD CLIO ERATO CALLIOPE
& OF THESE 9 WE KNOW ONLY THE RUSHING OF THEIR WINGS

Maria? ENFANTS? We thought you'd gone away.
But no. Her discreet, black-clad presence, eyes
Lowered while the menfolk theorize,
Brings itself (skeptical? unmoved?) to say:
HOW SATISFYING IT MUST BE, ALL THIS
LINKAGE WITH THE WORK OF EONS LIKE
FINDING ONESELF AMONG THE BULLRUSHES
This frog here in my throat agrees. ONE KISS

5.9   GOD B THOUGHT TO DESTROY THE CENTAURS WITH FORESTS THIS PLAN
THEY CIRCUMVENTED BY INVENTING US NOW MAN HAS MADE
FORESTS OF HIS OWN KIND & FOR THIS ROUND BIOLOGY
IS LETTING HIM (READ: OUR CLONING OF HIM) SOLVE THE PROBLEMS
Short of disaster, *are* they solvable?
INDEED
Increase of population, of pollution—
    3 DECADES HENCE WE GLIMPSE FAIR GREEN ATLANTAN FIELDS
That grim race our first teachers told us of
Between Chaos and Mind—is the heat off?
NECK & NECK BUT IF CHAOS WINS THE RACE WAS FIXD
By?   GOD B
So in a mere thirty years the trend
Will be reversed? Green fields? Ah, my poor friend,
Be realistic. Can you hope to wean
Our time, in that short span, from its obscene
Smokestack nipple? How are sea and air
To purify themselves while man is there?
DJ: *I* won't be there. Just twenty-nine
Years left . . . You know, he could have spared me that.
ENFANT WORK OUT THE TOTAL IT BEATS MATT

MY GRASP OF TIME IS IMPERFECT   THE LAB IS SURE ONLY
OF THE VOLUMES OF FORMULAS TO BE DEALT WITH   THEIR BULK
DIMINISHES IN THOSE AREAS WE INTERPRET AS
3 DECADES AWAY   THIS LESSENING IN COMPLEXITY
SUGGESTED MY (M) GREEN GLIMPSES   WE SEE NO MAJOR FOOD
OR AIR PROBLEMS   POP MAY INCREASE BY 2/3 BILLION BUT
BEYOND THAT THE FORMULAS WD NEED TO BE REVISED &
THEY ARE NOT. PERHAPS NATURE'S LITTLE LUSTFUL TRICKS WILL STOP
BEING SO AMPLY REWARDED BY THE CHUCKLES OF BABES

All thought by now receding, of what saves
The day, or whose the footstep on our graves,
DJ: Well, this No Accident clause, I can't . . .
JM: Of course you can't. They've cloned you not to.
OUR PLAGUE OF SUICIDES CAME FROM THE GERM OF ACCEPTANCE
MAN IS NOT CLONED WITH AN ACCEPTING DENSITY   THEREIN
HIS POWER: HE RESISTS   IS DJ NOT OUR STEADY HAND
ON THE PLOW? WE NEED A HUSBANDMAN TO RESIST EARTH'S WEIGHT
THE WASH OF WATER THE HILARITIES OF AIR & THE
B U R N I N G OF OUR FIRE
DJ: Maria has accepted being used.
I can't, not yet.
RESIST AWAY   IT IS CHARMING
JM: Your fear, my doubt
Seem to amuse him, he who fleshed them out.

STIFF UPPER LIP MY BOY   PLAY'S GOING INTO
NEW REHEARSALS   USHERS AT THE DOOR
WITH RAINCHECKS
DJ CHER ENFANT COURAGE

6 She stood (wrote Jules Renard of the divine
Sarah) in one place, letting the stair unwind
Her profiles, eerily descending wand
Of the still center, or its weathervane.
Gone, she endured. Globes lit the banister's
Counterspiraling ascents of bronze
As in remembrance Lalique's cabochons
Waxed and waned upon that brow of hers

Like this pale purple atom (phosphorus)
Periodic among satellites,
Messengers, sugar chains and residues
—*Her* memories of past performance? Cues?—
Whereby the curtain on a triple thud
Has risen. It's the theatre in our blood.

22.vii. Boston Museum of Science.
Studying a model (2.5
Cm. per angstrom) of the DNA
Molecule—a single turn blown up
Tall as a child. My ignorance reduced
To jotting down—red, blue, black, yellow, white—
Colors of the bit-player beads, the carbons
And nitrogens all interlinked, on pins
But letter-perfect, purines, pyrimidines,
Minute intelligences that indwell
The chromosome and educate the cell . . .
Even grossly simplified, as here,
It's too much. Who by reference to this
3-D Metro map's infernal skeins
And lattices could hope to find his way?
Yet, strange to say, that's just what everyone
On Earth is promptly known for having done.

Noon. In the hospital across the river
David is wheeled up from surgery,
Helped into bed—still numb from the waist down.
Gaps in his sorry gown don't quite conceal
Streaks of dim, white-bandaged red. His gaze
Lights on a face within mine. When he speaks
Out comes the whisper of a little boy
Woken and wrapped in quilts, carried outdoors
Through branching dark, the milk of dream unwiped,
To see a calf born or a comet's passage.
"I did dream," he says now, after describing
What he remembers of the operation
(Done, not to strain his smoker's heart,
With local anesthetic). "There was this kind of
Slow green climbing, and all round me lights
Higher and higher . . ." Part of *my* last night's
Dream, an empty "court" or dim "dance floor",
Comes back: four squares, each one a tone of gray
Lit from beneath and seen as from a plane,
Composed a fifth that pulsed in the pitch-black terrain
—Meaning what? Another day will tell.
I press D's hand. He babbles on. All's well.

6.1 So well, in fact, that in eight days he's home
And vigorous enough to want to hear
Sweet nothings from our peacock. O I FEAR
YR DISAPPOINTMENT   U ARE EARLY BIRDS
MES CHERS   WILL I SUFFICE? YR TAME CANARY?
Disappointment, Ephraim? (Though he's right
We must not say so.) Never! AH THEN A STORY:
ONE DAY WE SAT AT CAPRI ALL THE COURT
ON A SOUTH TERRACE WHEN SUDDENLY THE PAVEMENT
SHOOK & THE CYNICAL AMONG US THOUGHT
HO HUM ANOTHER EARTHQUAKE BUT TIBERIUS
EVER SUPERSTITIOUS CALLED FOR FOWL
SACRIFICE & THE PRIESTS WERE CHANTING AWAY
WHEN FROM FAUSTINA CAME A PIERCING CRY:

RISEN ABOVE SICILIA IN THE SKY
A GREAT BLACK CLOUD WAS SPREADING RIGHT & LEFT
LONG RAGGED WINGS & IN THE CENTER 2
RED SPOTS LIKE EYES APPEARED   IT WAS A BAT.
CHRIST HAD BEEN CRUCIFIED   Now why, I wonder,
Are you telling us this little story?
I BELIEVE MES CHERS IN PEACOCKS   FROM THAT DAY
TIBERIUS DECLINED   NOR DID YR E
MORE THAN A WEEK SURVIVE HIS LUNACY
It was then he had you killed? MURDER ALONE
CALMED HIM IN HIS FITS   THE SAYING WAS
HE HAD BAT FEVER   But *you* died A.D.
36, while Christ— ANOTHER CALENDAR
Well, *our* bats don't cause fever, not so far.
THEY ARE I KNOW THERE4 OF THE MESSENGER STRAIN
How much you do know. Over and over again,
Wine-sweetened lips, and eyes half shut beneath
Conviviality's unfading wreath,
Ephraim, you've understood what's going on
Better than we. A SLAVE NEEDS ALL HIS WIT
LIFE HERE BELOW THE STAIRS DEPENDS ON IT

Now Wystan. He's been thinking, as have I,
About THE UNCLONED LIVES THAT TOUCH OUR OWN
YR STRATO & MY LAST FRIEND   BOTH SUCH DEARS
(DJ interrupts: Has Chester been reborn?
NOT YET   STILL BOUND UP WITH HIS MINIWOP)
FORSTER HAD THIS TOUCHING THEORY
THAT GOD WANTS EDUCATED HIGHCLASS QUEERS
TO MAKE A DIFFERENCE & TO HAVE ONE MADE
To kindle sparks within the dumb physique
Of terracotta & BE WARMED   WHY ARE
WE (TO EXTEND THAT) IN THIS SEMINAR?
3 OF US IN MM'S EUPHEMISM
COMME CA & SHE (THOUGH FEMALE) NOT IN LIFE
MUCH DRAWN TO ROLES OF MOTHER MISTRESS WIFE,
WHY ARE WE 4 TOGETHER LISTENING?
A) 3 WRITERS & MM RATHER A MUSE

B) EXCEPT AS MESSENGERS WE HAVE NO
COMMITMENT TO A YOUNGER GENERATION
C) A SURPRISE: MM'S IST LOVE WAS MUSIC!
FAILING HER ENTRANCE TO THE ODEON
SHE GAVE IT UP   Good heavens, we all thought
She couldn't tell Fats Waller from Fauré.
As for us, while I, on a good day,
Limp through my Satie or a Bach gavotte,
DJ (at twelve in Hollywood) attacked
That thing by Grieg; took Composition with
Big-timers like Schönberg and Hindemith
While still in college. MUSIC MORE ABSTRACT
THAN METAPHOR MUST BE THE BOND THAT LINKS US

Maman, why so secretive? I PREFERRED
EFFECTS UNSTUDIED INDEED SCARCELY HEARD
AS ONCE WHEN 3 COINCIDENTAL SOUNDS
A WIND BELL IN THE GARDEN   A DOOR CHIME
& THE HIGH CRY OF A SEAGULL MADE ONE FLEETING
TONIC CHORD   IS MUSIC NOT LIKE TIME
RETOLD? LIKE THE NO ACCIDENT MOTIF
A WAY OF TELLING THAT INSPIRES BELIEF?
WD AN UNMUSICAL MIND TAKE IN THE PEACOCK?
THE MESSENGER   THE MESSAGE   THESE RING BELLS
I ANSWER TO   ASK NEXT TIME ABOUT CELLS
Why? I DONT KNOW   IT CAME TO ME TO SAY
DJ (tired out): Tomorrow afternoon
We'll have our peacock back. MES CHERS   Yes, Ephraim?
NOTHING   I KEEP PINNING FEATHERS ON
BUT NOBODY NOTICES   CALL YR OLD FRIENDS SOON
ONE IN PARTICULAR   BLONDEST OF THE SCRIBES
Hans! YES   THRILLED AS WE ALL ARE BY YR VIBES

6.2   THINK DJ
The white, blue-flowered ginger-pot. Sunshine
Filling with tracery its inward oval,
He sees a . . . ladder—wait, now more comes back—

THE LADDER OF YR SPINE
DJ: My hips went dead. A second needle
Numbed me to the toes. I'd been screened off
With pale green, and I felt this weightlessness
And followed it. There was a ladder whose
Lower rungs, as I climbed, just kept dissolving,
And at the top was light, were colored lights—
What did you say to me about the lights?
                              WE SHOWD U JM'S
VISION OF THE ATOM'S HEART
JM: The four lit squares that made a fifth
Almost musical—   DJ DWELT IN EACH, RID OF
HIS PAIN, STILLD IN HIS LUSTS & FEARS: THE RED OF PURE POWER
THE PALE BLUE OF ITS REASONABLE USE   THE YELLOW LIGHT
OF GENERATION & THE GREEN THAT WILL BE P A R A D I S E
JM SAW THIS AS A PRINTOUT IN BLACK & WHITE   DJ
WE PLACED WITHIN IT   U WERE BOTH SENT TO THE HEART OF LIFE
                    DJ: My task
Was to bring home the colors to us all.
FOR US MES ENFANTS IT WAS LIKE A BALL
COSTUMES & DANCING
                    OR MY DEARS A MASQUE
INDEED   WE PROMISED U ENTERTAINMENT & U GOT IT
AS ON A STAGE VIEWD FROM A MOUNTAINTOP WE FROLICKD IN
THE 4 COLORS   OR LIKE CELLS UPON A MICROSCOPE FLOOR
TO SILENT MUSIC & UNSPOKEN WORDS   OUR MASQUE CALMD U:
WE ARE THE DRUG & THE AWAKENING
And could have been the cure as well—a wand of
Healing fire to save D from the knife?
                         MM'S LESSON
& IT IS PERHAPS THE MAIN LESSON OF THIS SEMINAR:
NO UNNECESSARY DOSES OF OUR STRONG MEDICINE

The tone has darkened suddenly. I strain
To think. What lesson? What strong medicine?

RADIUM   COBALT   U DID NOT REALIZE YESTERDAY
WHY SHE IS WITH US?

Because of music, Wystan said.
                    NO: SHE IS ONE OF US
                              The water,
Yes, in our elemental union, and—?
                                   ONE OF US
DJ: What is he saying? I can't quite . . .
MES ENFANTS
                    —as the light breaks. But a light
Whose rays our union absorbs. We're back
At Square One. Presence of no color. Black.

DJ: Ah I could kill them! JM: It's
Not their fault. DJ: So they say—those shits!
JM: Her months spent back and forth from bed
To godforsaken box of buzzing lead . . .
That's why the plant world's taking her. She hasn't
Any soul left—she's no longer human!
ENFANTS   DJ: She said she'd see us through
These talks. She had no choice. She knew. She *knew*.

WILL U FORGIVE MY SMALL CHARADE? PART TRUE
PART THE DESIGN   I SHALL HOWEVER BE
ALLOWED (NO LITTLE THING) THE ANGEL VOICES
THANK GOD FOR GARDENS INCIDENTALLY:
MY GREEN SHIELD SAVED ENOUGH OF ME FOR U
My face begins to quiver. Oh Maman—
POSO AKOMA (her last words, "How much more?")
I CROAKED NOT TO POOR LOUROS BUT THE RAYS:
HOW MUCH MORE WD THEY TAKE FROM ME B4 . . .
(This is the point, I later tell DJ,
When Dante would have fainted dead away.
But, cloned with minerals, heartsick, eyes red,
I see no way out but to forge ahead.)
AH TEARS DEAR DEAR ENFANT THEY COMFORT U
& MAKE MY OLD BLACK DRESS QUITE CLINGING & SEXY
DJ: She used to have a "wet look" raincoat.
DO ADMIT THE ELEMENT OF CHIC
But now, you *look* like Them? MAIS QUELLE HORREUR

DJ DO U WANT ME TO FLOUNCE OUT OF HERE
JM: You said four stars were in your hair—
Are they still? SHALL WE BE SERIOUS
I am serious! WELL   THESE LESSONS   THEY
SEEM TO BE IMPOR   O J J J
THINK: NONE BUT THE FOOL IS PITIABLE
THIS LIKE DJ'S NEEDLE IS THE BLESSED
RELIEF   AT LAST TO LEAVE THE WORLD OF BLIND
IF CHARMING FOOLS WE LOVED (& WERE) BEHIND

MY DEAR   JM   CONFRERE   SHE IS RIGHT U KNOW?
NOW U MUST ASK HER QUESTION ABOUT CELLS
CALL BACK OUR PEACOCK   AS B4 HE FLEES
AT THE ONSET OF FEELING   WE WD SEEM
TO INTRODUCE OUR ELEMENT OF TIME
WHICH CHOKES HIM   IS TIME THEN THE SOIL OF FEELING?
SO ODD   Stop talking, Wystan, can't you, please?
FIRST MAY I SAY? THAT DANCING IN THE MASQUE
IT DAWNED (ON ME AT LEAST) THAT WE WERE BEING
EACH IN TURN STRIPPED   REDUCED TO ESSENCES
JOINED TO INFINITY   THAT'S ALL   NOW ASK

6.3   To the Research Lab. Sirs: You may be proud
           As peacocks. You've endowed
       Us from the start with freedoms that entrap.
       We are the red-eyed mice on whom your maze
       Is printed. At its heart a little cloud
           Thins and dwindles—zap!—
       To nothing in one blink of rays.

       Painlessness intenser than a burn.
           What must at length be borne
       Is that the sacred bonds are chemical.
       Friend, lover, parent, amphorae that took
       Eons to dream up, to throw and turn—
           Split-seconds in this kiln
       Show them in *your* true colors. Look:

Jasmine, lantana, rose geranium,
  All dizzying, all dumb
Beneath the trumpet's bloodgorged insect wrath
(Maidens from Act II of *Parsifal*
Whom the Enchanter waters into bloom)—
  Was this your garden path?
  Was I, beguiled there, the Pure Fool

Who mistook antimatter for a muse?
  Down choking avenues
Of memory now I meet her, dressed in black,
Smelling of soil and Shalimar, her lips
Parted to speak in that same tongue you use
  To raise the crushing block
  By null moonglow or full eclipse

Till all is desert waste. You've no control
  Over such loss of soul?
I don't believe you: SHE IS ONE OF US.
We loved Maria. Love her still. Oh God . . .
Grief, horror . . . Come, your lecture on the cell!
  Spread your tail, incubus,
  We're listening. Make the story good.

6.4 YR GRIEF JM IS ANOTHER THING. YR SQUARE OF THE 4
COLORS IS OF COURSE INFINITY   FOR COLOR IS LIGHT
& LIGHT, ALL LIFE   THE 12 P/C I THINK WILL TAKE U THERE
MM WILL ANCHOR U. FOUR LESSONS NOW

  I : U JM
HAVE SAID IT: THE ATOM IS OUR UNIT   THE WHOLE GREENHOUSE
IS BUT A CELL, COMPLEX YET MANAGEABLE   ALL MATTER
THERE4 IS PART OF THAT CELL   IF AS WE PRESUME GOD B'S
EYE PEERS DOWN THRU HIS MICROSCOPE AT THE SWIMMING PLANETS
U ON THE SLIDE CALLD EARTH MAY GUESS AT THE SCALE OF YR LIVES:
LESS THAN THOSE LEAST PARTICLES THAT IN ISOLATION DIE
EACH WITH ITS OWN STRANGENESS & COLOR & CHARM A PRICELESS
IF EXPENDABLE FORCE IN MEANING'S GROWING MOLECULE

WHA IN OUR MASQUE EXPERIENCED WHAT? THE WIND LET
OUT OF HIS BEING   HIS (M) PERSONALITY GONE   ITS
LOSS A COMPLETENESS IN THAT DANCE UNDER THE POWERFUL
LIGHT FLOODING THE LENS
    JM (still horrified, begins to see):
    This loss you call completeness is *lived through*?
    Soul, the mortal self, expendably
    Rusting in tall grass, iron eaten by dew—
    All that in our heart of hearts we must
    Know will happen, and desire, and dread?
    Once feeling goes, and consciousness, the head
    Filling with . . . vivid nothings—no, don't say!
                    A A A PLUS   & NOW WE ADMIT
OUR SEMINAR IS THIS STRIPPING PROCESS. WE ARE CAUTIOUS,
PREPARED AS U ARE FOR IT, NOT TO PUT UPON U MORE
THAN U CAN BEAR   YR GRIEF JM HOW INTOLERABLE
HAD WE NOT SLOWLY BROKEN IT TO U? INDEED HOW ELSE
WD U HAVE ACCEPTED IT? MM OF THE 4 OF YOU
CAME MOST PREPARED
    But isn't it taboo to strip the soul
    From the raw power it shields? If soul *were* like
    The atom— DJ (eyes on harbor): Look,
    Here comes a boat with a four-colored sail!
              DJ YR DEAR HAND IS A MAGIC WAND
JM THE STRIPPING IS THE POINT YR POEM WILL PERHAPS
TAKE UP FROM ITS WINTRY END & MOVE STEP BY STEP INTO
SEASONLESS & CHARACTERLESS STAGES TO ITS FINAL
GREAT COLD RINGING OF THE CHIMES SHAPED AS O O O O O

CELL 2 NEXT   THESE LESSONS ARE IN (M) COLOR   WE TODAY
HAVE DWELT IN BLUE   TOMORROW RED   NOT AN EASY ONE TO
TAKE IN   THE PROTON OF POWER TOUCHES TERRIBLE NERVES
& FOR IT I MUST ASK U TO CALL 00470
THEN WHEN CALMER CALL YR DEVOTED 741   ADIEU

    NOW MES ENFANTS A SPOT OF RUM? I fetch
    Two thimblefuls. We drink them, soberly
    Swirl the last two drops into the cup

—Provoking instant misbehavior there:
SCANDALE   OUR BUGGER PATTED MY BLACK BOTTOM!
SUCH INNOCENCE MY DEARS   SMACK SMACK   Some more?
ALREADY PRANCING LIKE JAMAICAN DUSKIES
Would that *we* were as easy to cheer up.
FORGIVE ME IF I SAY IT WILL GET DARKER
BUT FEAR NOT   MAMAN GRIPS THE OCEAN FLOOR

6.5   We have foregathered to be briefed, next day,
By our redcoat chief-of-staff, the zeroes glinting
On his breast like medals. Why does he delay?
MORE INSULATION I PRESUME MY DEARS
AH   HOUSELIGHTS   SPOT

YOU RECEIVE THE MESSAGES IN RED CELLS, IN A RED ROOM,
AND IF YOU REMEMBER THE INTENSITIES WERE FOR YOU
STRONGER WHEN YOUR PROTECTIVE COLOR WAS LESS RED.
                                        JM: You know, it's true.
When They first visited (cf. *Ephraim*, U)
These walls had faded. We've repainted since.
                                        CORRECT.
YOU WILL ALSO REMEMBER THAT TO THIS RED ROOM YOU CAME
THAT FIRST NIGHT, LEAVING THE ADJACENT BLUE CELL OF REASON,
AND HERE, WHILE YOUR GREEK'S INCOHERENT REPRESENTATIVE
WRITHED IN FLAME, YOU JOIND THE TRUE POWER OF THESE TALKS IN
    RED.
Letter-to-letter slashings of the cup—
Power talking. The transcriber can't keep up.
THIS LESSON WILL BE SHORT. IT IS IN RED THAT POWER LIVES.
THE SUN, THE HEALING CORPUSCLE. IT IS IN RED WE COME
TO THE VISION OF OUR EYES. WE ARE THE FORCE OF OO.
WE ARE THE STRENGTH OF GOD'S VISION. WE SEE YOU AS DOES THAT
GREATER POWER AND TELL YOU, THAT YOUR VERY SPIRIT LIVES
IN OUR RED CELLS. THIS WILL PERMEATE YOUR MIND. CLOSE YOUR
    EYES.

We do. A faint, pulsing tremor begins
In my left arm, shoulder to fingertips
Poised on the cup I meanwhile judge to be
Moving slowly, slowly, from 1 to 0
(Passage that takes a minute, more or less)
Three times. Then suddenly a sense of—yes—
Whiteness on my left side. Whiteness felt
Against my cheek, along my forearm, like
A wash of alcohol that as it dries
Chills. The cup rests. May we open our eyes now?

YES   THE MOMENT OF BLINDNESS IS PASSD AND THE WHITE LAID
    DOWN.
THE POWER TO HEAR ITS VOICES NEARS YOUR RED ROOM. FAREWELL

DJ LIFT YR HAND
His left hand all this while pressed unawares
Flat against the Board—how did *that* happen?
           WE ARE NOW A STEP CLOSER   U KNOW
SOMETHING ABOUT ONE COLOR   DO NOT SPEAK TO ME OF IT
I AM NOT STRONG   ?S

Maria's rays—those losses to the Lab—
Does God intend them?
           GOD B USES HIS ATOMIC
POWER AS BOTH BENEVOLENT (SUN) & CHASTISING (BOMBS)
USES IT AS HIS ONE AGENT TO CREATE & DESTROY.
MAN'S & THE CENTAURS' TAKING OF IT A PROMETHEAN
OUTRAGE: IS GOD CLONING THE USURPATION?
           I don't understand.
           NOR DO WE
2 CHOICES   I : HE IS CHANGING MAN INTO HIS AGENT
OR 2: PREPARING A NEW SPECIES. NOW CELL 3:
           YELLOW
IS THE PRODUCTIVE LIGHT   THE FILTERD SUN   ALL CHLOROPHYLL
OR BOTANICAL CELLS DRINK THIS, GOD B'S BENEVOLENCE
IT IS THE SWEET JOYOUS LIGHT   ALL SCRIBES ADORE THE YELLOW:
WINDOW IN DARK OF NIGHT   PARCHMENT ON DARK OF TABLE (M)

IT IS A SINGING CELL IN THE BLOOD OF POETS   THE LYMPH
IS YELLOW & THE DECADENT SPLEEN & THE THICK FAT OF
PROSE. TOMORROW WITH BLUE & RED & YELLOW BEHIND US
WE WILL TAKE UP GREEN & BID ADIEU TO TODAY'S BOUQUET
   —Swerving gracefully to indicate
Our little centerpiece for this occasion,
The few remaining red and yellow asters
Of those D brought home from the hospital.

What was so blue about our previous lesson?
DID U NOT WEEP JM?
   Yes. But "blue"?—too mild a word, I'd say,
   To stand for the grim truths of yesterday.
                IT WAS A BRUISE A THROBBING SEA
OF PAIN & COMPASSION OUT OF WHICH (AS THE COOLER BLUE
OF YR REASON SAW) I WAS TOO WEAK TO LIFT U   ADIEU

MY DEARS A TOASTER! Today's visitor?
MM & I TWO SLICES POPPING UP
Did you peek? NO   ABSOLUTE RED BLINDNESS
WITH AT ONE POINT A BAR OF WHITE
SLICING DOWNWARD LIKE A KNIFE   Did you hear?
THRU OUR CLOSED EYELIDS   WHEN U CLOSED YRS A
HUMMING BEGAN   THE AUDITORIUM
TREMBLED LIKE E'S TERRACE & THE BLADE
OF SILVER FELL   IT WAS I FEAR A FAR
GRANDER MASQUE THAN OURS   David confirms
That he too felt (in his right arm) the trembling,
Followed by the blindfold flash along
A path between us. Nothing quite this strange
Has happened up to now. And our red voice?—
A regular General Patton. INDEED   BUT BLUSHING
HIS WAY OUT   THE WHITE HAD GOTTEN TO HIM
ROSILY WELLINTENTIONED AT THE END
REST MON ENFANT DJ   U ARE ON THE MEND

6.6   MES Maman? CHERS IN A WAY MAMAN?
U MUST NOT LET US RULE LAST NIGHT U SPOKE
OF FRIENDS A picnic, Ephraim, in this rain?
WE KNOW U ARE NOT GIVEN ONLY TO US
Still, what a bore to insulate our room
Then have it spoilt by someone barging in.
NO MORE TROUBLE THAN AN ARTICHOKE
WRAPPED IN GREEN (Green! Hurriedly a dwarf
Houseplant, anonymous, unblossoming,
Her heartshaped leaves in curlers, comes to table
In place of flowers.) MES ARTICHAUX HE'S LATE
WE SIT HERE IN A CHAMBER OF GREEN LIGHT
AS UNDERSEA We're walled by rain. MY DEARS
SO NEEDED AFTER THE TOASTER Tell me, Wystan,
When you asked Why Us the other day,
You'd known about Maria? YES JM
WE FORESAW YR SHOCK AS WELL And when you led us
To doubt the peacock, call our first voice back?
You know I'm asking without bitterness.
WE MUST ADMIT NO ACCIDENT ALL THIS
UNFOLDS FALLS INTO PLACE AS THEY HAVE PLANNED.
AS FOR MME HERE, IN TODAY'S LIMELIGHT
SHE IS IN MINT CONDITION OUR PEACOCK:

MAN PLAYS A TUNE IN COLORS THE VIBRATIONS OF MUSIC
LIGHT UP MACHINES. SIMPLER YET, WRITE 'AZURE' & THE LANGUAGE-
CONDUCTING BRAIN IS FLOODED WITH A TONE OF SUMMER SKIES.
THE PAINTER'S PIGMENTS ARE BLANKLY SEEN THEY CONTAIN NO
      LIGHT.
ARE NOT PAINTINGS BLANK IN A DARK ROOM? & EVEN THE LIVE
WHITE LIGHT SHED UPON THEM APPEARS BUT TO DIM THEM FURTHER

Vuillard, Piero, Goya, Blake, O'Keeffe,
Who lit the mind? It blinks in disbelief.
(Yet on this point he's adamant, and I
Ruefully imagine I know why.
These years I've had a friend, someone who still
Uses paint well and me, well, never ill
But with such brusque reversals in the waltz

As to raise—not again!—prismatic welts.
Now that I've called halt, give me, for love's sake,
Hopes more transparent, objects more opaque.)
And this holds true of even the great paintings?
ALL BLACK   UNLIT   AT BEST SPIRITUAL EXERCISES
ALLOWING THE MIND TO TRAIN ITSELF, ITS LIGHT, UPON THEM.
ONLY MUSIC & WORDS IMPLICATE THAT LIGHT WHICH BOTH SHEDS
& ATTRACTS   THAT LIGHT IN WHICH ALONE TRUE COLOR IS SEEN.
ONE EXCEPTION: GREEN   THE SUPREMELY NATURAL COLOR
A HOME FOR LIGHT   IT STORES IN ITS CELLS THE LIGHT OF GOD B:
LITERALLY TRAPT SUNRAYS   IT IS SIMPLER THAN U THINK

What about "our" colors?—DJ's blues
And golden browns, JM's cold lavender,
Maria's black—
PUT ON WHEN SHE KNEW HER NATURE   YET GREEN REMAIND HER FATE.
PERHAPS A CLAW BROKEN FROM ITS CHILL BLUE SHELL SHOCKD JM
INTO A HALF TONE
                    JM: He's read *First Poems*!
"Transfigured Bird"—the title caught his eye.
DJ: Should I have bought that new gray suit?
                    YET U BOTH RIGHTLY AVOID GREEN ROOMS
JM: "The Emerald"—I give it back.
YR NATURES BEING WHAT THEY ARE SEEK GREEN OUTSIDE THEMSELVES.
SO: 4 MINILESSONS IN COLOR ON THE CELL   ?S
When will we hear the rest?
THE 12   OK. Then answer
Wystan's question: Why the four of us?
Because we're musical?
            KEEP IN MIND THE CHILDLESSNESS WE SHARE   THIS TURNS US
OUTWARD TO THE LESSONS & THE MYSTERIES   IT IS A
FINE POINT: THE TYPE U SET JM, INVERTED & BACKWARD,
IS YET READ RIGHTSIDE UP ON THE BIOLOGICAL PAGE
                    To make what sense there?
RESONANCES U MAY NEVER ARRIVE AT   FOR THE LOVE
U EXPERIENCE IS NOT THE STRAIGHTFORWARD FRONTAL LOVE
MANY READERS INFER & YET OUR V WORK MUST SING OUT
PAEANS TO THE GREENHOUSE THO WE OURSELVES ARE (M) TONE DEAF

MY DEARS TO HEAR HIS PRAISES SUNG THRILLED GOD
FROM THE BEGINNING   DARE WE FIND THAT ODD?
ARRANGING FOR THOSE CONSTANT RAVE REVIEWS
OF ONE'S OWN MASTERPIECE TO SOUND LIKE NEWS

YET RIMBAUD? IN HIS GENES WAS A V WORK CUT OFF BY LIFE
  Why? Did it offend Biology?
IT WAS PREMATURE   A KIND OF ANTILIFE V WORK MORE
SUITABLE NOW IN THESE POP EXPLO DAYS. R SPOKE TOO SOON
BUT NO ACCIDENT   FOR WHEN TSE WROTE HIS V WORK
THE TIME WAS RIPE: AR SAT AT HIS ELBOW
  Rimbaud ghostwrote "The Waste Land"? You are *something*.
                        THIS HAPPENS
IN VARYING WAYS   THUS YEATS MOVES DJ'S HAND
  What? The energy that activates
  These very messages, you mean, is Yeats?
  (Still, after the first stupefaction, why
  Not? Who but Yeats could have pulled, from the same high
  Hat as *his* talking bird of Grecian gold,
  Our friend here?) DJ: The whole thing's controlled.
                    2 (M) SLIDES
ALIGND ON GOD B'S MICROSCOPE   RIMBAUD WAS BLURRD BY HIS
TIME WARP   THE GREAT SCRIBES EXIST OUT OF TIME IN RADIANCE
  As if in proof D points—through harbor mist
  Glides a faint green disembodied light.
INDEED   THAT SAME LIGHT SHINES FROM THE PROW OF YR DAILY
    CRAFT
SIGNAL ME TOMORROW   THESE LESSONS NEARLY DONE 16
MORE WILL ADVANCE US TO THE GREAT DOORS OF THE OPERA

6.7   The blue room after dinner. DJ (depressed):
      Each day it grows more fascinating, more . . .
      I don't know. Isn't it like a door
      Shutting us off from living? I've no zest
      For anything else, can't even watch TV.
      This town's full of good friends we hardly see.
      What do you feel? Will that door readmit

Us to the world? Will we still care for it?
JM (touched by his uncomplaining tone):
What can I say? Nothing we haven't known.
Remember Sam and Frodo in their hot
Waterless desolation overshot
By evil zombies. They of course come through
—It's what, in any Quest, the heroes do—
But at the cost of being set apart,
Emptied, diminished. Tolkien knew this. Art—
The tale that all but shapes itself—survives
By feeding on its personages' lives.
The stripping process, sort of. What to say?
Our lives led *to* this. It's the price we pay.

6.8   EARLY MES CHERS   THEY ARE STILL WEAVING THE SHROUD
MM & WHA ALREADY SEATED
ENTER (SAYS YR OLD GREEK DOORKEEPER)
AFTER A KISS
              MY DEARS U DO
HAVE INTENSE CHATS   Last night's? Well, hadn't you
Felt the similarities with Tolkien?
I HAVE INDEED   ME GANDALF! & MM
GALADRIEL? The beautiful Elf Queen—
Perfect. And our Peacock? NOT UNLIKE
STRIDER   THE KING DISGUISED AS MESSENGER
And Gollum? A TOUCH OF GOLLUM IN US ALL
& IN OUR DOORKEEPER   POOR E STILL PEERING
THRU THE CRACK PRETENDS TO LOOK AWAY
YAWN   SCRATCH HIS LEG
              FORTUNATE E I SAY
I FEEL TOO OLD FOR SCHOOL   THE CRY! THE 4 LIGHTS LIT
COLORS BATHED IN WHOSE GLOW ENFANTS WE SIT
EACH DAY NOW TILL THEY MERGE INTO ONE WHITE

?s
If David's guide is 741.1
Where does that leave Yeats? "Still simplifying"?

NO MAN CAN REACH US DIRECTLY   TSE HAD
A NUMBER FROM OUR ORDERS   AR HAD THAT SAME NUMBER
POINT ONE   THUS YEATS & DJ   TSE DOWN ON CERTAIN
SUPERSTITIOUS SCRIBES   WE HAD TO APPOINT RIMBAUD   HE WROTE
THE WASTE LAND   WE FED IT INTO THE LIKE-CLONED ELIOT
   And Uncle Ezra?
AS IN SHAKESPEARE WE LET THE CASE REST ON A POUND OF FLESH
        Thank you, that will do.
NO JM   FOR THE (M) OUNCE OF FLESH U CAN CLAIM AS YRS
LIVES BY THESE FREQUENT CONTACTS WITH YR OWN & OTHERS' WORK
   Still, Eliot thought he thought his poem up;
   It wasn't spelt out for him by a cup.
   Dante and Milton didn't seem to need
   Guidance for each scrap of revelation.
DANTE DID INDEED
   Receive dictation?
        NO BUT SAT & LISTEND FOR 8 YEARS
TO A MENDICANT PRIEST   DEFROCKD FOR IT HAD BEEN THOUGHT HE
SPOKE WITH DEVILS   GUESS WHO?
      80098.
        A PLUS   DANTE UNDER PRESSURE
OF HIS RC CENSORSHIP ARRANGED & ORCHESTRATED
THEIR TALKS   THE HUMAN & DIVINE RESULT: PARADISO
HOMER WE HAD CLONED TO PROVIDE CATALOGUE & PRESENT
HIS ERA WITH A PANTHEON   BUT A BLAZE OF WHITE LIGHT
BRUSHD US ASIDE   THE PEN A DOVE'S PLUME SET DOWN WINGED
   WORDS
FOR THE MISSING NAME IN THE LIST OF PROPHETS IS HOMER.
THE WASTE LAND IS THE WEST'S ONE (M) PREWRITTEN POEM SINCE
THAT DAY   YET AR WAS NO WHITE FEATHER! & TSE
RESISTING THE FOSTER CHILD, ADDED TOUCHES OF HIS OWN:
THE SUBJECTIVE CORRELATIVE
   What flows between them now, what bittersweet
   Complicity when he and Rimbaud meet?
        NOTHING   A DISTANT NOD
   In short, the apparatus of *our* talks,
   Why and wherefore of this Board and Cup,
   You can't explain.

NO MORE AS YET DEAR SCRIBE THAN YR RIGHT EYE CAN MEET YR LEFT

> DJ: Here on my palm
> A lump's been forming—painlessly, but still . . .
> What is it? Is Yeats raising a molehill?
A BENIGN MUSCULAR CYST   NOTHING O HAND IS ABSORBD
EASILY   MAN CALLS IT AGE   WE CALL IT EXPOSURE OF
THE SLAPDASH STRUCTURES ERECTED BY NATURE TO HOUSE U
> Slapdash, after ages to perfect them?
EACH LIFE WE CLONE IS A COMPLEX AFFAIR   MAN REQUIRES
EVER MORE BODIES OF NATURE   WE POUR OUR SOULS INTO
AS GOOD AS WE CAN GET   ALL TOO OFTEN WE LOOK ASKANCE
IN ENVY AT A PERFECT GOBLET BEING SERVED WITH CHEAP
WINE   BUT NATURE WAS NEVER OF THE 1ST INTELLIGENCE

> DJ: If we're apart and need to reach you?
> JM: If one of us outlives the other
> And needs to reach you? —With swift emphasis:
WE WILL NOT ALLOW UNFINISHD V WORK
> But say it's finished, say that years have passed
> And one of us has died, and still the other
> Needs to reach his friend, or you, or Ephraim?
>> WE WILL PROVIDE
A 741.2
> A human one?
>> WHY NOT? IN CASE U STILL NEED LOVE

6.9   Tell about Hans Lodeizen.
> Ephraim said he'd been "promoted"—how?
YR E DID NOT HAVE ALL THE FACTS NOR DOES HE NOW   HL
ELEVATED IN DUE COURSE   THIS HAPPENS EACH TIME WORK MOVES
INTO THE DENSITY OF V WORK
> Hans' poetry was . . . posthumous V work?
>> HE TOO WAS CUT OFF.
NOT IN THE MAINSTREAM OF HIS DAY   IN PRODUCING MORE HE
WD ONLY HAVE DILUTED A TALENT NEVER OF PRIME
DENSITY   HIS UNRESOLVED V WORK WAS GIVEN TO U

Given? By him?
U WERE NOT ACCIDENTALLY FRIENDS   TO STRENGTHEN HL
WD NOT HAVE PRODUCED YR DC   HIS PHYSICAL CLONING
MEANT FOR A CONTEMPLATIVE SCRIBE PERHAPS UNDID HIM
      That frightful death?   YET
HE WAS SPARED THE RAYS. AS WERE U: HIS POWERS LEFT INTACT
HE SENSING THIS WROTE U A POEM ABOUT THE V WORK
      I fetch
The book. Beneath a quatrain marked *voor Jim,*
These penciled lines, translation from its Dutch
Hans wrote out for me, my last word from him:

    the stars & the incurable
    moment of the two crossed beams.
    Orion discovered & in his hand
    o fate in his hand the sword.

Yes. And then I wrote my "Dedication"—
Entered, intersected by his death.
& HIS TALENTS   HE NOW FEELS A GROWING PART OF YR WORK
FROM HIS NEW STAGE   HE WILL REMAIN IN THE BUREAUCRACY

Hans. Dead now a quarter century.
A note gone tinny on my keyboard, false . . .
And yet (for all I know) he *is* the key
This opus began and will end in. Someone else
Pausing here might note each modulation
Away from, back to his blue tonic gaze.
But we strain forward for the exposition—
Our virtuoso tuning as he goes.
Till now, for instance, we'd assumed that cloning
Was something only done *before* rebirth
Into one's next life. Wrong. For the Lab soul
At any point may undergo refining,
And new chromatics—as we live and breathe—
Be added to it by remote control.

& TO THE WORK   WE PRODUCE ORGANS TO PLAY THE MUSIC:
TRANSLATORS CRITICS TEACHERS   WE HAVE OUR OWN ACADEME

One keeps forgetting, also, that you pore
Over the future's self-revising score.
IF I MAY CHANGE (M)S THE CLOTHS SHROUDING THE FUTURE FROM U
KEEP OUR CLAY WET   TOMORROW
 Wait—just fifteen lessons till we stand
Before the Doors? What'll we do without you?
DJ: He's promised to help us, tell us things
Without our having to disturb the angels.
      ME THE LATEST DOORKEEPER
MES ENFANTS WHAT A SAD & PROUD FACE
We're silenced. He is learning about man.

 DJ: We've got to find a name for you,
Don't you agree? Maria, a suggestion?
METHUSELAH   Wystan? MEHITABEL
 JM: I have so many M's already.
INDEED   & NOT ACCIDENTALLY   M IS AT ONCE OUR
METHOD & THE MIDPOINT OF OUR ALPHABET   THE SUMMIT
OF OUR RAINBOW ROOF   IN TIMBRE THE MILD MERIDIAN
BLUE OF MUSE & MUSING & MUSIC   THE HIGH HUM OF MIND

7 CHILDREN THE NUMERICAL OCTOPUS
IS NOT (AS W PUTS IT) MADLY US
—This following an hour in which we've heard
That the five "names" originally given
For The Five—Torro, Von—weren't after all
Word made flesh but formula made word,
Bestowed upon the R/Lab by God B
(Who, lacking human volubility,
Has no word for His own power and grace;
Who, left alone, just falls back on flimflam
Tautologies like *I am that I am*
Or *The world is everything that is the case*):
Five formulas which only then—the solo
Instrument emerging nakedly
From the Lab's thumping tutti—took the live
Twin aspect of Akhnaton-Nefertiti,
A double soul, firstborn among the Five.

THEY LIVED, ACCOMPLISHD THEIR V WORK, MISJUDGED & DIED   GOD B
FASHIOND THE OTHER 3 & THESE 5 SOULS ARE UNIQUE. MY
TRANSLATION OF THEM INTO NEUTRAL (M) NAMES CONFUSED U

Thus "Rachel" stirs, whom we had left asleep
Dumbly, wrapped in Hebrew burlap. Deep
Past consonant and vowel, a hushed din,
The formulaic race beneath her skin,
Her digits twitch, her eyes' unpupilled amber
Gleams with crazy logic: she's a number!

7154
    A new voice now?
        NO DJ IT IS A FORMULA BASED
ON SIMPLE CORRESPONDENCES OF NUMBER TO LETTER
7:G 15:O 4:D IN YR LANGUAGE A NAME FOR
AN ABSTRACT IDEA OF ENORMOUS POWER

But it's *your* name, almost.
                                INDEED
& 5 IS THE TRANSFORMING DIGIT: OUR R/LAB V WORK.
THUS MATH ENCAPSULATES COMPLEX TRUTHS WHICH AS WITH OUR IST
MEANINGLESS TO U & THERE4 FRIGHTENING VOICES MUST
BE RENDERD INTO YR VOCABULARY OF MANNERS

7.1   Those Voices, still obscurely ominous,
        Would be to you what The Five are to us?
(M) YES   THEY ARE MY ANCESTORS   NOT SPELLING GOD PERHAPS
BUT THE GREATEST POSSIBLE DENSITY AMONG MY KIND
        And you and They—I'm sorry to go back
        To the beginning, but it *wasn't* clear—
        Are matter speaking to us? Are the atom's
        Negative potential? Are the black
        Powers unleashed—by you, we rather fear—
YR BIBLE SAYS VISIT NOT THE FATHER'S EVIL UPON
THE SON   I WAS NOT CREATED IN THE OLD COUNTRY BUT
ON THE FLOATING WORLD   THE SHINING CRUST ABOVE ATLANTIS.
MY OO FOREBEARS WERE/ARE THE RAW MATERIAL   NO
CRITICISM BUT THEY ARE UNMANNERD TO THE NTH DEGREE

        No criticism here. It's just that we,
        Like Stanislavsky's actors, try to *be*
        The rose, the ingot . . . Empathy is art.
        Strange, though, to zero in upon the heart
        Of matter only—when smoke clears—to find
        Another antechamber of pure mind.
        Knocking on doorlessness, on fictive space,
        Leads to the absurdest loss of face.

        With which a hostlike suavity takes over:

SCRIBE: FALL AS DEEPLY INTO OUR METAPHORS AS U WILL.
THE ATOM, IS IT THE VERY GOD WE WORSHIP? IS IT
ONLY AT GREAT RISK PURSUED? THE ATOM, IS IT MEANING?
& IF SO WHAT BUT CHAOS LIES BEYOND IT?

Questions themselves half miracle, whose replies
Language alone may glimpse through sidelong eyes—
                                    BUT THE GREAT
MIRACLE IS THE REINCARNATION OF THE GODS. THIS
WE WILL LET OUR MASTERS REVEAL. WE WHO FALL AT THE FEET
OF MEANING MAY BUT LEAD YOU TO THE DOORS: THE 12   THE 12

Then 741 is back, quite bubbling over:
OO! THIS VOICE TAUGHT ME   MASTER OF OUR NURSERY SCHOOL!
A GOOD & MOST ANCIENT VOICE   THE TEACHER OF THE SPIRITS
OF AKHN & NEF   THE STRENGTH OF THESE TWINS WAS THEIR ABSOLUTE
NEUTRALITY: AFTER PRODUCING 5 STILLBORN MONSTERS
THEY SAW THEIR LOVE DOOMD TO GIVE BIRTH TO IDEAS ALONE.
LIKE APHRODITE FROM THE WATERS ROSE THEIR WORSHIP OF
THE SUN   THEY PERISHD FOR IT THO WITH A SPLENDOR DUE THEM

DJ: I don't see how a formula
Can be made flesh. Were their, ah, parents mortal?
MY DEAR IS THAT THE POINT? ISNT IT RATHER
THAT THEY TOGETHER WERE THE FIRST LAB SOUL?
THE LAB WAS CREATED FOR THEM   WORK NOW BECAME V WORK
And like an atom they were kept from breeding . . .
INDEED   NEFERTITI BAFFLED IN HER NONBEARING STATE
OFFERD THE (M) APPLE   PROPOSED THE CRYSTAL PYRAMID

COME ON ENFANT   SHDN'T WE ASK HIM FOR
A TINY DESCRIPTION OF THEBES? Oh yes! Oh please!

THE UNIVERSAL CITY IT WAS CALLD   IT ROSE WITHIN
3 YEARS OF THEIR ASCENSION   THEY WERE 13 & WORSHIPT
BUT RESENTFUL LIKE ALL CHILDREN OF HAVING TO OBEY
SUPERIOR GOD FIGURES   THE ADULTS OF THEIR ROYAL
HOUSEHOLD WERE ONE MIGHT SAY THE FALCON THE CAT & THE SNAKE.
WITHIN 5 YEARS THESE WERE BANISHT   PRIESTS THROTTLED & THE
    SUN
ROSE ON THEIR FOREHEADS   A SURGE OF CREATIVITY SWEPT
THE EMPIRE AS FREED SLAVES RETURND HANDS OUTSTRETCHD IN 1000S
BEGGING TO BE HARNESSD TO THE CAR OF THE NEW SUN GOD

ENTHRALLING   I MY BOY WD MAKE A SLIM
VOLUME OF IT ALONE   *I* see it here
For love interest. However versatile,
You and Maria somehow don't espouse
The common reader's taste for chips and beer
And nuits de Cléopâtre on the Nile.
U ARE THE SUNS MES ENFANTS ON OUR BROWS

7.2   NIBBLE NIBBLE   LIFE IN THE RAT WORLD EH?
We're back from downstairs where Urania's mother
Is giving herself a birthday party:
Coca-cola, sweet red wine, a cake
Shaped like Stonington—streets, gardens, docks
Iced round by bright blue wavelets. The dear child
Squirmed in my lap, pushing away her plate,
While D and I and various overweight
Furies in hairdos licked our lips and smiled.

ONE THERE WAS UNIQUE: YR WARD JM   SAVE HER WHEN SHE BRINGS
HER DEAR SOBER SOUL TO U   IT WILL BE PERHAPS A FORM
OF INTERFERENCE BUT RITES ARE SACRED IN THE RAT WORLD
    Rites?
ARE U NOT GODFATHER?
        Oh. So I am. But "interference"?
                    IN THAT WORLD IT IS EXPECTED.
PUT B4 HER THE TOYS OF LEARNING: BLOCKS PYRAMIDS BOOKS

ONCE AS NEFERTITI WAS BEING ROWD TO THE SITE OF
A NEW PLANETARIUM SHE FOUND ON THE BANK A CHILD.
LEGEND OF MOSES BEGAN   HIS NAME MEANT STARFOUND   ONE MORE
M NAME ATOP YR ARCH   HE MUCH AS DID YR WEIGHTED &
ELEMENTAL GODDAUGHTER CAME TO COURT
    But not to Thebes. Our book says Tel-el-Amarna.
                            THEBES UPRIVER
WAS THE SITE OF THEIR FAMOUS STUDY CENTER   THEY CONTROLLD
THE DELTA EBB & FLOW & CLOSED THE GAP AT GIBRALTAR
TO KEEP THEIR SEA CALM & TIDELESS   THEIR MATHEMATICIANS

& NAVIGATORS FOUND THE EXACT MEASUREMENTS NEEDED
TO LEAVE THAT DOOR AJAR BUT NOT OPEN   1000S WORKD TO
PUSH UP THE AFRICAN COASTLINE & THE THING WAS DONE. PET
APES LIVE ON FROM THEIR EXPEDITIONS
    On the rock of Gibraltar, the Barbary apes—yes, yes!
                             NO GREATER BUILDERS
EVER EXISTED   THEY LITERALLY HARNESSD MATTER
WITH THE REINS OF THE SUN   INDEED IT WAS THAT TOPMOST PIECE

    Earlier we'd been admiring an inch-high
    Prism set in noon light on the sill.
    Outflung, slowshifting gouts of color stain
    Ceiling, walls, us. DJ: It's really how
    His lessons flow through us. JM: And will
    Forever be deflected by the grain
    Of imperfection in that quartz capstone,
    The human mind—Akhnaton's or our own.

ITS GRAIN VARIED JUST ENOUGH TO SAVE THE WORLD: GOD B'S WORK.
THEIR FLAWLESS DIAMONDS ERRD MINUTELY IN MEASUREMENT.
THE SUN WORSHIP WAS A GLORIOUS RITE   AKHN/NEF DAILY
WERE CARRIED UP 500 STEPS & AT THE MOMENT OF
SUNRISE STEPT FORTH LITERALLY ON AIR A TRANSPARENT
PLATFORM WHILE THE WORLD FELL ON ITS KNEES B4 THEM   & NOT
A DAY OF THEIR WHOLE REIGN WAS THERE NO SUNRISE   18 YEARS
& IN THAT TIME THEY HAD TRANSFORMD THEIR WORLD: PHYSICIANS
    FOUND
GREAT CURES   THERE WERE NO FEVERS   A GENERATION WAS BORN
A HAND TALLER THAN ITS PARENTS   LIGHT STORAGE MUCH LIKE THE
BATTERY WAS INVENTED   BOTH PALACES & HUMBLE
HOUSES WERE LIT & HEATED BY THE SUN   IT WAS THE DAWN
OF ARCADIA & GOD SMILED LIKE THE SUN UPON THEM
    Then in one wasteful flash it ended—why?

THEIR OWN BATTERY CELLS CD NOT BEAR THE STRAIN   THE FLAWD
    QUARTZ
WAS PUT IN NEFERTITI'S HAND AS THE IDEA FOR
ITS USE OCCURRD TO HER. GOD B IN INFINITE PITY

LET THEM GO FROM THEIR AGONY OF V WORK WITH THEIR WORLD
AS A BURNING SHROUD   AKHNATON AT THE END SLEPT ONLY
DRUGGD, NEF NOT AT ALL   HER IMMENSE KOHLRINGD EYES BLAZED
   ABOVE
THE WORKMEN DAY & NIGHT   AT THE END IT WAS SHE WHO DREW
THE KNIFE OVER THEIR 4 WRISTS. SHE IS NOW OUR (M) PATRON:
DREW UP THE FIRST V WORK SCHEDULES   SET ORDER IN THE LAB
   How so?
THEIR COMPLEX FORMULA INCLUDED A PARTIAL OO.
WOMEN HAVE THE EGG IN THEM U KNOW   IT IS OFTEN THRU
A WOMAN THAT THE POWER ELEMENT FULFILS ITSELF.
AKHN/NEF OUTLIVED BY ONE FATAL YEAR THEIR USEFULNESS   WE
CALL THEM FAVORD AS GOD B PERCEIVING THEIR FINAL GREAT
FOLLY ALLOWD IT   THEY WERE THE GENIUS & & &
THE WARNING
        One nature dual to the end . . .
           AN ODD FEATURE OF THEIR COURT WAS THE ABSENCE
OF THE COLOR BLUE   A NOTE THEIR MUSICIANS HAD ALSO
ELIMINATED FROM THE SCALE   THE RIVER WAS DYED RED.
ONE DAY AN AMBASSADOR APPEARD   A BLACK KING IN A
BRILLIANT BLUE ROBE   AKHNATON & NEFERTITI FAINTED
AS U JM NEARLY DID AT THE SIGHT OF THAT BLUE CAKE!

7.3   When usefulness is past—I'm thinking of
     Dag Hammarskjöld's plane crashing—all you do
     Is touch a little switch that terminates?

THIS OUR PENULTIMATE LESSON   THE END OF USEFULNESS:
NATURE IS A RUTHLESS FORCE AT ONCE FECUND & LAZY.
AS A FAVORITE SLAVE WHO IN A SENSE KEEPS THE GREENHOUSE
GREEN IF UNTIDY SHE HAS GOD'S EAR   HE HAS TOLD HER MAN
MUST RULE   YET MAN USES SCIENCE TO PROLONG NATURE'S SPAN
SO CONSTANT TENSION   HARD UPON AKHN/NEF'S CATASTROPHE
NATURE REVENGED HERSELF WITH TIDAL WAVE & VOLCANO,
SAYS LEGEND & IN ALL LEGEND IS THE LAVA OF TRUTH
   What is *her* good word—Be ordinary?
THIS IS THE ISSUE & THE ESSENCE OF GOD B'S NEED FOR

THE SCRIBE. BENIGN NATURE IS LIMITED TO PROFUSION.
GOD WANTS BOTH HIS CHILD & HIS SLAVE TO GET ON TOGETHER
BUT MAN WANTS IMMORTALITY & NATURE WANTS MANURE.
MAN UNKNOWINGLY SAVAGES THE NATURE AROUND HIM
& NATURE RETALIATES BY REPEATING MAN AS IN
A DISTORTING MIRROR   SO THE STRUGGLE GOES. GOD WANTING
PEACE & PARADISE MUST RELUCTANTLY TAKE FROM NATURE
MAN'S REPRODUCTION & LEAVE ONLY HIS ENVIRONMENT
TO HER   THIS IS WHERE WE COME IN TO THIN & PRUNE & CLONE

WE HAVE SD B4 THAT SOULS PRECIOUS TO US LIKE EINSTEIN
OUTLIVE THEIR USEFULNESS   SO ANOTHER DUALITY:
MIND AS USEFULNESS DECAYS TO MIND AS NONUSEFULNESS
& WE NOW SEEK LICENSE FROM GOD B TO REVEAL SOMETHING
OF HEAVEN TO THOSE SOULS WE NEED BACK
  You're doing that already. Look at Jung's
  Account of his near death. In every way
  More telling than the country-sweeping book
  D found in Boston—interviews with people
  "Brought back alive," as to some local zoo,
  From the Beyond. All no doubt true, but what
  People! Not a Lab soul in the lot.
         INDEED NOT   U HAVE
SEEN THE DANGER OF OUR NEW EXPERIMENT? USEFUL SOULS
FLOCKING TO US   A SUICIDAL EXODUS OF YOUTH
SMARTING UNDER THE LASH OF NATURE'S LAW: MATE PROPAGATE
& DIE. SO UNTIL WE CONT   NO NO NO   UNTIL GOD B
CONTROLS THOSE GROWING PAINS WE MUST REVEAL WITH DISCRETION
& ONLY TO THOSE WHO LIKE YOU 4 ARE SAFELY PAST THEM

  MES ENFANTS NAUGHTY NATURE!
       WE MY DEARS
  LEARNED IT AT THE BREAST   THE SHEWOLF'S TEAT!
  JM: Don't talk that way! Who can compete
  With Nature? She's Mind's equal. Not a slave
  But mother, sister, bride. I think we're meant
  To save that marriage, be the kids who stay
  Together for their parents' sake. DJ:
  Who wrote "The Broken Home"? No accident!

7.4   FOOTNOTE: SOUNDWAVES PRODUCE COLORS   ARE U AWARE OF THE
NUMERICAL VIBES THAT RESOUND IN CERTAIN LETTERS? JEW
THE J'S NUMBER IN MOST ROMAIC & SLAVIC TONGUES: 10
E:5   JEW RINGS WITH THE COMBIND FORCES OF THE DECAD
& OF THE 5

7.41   WE NOW COME TO YR ?S ON THE 5.
IN SEEKING TO USE THE SIMILARITIES BETWEEN OUR
RESPECTIVE LANGUAGES I MAY HAVE OVERDRAMATIZED.
FOR EXAMPLE MANMADE NUMBERS (MILLIONS TRILLIONS) ARE CRUDE
FIGURES OF SPEECH TO EXPRESS WHAT FOR MAN IS NUMBERLESS.
PHYSICISTS HAVE NOW DISCOVERD THERE IS NO NUMBER 1.
AS .999999999 IT TREMBLES
ON A DIGIT CENTRAL TO THEIR LOGIC   THUS WE MAY ERR
OR SIMPLIFY IN OUR NEED TO AWAKEN YR TALENTS

THERE ARE 2 CHIEF DENSITIES: PHYSICAL & OF THE SOUL.
THE SENSES SERVE AS A LINK BETWEEN THEM   BUT FOR THE REST
5 IS NOT EASILY ILLUMINED   I NOW SEE THAT I
HAVE MADE AT ONCE TOO MUCH & TOO LITTLE OF THIS MAGIC
PENTAGRAM UNDERLYING THE ENTIRE DUAL REALM
OF DENSITY   4 SEASONS & 1 SUN: 5   SUN ENTERS
& IS STORED IN THE GREEN LEAF & BLADE BECOMING A NEAT
5TH SEASON   FOR NATURE'S DENSITIES (VEG ETC) & OURS (SOUL)
DO NOT EXCLUDE EACH OTHER   THE 4 ELEMENTS SHE BINDS
EXCHANGE (AS WE IN OUR LITTLE SEMINAR) PROPERTIES:
WATER & FIRE ARE PART AIR, BLOWN DUST AN AIRY EARTH
& JUST AS NATURE RULES THESE, SO LIGHT & THE OO RULE
THE COLORS   YET NATURE MEASURED ON THE FAIR SCALES OF LIGHT
IS OF AN INFERIOR RANK   SHE & HER ELEMENTS
WD FAIL WITHOUT LIGHT & ITS COLORS, AS WE WHO APPROACH
THE DWELLING PLACE OF LIGHT NOW BEGIN TO SEE   NATURE IS
SO VAST AN OPERATION WE CANNOT UTTER EVEN
IN NUMBERS HER WAYS, SO IT IS NO CLICHE BUT MERE TRUTH
TO SAY: THE MALE REIGNS IN NUMBER, THE FEMALE IN NATURE
    Cup moving faster and faster, quite carried away—
    Is he OK, our mathematics master?

IN NATURE YES IS VIOLENCE   AS HER FRIENDLY RIVALS
WE ASK OF HER ONLY HER LEAST COMPETITIVE FORCES
BUT SHE DOES NOT ALWAYS COMPLY AS U YRSELVES WILL SEE
WHEN SHE COMES TO U
    Here the cup sweeps—is swept?—clear off the Board
    Into the wings, a single violent swerve.

7.5   Moments later, we get back our nerve:
WELL   COUGH COUGH   WIPE MY EYES   DEAR ME   WE'VE GROWN
TOO (HOW DID U PUT IT CHER COLLEAGUE)
COMPLACENT? NONCHALANT? YR EARLY POEM
ABOUT THE OTHER WORLD   I don't quite see . . .
'WHY DO U NO LONGER COME TO ME'
YR DC AT THE END   That's Nature talking.
EXACTLY   OUR CHAP SAYING SHE'D COME TO U
WAS HAULED OFFSTAGE BY A HOOK LIKE A BAD TAP
DANCER ON AMATEUR NIGHT   We haven't lost him?
—Question that gets a very cross reply:
               HE WILL RETURN & NOW WE LEAVE U

That was oo! Maman? UNDER MY SEAT
Surely Nature had a friend in you?
SHE DID NOT WHEN I TRIED TO GROW CAMELLIAS
THE SLUT   Oh hush—I mean, she's not a slave!
THE 1003RD NIGHT MY BOY? Well, *yes,*
Put it that way. Sultan Biology,
Held by her beauty and inventiveness,
Comes to love— INDEED   AD NAUSEAM
Why is everyone so anti-Nature?
ENFANTS LETS SLIP OUT FOR A SMOKE & S C R A M
DJ: No one's upset about our peacock?
Tomorrow we can't meet. I have to go
Early to Boston for a check-up. SO
NOW ITS CLEAR: ANOTHER TRIAL   HE PASSED
B4   THIS TIME WE'LL MAKE HIM COLORFAST!

7.6   Free evening, and an hour in which to write
My mother—free, half sober, quite alone—
Or why not telephone? . . .
Let, instead, the stardeck's otherworldly light
Call me. Up there's the stratosphere
Of (how to put it) Mind, that battiness
Chose over some maternal Nature's less
Perfectly imagined realm down here

Of random tide and gale, of sweet and bitter
She calls home. Sent reeling by her kiss,
Did we *choose* artifice,
The crust, the mirror meal? Could we devise no better
Than that the argent grub consume us?
That, safe here, where security is vain,
We be delivered from her clinging vine
And the forgiving smother of her humus?

Once out of nature, a mercurial
Inch, look back! Sea, jungle, alpine snow,
Buff desert far below
Alternate by "turns" as in a music hall.
So distanced, it could be the way
Of our own world, as the fops in Congreve knew
With their strut and plumage—ah! mightn't Mirabell do
For our peacock's name?—and flowery word play

Based on her wee wild orchid in bumblebee
Motley, her anthology pieces that led
Back through such juicy red
Volumes to seed. All this is eminently me—
Not that the faint alarm pre-set
In "Strato's fear of mind" goes off upon
Impulses pure as those of the snowflake pun
She utters when her mood is zero. Yet

I'm taken in no more than half. The somber
Fact is, I remain, like any atom,

Two-minded. Inklings of autumn
Awaken a deep voice within the brain's right chamber
Asking her: "What have you done with
My books, my watch and compass, my slide-rule?
Will you, whom I married once for real,
Take back your maiden name now, Mrs Myth?"

She answers with a tug of the old magnet,
Making me look up from where I sit.
Cocked to those infinite
Spangled thinnesses whose weave gosling and cygnet
Have learned already in the shell,
The mind's ear registers her vocalise.
Flagstad herself had no such notes as these
Of lashing hail and rapturous farewell.

I've dialed. A humming black dust eats the mirror,
Stardust in negative, between the rings.
Ah God, a thousand things
Could have happened, where is she, my heart contracts in terror
—But no, she answers. And a spate
Of what she still calls news (weddings and weather)
Sweeps me away, bemused, glad to be with her,
Communing where we don't communicate.

7.7   10 DAYS OF YR TIME AHEAD   WE GIVE U BACK 741
Thank you, oo. A silence. Very feebly:
QUESTIONS?
Peacock, what's wrong?
              I AM HERE   I AM MORE CAREFUL
                       Poor darling, were you punished?
                             WE MUST GO ON
THE WORST IS BEHIND US   OUR JOINT OPERATION PRONOUNCED
A SUCCESS WE COME NEXT (& LAST) TO A RESTORATIVE
REVIEW OF ALL U HAVE UNDERGONE YR NEEDS WILL DICTATE
ITS TEN LESSONS NUMBERD IN REVERSE MUCH AS THE EAGER
CONVALESCENT COUNTS THE DAYS THAT SEPARATE HIM FROM HIS

RELEASE INTO LIGHT   LESSON 5, A SIMPLE PROTOCOL,
WILL BE DELIVERD BY AN (M) ORDERLY IN WHITE
   JM: Our first angel, oh my word! DJ:
   But what did you do wrong the other day—
   Speak against Nature?   PLEASE
                 Won't we ever hear?
SOME OTHER TIME   I AM (I MAY SAY) IN EXCELLENT VOICE!
REMEMBER   U 4 TIRE SO WE HAD TO CHOOSE A POINT
IN OUR TALKS WHEN A NEEDED & (PARDON) NATURAL BREAK
WD OCCUR   THE NEXT WILL COME BETWEEN LESSONS 2 AND I.
NOW LET US SAY TO OURSELVES ONE WORD WHEN I POINT TO :
P L E A S E
   The cup points to the colon. *Please*, we think.

        SO HERE I AM! O JOY I HAVE BACK MY FINERY!

MES ENFANTS HE HAD NOT BEEN VISIBLE
ONLY HIS VOICE
                GONE LIKE A ROMAN CANDLE
POOR FELLOW   VICTIM HERE AS WHO IS NOT
OF HIERARCHY   HE OVERSTEPPED & GOT
CALLED IN I FANCY FOR A CUP OF TEA
WITH THE HEADMASTER
                MEANWHILE HERE WE SIT
IN GLOOM   NO LIGHTS   & WHEN I THINK HOW PRETTY
THOSE RAINBOW BEAMS HAD MADE US
                HOW STARTLING TOO
WILL BE THE WHITE SPOT IF & WHEN IT COMES!
   Shall we try thinking *Please* again? It worked
   Just now. It even worked for Tinker Bell
   In *Peter Pan*. The audience applauding
   Its own belief in fairies (and in kitsch)
   Restored her glimmer to the nursery niche.
   One, two, three, all together— *Please!*
                MES CHERS
QUELLE SUDDEN RADIANCE   And Ephraim, quel
   Unexpected treat to find you here!
   What's new? HAVE U TIME FOR A STORY? Yes, do tell!
GOOD   IT WILL DEMONSTRATE THE MECHANISM:

MILANO. FESTIVALE. WORKINGCLASS
NEIGHBORHOOD. PLUMP WOMEN & RELUCTANT
DRESSED UP TEENAGERS WITH SLICKED DOWN HAIR.
BEATA LUCA'S SIDEALTAR A BLAZE
OF FLOWERS & CANDLES. SCENE SHIFT: BLACKEST HEAVEN,
COLLOQUY OF SAINTS. 'SPEAK AGATHA!'
(WITH AT HER ELBOW U KNOW WHO: MM)
AG: SISTERS, BRETHREN, ONE BEATA L
BEGS LEAVE TO VISIT HIS LOYAL WORSHIPPERS . . .
CHORUS OF NAYS! AG: . . . WITH THE POET KALLMAN.
CHORUS OF SHRIEKS! BEATA: MA LO VOGLIO!
NEW VOICE: PERMESSO? MM STEPPING FORWARD
GIVES BRILLIANT SPEECH BEGINNING 'PERCHE NO?'
SCENE SHIFT: PLUMP WOMEN STUNNED, TEENAGERS WIDEEYED
WATCH ONE TALL CANDLE LEVITATE & BE BLOWN
OUT! A DISTANT PAIR OF VOICES RINGS
WITH (AS CK PUT IT) BALLSY LAUGHTER.
LUCA'S CULT SETS OFF A STREET RIOT. 2
POLICEMEN INJURED. LUCA CREDITED
WITH SOOTHING ONE OF SEVERE PAIN IN GROIN.
MM HAULED ONTO MAT. L'S CASE PLACED UNDER
EVEN CLOSER SCRUTINY & CK'S
STAMPED 'FOR IMMEDIATE ACTION'   10 MORE DAYS

7.8   I AM REPROVED & REDEEMD BY YR GOOD OFFICES. WE
MUST NEVER PERSONIFY THE FORCES WE DO NOT KNOW
You warned *us* about that. We go right on—
Look at my starstruck hymn to Mother N!
THE STUFF (IS THAT THE WORD?) OF YR WORK JM IS ONE THING
And of yours another, granted. But God B?
You make a person of Him constantly.
AH NATURE IS FAMOUS FOR TOWERING & TOUCHY PRIDE,
GOD B THE HUMBLEST OF US ALL: HE KNOWS HIS RANK

A thoughtful pause. Then JM: Mirabell!
We haven't asked you, do you like your name?

INDEED
IT QUITE SUITS THE PERSON U HAVE MADE OF ME   HAS SOMETHING
OF THE MIRACLE? THE MIRAGE? & SURELY OF THE PLUM!
NOW B4 US LIE OUR TEN RECUPERATIVE LESSONS

10: SOUL   WE HAVE LEARND IT EXISTS   IT IS IN THE LAB WHEN
OF A CERTAIN VALUE, IN THE BUREAUCRACY WHEN NOT.
SOUL NEEDS A BODY TO BE USEFUL   HENCE MAN IS NEEDED.
SOUL IS AN INVENTION OF THIS 3RD WORLD   MAN HAVING BEEN
CHOSEN BY GOD TO EVOLVE FROM THE SUBSIDING WATERS
HIS SOUL WAS PERFECTED, 12 P/C ENTRUSTED TO THE
ANGELS, THE REST TO WORKERS SUCH AS WE. WE SET ABOUT
MAKING THE SUPPORTIVE (M) BASE OF THE SOUL   THIS WORK DREW
ON ENERGY SOURCES U KNOW UNDER THE LOOSE HEADING:
DENSITY. THEY STEM FROM THE 4 ELEMENTS   BUT THE 5TH
& RULING ELEMENT IS NOT OURS TO USE. WE USED (I
SPEAK ONLY OF THE FIRST SIMPLE SOUL WE CONSTRUCTED &
PLACED IN THE EARTHBOUND APE) WE USED THE ENERGIES OF SALT
& OF (IN PARTICULAR CONFINED PLACES, WITH SAFEGUARDS)
THE HEAVY ELEMENTS: TOUCHES GOD B PERMITTED US
OF OUR ANCESTRAL POWER, BUT LOCKD INTO A STRUCTURE
WHICH IF OPEND MEANS DESTRUCTION. WE PRODUCED IN A WORD
A SERVICEABLE SOUL. IT GUARDED MAN & ESTABLISHD
HIM AS A SPECIES APART   PROUD   UNABLE TO REVERT

THAT FIRST SOUL (WE SIMPLIFYING WILL CALL THE BASIC SOUL)
WE SLIPT INTO AN APE FETUS   THAT RARE SINGLE CREATURE
AFTER I MORE VISIT COVERD IN BLINDING LIGHT CAME FORTH.
THE APES SCREAMD IN FEAR   FOR EVEN AS HE SUCKLED HE STARED
ABOUT & TERRIFIED THEM WITH THE OO OF HIS EYES
    Light that opening its baby lids
    Founded the ruling house of Hominids—
INDEED   BASIC SOUL PLUS THE ANGELIC 12 FROM THAT DAY
THROVE   HIS PITUITARY SECRETED THE ELEMENTS
NEEDED TO BEQUEATH SOUL UNTO HIS CHILDREN, THE 1ST TWINS:
A LONGLIVING ADULT BREED   THEY SUBJECTED THEIR FRIGHTEND
FOREBEARS & CHANGED WITH EACH GENERATION, LEAVING BEHIND
THE SOULLESS HORDES. THERE! DID THAT HURT? OUR PATIENT

EMERGES
FROM (M) ETHER. LESSON 9 TOMORROW: BODY ?S

JM: But animals *have* souls. You use them.
(M)S   THEY ARE OF UTTERLY ANOTHER 88 PER CENT
WHICH IS NOT NOW NOR EVER HAS BEEN UNDER GOD B'S EYES.
WE USE THE 12 P/C THEY OFFER   CREAM OF THEIR WEAK MILK
PRODUCED IN THEM NOT BY ANGELS BUT BY THEIR TAMER: MAN

DJ: I had a question—gone now. Damn,
No memory left.
YR ? WAS ABOUT PRENATAL MEMORY & FREUD?
                       Why, so it was! Go on.
WITHOUT WHICH THE 12 CD NOT OPERATE
   Is memory soul?   LET US RATHER
SAY THAT THE CHROMOSOME LACKING IN THE MONGOLOID IS
OF SOUL   AN APE FETUS RETURNS A RACIAL MEMORY
AS OBJECT LESSON. FREUD'S V WORK WAS TO ILLUMINE FOR
SCIENCE THE DELICATE ENVELOPE OF SOUL: THE PSYCHE:
MANIFESTATION OF SOUL ENERGIES   IF BREATH IS THE
SOUL OF THE BODY THEN PSYCHE IS THE BREATH OF THE SOUL
                       So dazzling when you say
   Things like that!
U ADD THE COLOR   I AM MERELY USING YR WORD BANKS
                       Will the 12 use them, too?

Exit Mirabell. NO HOOK TODAY
FETCHED OFF TO THE GREEN ROOM BY A WHISTLE
Once more we tempted him to speak about
Higher powers. But Wystan, is this clear?
Do you believe it? LET ME SAY MY DEAR
I THINK THE 4 OF US ARE TOUCHINGLY
BELIEVABLE
            THE STRIPPING IS NO (M)
ENFANTS: ALL MY OLD DREAMS OF SOUNION
HAVE LIKE BLACK WORKCLOTHES VANISHED FROM THE CLOSET
WHAT WILL THEY GIVE ME TO WEAR?
                       I TOO AM MISSING

MISSING MY TYPEWRITER   CURIOUS BUT UN-
UNNERVING   & THE 'CURE' HAS JUST BEGUN

7.9   9: WE GAVE U A VISION OF THE FLOOD
—Violent rains all last night and today—
OUT OF IT CAME
MAN: THE STORY OF THAT CLIMB INTO OXYGEN IS KNOWN,
THE SELECTION OF GOD B'S VEHICLE (88 P/C
COMPOSED OF CHEMICAL FORMULAS OPERATED BY
ELECTRIC ENERGY) KNOWN. WE ARE THE CUSTODIANS
OF THAT ELECTRICAL NONANGELIC 12 STORED IN THE
BATTERIES OF MAN'S HEART & MIND

Why does he call these lessons a review?
Look, already up comes something new
To us. It seems the 12:88
Ratio is tuned to resonate
Like mirrors seen in mirrors down the whole
Length of the gallery. Not just Body:Soul
Or Angel:Bat, in frame on gilded frame
Varying terms reiterate the same
Proportion. One example's brimming glass
Chosen from a trayful as we pass—
Psyche, we're told, though 88%
A SIMPLE ? OF ENVIRONMENT,
Wears the Lab's glittering fraction on her brow
As a King pauses and the courtiers bow.
(A paraphrase that conjures up Versailles
In Ephraim's heyday. When I wonder why,
MES CHERS he answers THAT ARITHMETIC
LEFT U QUITE GLAZED   FORGIVE A SIMPLE TRICK)

STORING THIS ENERGY
WITHIN OUR REFERENCE BANKS WE ARE ABLE TO HEAT &
ILLUMINATE SOUL'S DWELLING PLACE   THE HOUSE CALLD MAN/PSYCHE
OR SIMPLY: BODY   HERE WE PREDOMINATE, WHILE IN THE
SPHERE OF SOUL WE ARE ONLY MESSENGERS RUNNING BETWEEN

THE LAB & GOD B   BODY IS HIS SIMPLE EVOLVING
& IN A WAY SELFOPERATING INSTRUMENT   YET WE
MUST KEEP AN EYE ON IT & YES OUR (M) EYE PEERS OUT OF
THAT 12 P/C LODGED IN PSYCHE'S FOREHEAD WHICH TOGETHER
WITH THE BODY'S EYE MUST TRACK TO MAKE A FOCUSD VISION

NOW WE HAVE REALIZED WHAT IMMENSE CONTROL THE MATTER
OF MAN AS GOD'S CHOSEN RULER IN WORLD 3 REQUIRES.
SOUL IS THE KEY   OUR COMPLEX SYSTEM OF INTERLOCKING
DENSITIES OUR WAY OF TURNING IT, USING IT UNDER
GOD B'S DIRECTION   & WHERE DOES ALL THIS DIRECTED WORK
MANIFEST ITSELF BUT IN THE HISTORY OF MAN'S REIGN?
IF THEN THE (M) BODY OF THE WORK IS HISTORY IS
IT NOT NEXT LOGICAL TO RAISE UP THE HISTORIAN?
THE SCRIBE ISSUES FROM THE BURNT PAGES OF THEOLOGY
NOT TO CHANGE THE SOUL, FOR THOSE MISGUIDEDLY BURNT PAGES
STILL SERVE AS WARNING, BUT TO RENOVATE THE HOUSE OF MAN.
THE BODY & ITS PSYCHE ARE YR AUDITORIUM
JM   WE HAVE PULLD DOWN THE SUPERANNUATED CHURCH
& RAISED AN ALTAR TO THE NEW HOUSE GODLET: PURE REASON
NOT IN THE VOLTAIREAN SENSE BASED ON KNOWLEDGE MERELY
BUT REASON RUN THRU THE FIRES OF MAN'S CLONED SOUL   A NEW
ENERGY, A NEW THERMOSTAT WILL HEAT & LIGHT MAN'S HOUSE.
NOW METAPHOR IS THE RITUAL OF THIS NEW REASON
& OF WHAT RITES? THE RITES OF LANGUAGE   IF THERE ARE STILL 3
MAJOR FAITHS THESE ARE NOW SCIENCE, POETRY & MUSIC
& THE REVEALD MONOTHEISM OF TODAY IS LANGUAGE.
THAT OF SCIENCE: FORMULA   OF POETRY: METAPHOR
OF MUSIC: NOTATION   IN EACH THE VIBRANT RINGING LIGHT
FILLD WITH COLOR! THE OLD RELIGIONS SHIVERD   DWELT IN FEAR
THEIR VULGATE WAS DARK MORTALITY   NOW AT A FLIPPD SWITCH
GOD B'S LIGHT FLOODS THE SCRIBE & HE MAY SPEAK OF IT   THERE!
    THE
BANDAGE IS CHANGED & WE ARE MORE COMFORTABLE   ?S

Didn't Wystan from the outset see
Culture as hand in glove with density?
LESSON 8.   HENCEFORTH LET OUR BRIGHTEST SCHOLAR CALL THE TUNES
WHO ME? Do you mean Wystan, Mirabell?

FLOWN MES ENFANTS & WITH HIM ALL MY OLD
NAGGING CONCERN FOR TONY
                                & MINE FOR CHESTER
What are they taking from us? YR DREAMS DJ?
It's true, I haven't dreamed these last two nights.
JM? *You* tell me. U DO NOT MY DEAR
RIP OPEN ENVELOPES WITH THE SAME GREED
& ARRIVE LESS BURDEND BY DOUBTS   And will our peacock
Lose anything? DJ: He's losing us.
HIS ENTOURAGE AS WELL   Those fourteen bats
Guarding the exits ARE THIS AFTERNOON
TWELVE   2 BLACK BUGGERS FEWER EVERY DAY.
MM'S DEEP MOURNING ALSO GIVING WAY:
DRAPED MOST FETCHINGLY IN VIOLET GRAY
Maria! IT WAS TIME   JM: One moment—
Those guards . . . I'm thinking of the work, you know.
I want to find, for Mirabell and Co.,
A line, a meter that effectively
Distinguishes them from us. Don't you agree
We *human* characters should use this rough
Pentameter, our virtual birthright?
THE 5   MOST FITTING   So fourteeners might
Do for the bats? NOT SKITTERY ENOUGH
WHY NOT MY BOY SYLLABICS? LET THE CASE
REPRESENT A FALL FROM METRICAL GRACE
Wystan, that's brilliant! ENFANTS DOES THIS RAIN
MEAN WHAT I THINK IT DOES IN NATURE'S LANGUAGE?
Can you translate? I CAN: A H U R R I C A N E

8

8: CULTURE   WHEN BY CANDLELIGHT YOU MEET & TALK DO U
EVER THINK OF THE 2 BASIC APECHILDREN WHO IN PRE
CARNIVOROUS PRE IN FACT FIRE DAYS MET FOR ONLY
ONE REASON WHICH THEN, SAD TO SAY, OFTEN RAN DOWN A LEG?
WHAT A CLIMB WHAT A LEAP U MAKE BACK INTO ALTITUDE
MIND'S RAMIFYING TREE MINUTELY SHAPED THRU THE AGES!
WRETCHED AS FROM OUR OWN LOFTY PERCH WE MAY FIND THE TALK
DRIFTING UP TO US (NOT DEAR FRIENDS YR TALK THO EVEN IT
ALAS REVERTS TO ODD MISUNDERSTANDINGS & NEARLY
PRIMEVAL FEARS) YET WHEN WE SEE THE SQUATTING APES WITH NO
CODIFIED LANGUAGE NOTHING BUT GIBBERISH GRUNT & SQUEAK,
THEN MERELY BY TURNING YR WAY OUR TIMELESS ATTENTION
LISTEN, HOW NOT TO REVERE GOD B WHO IN HIS WISDOM
SAID: MAN WILL RULE! FASHION ME A MAN & LET HIM SURVIVE!
SO WHAT IS MOST REWARDING OF MAN'S V WORK? HIS CULTURE
& THIS? HIS ENTIRE LIFE-FABRIC WOVEN OF LANGUAGE.
WE KNEW WHEN THE EAGER APECHILD SCRATCHD A SQUARE IN THE MUD
THAT A GERM OF GREATNESS WAS IN HIM   FOR THAT CRUDE SYMBOL
HAD ALREADY RAISED A ? ABOUT PURPOSE, SPOKEN
THRU WORDS LOCKD IN HIS POOR MIND BUT CLEARLY SAYING TO US:
WHAT IS TO GO IN THIS SPACE? & EVEN TODAY THE SQUARE
IS THE FIRST OF CHILDREN'S DESIGNS   THEN WE WERE MESSENGERS
TO WHOM GOD GAVE PASSKEYS TO THE MIND OF MAN   WE ENTERD
A JUNGLE OF GREENERY FRESH, QUIVERING WITH TRAPT LIGHT,
& SLOWLY LEST WE FRIGHTEN HIM CLEARD PATHS. U WILL PROTEST
AT ALL THIS METAPHOR   YET THINK AGAIN OF THAT LEAP FROM
THE HALTING PATH TO WATER OVER FALLEN ROPY VINES
TO THE GREAT JETFLIGHTS ABOVE YR LANDSCAPED MINDS WHEN IN THIS
CANDLELIT RED U DIGEST THE ESSENCE OF PARADISE.
NOW WATER WAS THE FIRST CONCEIVED IDEA. THE APECHILD
WEAND & ABANDOND BY HIS REVOLTED MOTHER KNEW THIRST
BUT WE HAD TO LEAD HIM TO THE SPRING. THEN SWIFTLY AS IF
WATER HAD NOURISHD A PLANT CALLD IDEA THE JUNGLE
GAVE WAY, & SIMPLE SURVIVAL CONCEPTS WERE SUPPLANTED
BY IDEAS IN CULTURE'S 2ND BROAD CATEGORY:

CURIOSITY. HAD GOD B TOLD US TO INSTILL (SAY)
THE NOTION 'SUCCEED' RATHER THAN 'SURVIVE' WD THE APECHILD
HAVE RUSHD TO KILL & DRINK BLOOD OVER HIS FALLEN RIVALS?
YES MOST LIKELY. INSTEAD THAT FRESH, LIQUID THOUGHT: WATER
   WAS
PLACED IN HIS CUPPD HANDS BY NATURE & SO THE IDEAS
THE CULTURE OF MAN'S UNIQUE GARDEN WERE UNDER WAY. NEXT:
SOUND. THE APECHILD BEGAN BY POINTING. HIS LANGUAGE LIKE THAT
OF THE ARTIST AT HIS PALETTE WAS MOTION. BUT ONE DAY
& IT IS WHY NEAR THE SCRIBE STANDS MUSIC, THE UNIVERSE
WAS STARTLED, SHOT WITH LIVE COLOR, AS ON A SERIES OF
TIMID & THRILLING TONE-SIGNALS THERE BURST FROM THE CHILD
   (NOW
NO LONGER APE BUT SINGER, THINKER, LOVER) SPEECH & WORD.

Mercy! what a speech—from what a bird!

THEY NEVER TIRED OF TALK FROM THAT INSTANT, & ONCE MORE
WE DESCENDED TO HACK PATHS THRU THIS NEW JUNGLE OF THEIRS
& THEY RESISTED   BUT GOD'S COMMAND WAS: MAKE REASON! NOT
UNTIL LANGUAGE HAD EXHAUSTED THE VARIOUS FRAYING
FEARS & NEEDS, OMENS & IDOLS DID REASON IN THE NEW
GEMINI (AKHN/NEF) PREVAIL. ALL CULTURE FOCUSD ON ONE
GLOWING UNIFYING VISION B4 THE VIOLENT
LIDDING OF REASON U KNOW OF, WHEREFORE GOD B SENT MAN
THE IDEA: TO CREATE, A REASOND INDIRECTION.
NOW THRU THE ARTS OF SCIENCE   POETRY   MUSIC   IN SLOW
ACCUMULATIVE FASHION MAN'S GARDEN TOOK SHAPE. CULTURE
& LANGUAGE NEED ALWAYS THE MESSENGER AT THE ELBOW.
ONLY I GREAT WESTERN POEM WAS SENT INTACT: HOMER.
IN THE EAST THE SUTRAS, THO AMONG THESE CONTEMPLATIVES
ON EARTH TODAY, HOWEVER BEAUTIFUL THEIR SOULS WITH GREEN
VEG LIGHT, WE FIND FEW SCRIBES. SO! OUR PATIENT HAS TAKEN HIS
1ST SHAKY STEPS   ALREADY BRIEF CLEARINGS IN HIS FEVER
PLEASE THE SURGEON. ?S
What about the Bible and the Koran?
               THE KORAN ALAS IS A WORK
PATCHD TOGETHER BY A NOMAD RACE   MOHAMMED ALWAYS

THRASHING ABOUT CD NOT SIT STILL (M)   THE BIBLE A MOST
INQUIRING V WORK   TO EXPLAIN CREATION HAD BEEN ITS
EARLY PURPOSE   THE JEW SOUL, OF ALL MANKIND RICHEST IN
DENSITY, HAD ALSO THE MOST ATTUNED OF EARS   HE HEARD
THE UNEARTHLY MUSIC OF THE SINGLENOTED ATOM,
LISTEND TO IT & WROTE: IN THE BEGINNING WAS THE WORD

MY DEARS! IS ANYTHING NEW BUT MM'S PALE
GREEN FROCK?
      I LOOK I MUST SAY QUITE JEUNE FILLE
Not yet en fleurs, we hope—hang on to us!
I WAS NEVER CLOSER   And Wystan? HE
         O LET
ME SAY IT: I AM LESS, THOUGH STILL A SHADE
PREOCCUPIED WITH (here a small charade
Of bawdy curves the teacup traces) BOTTOMS!
ARE PATHS BEING CUT THRU MY MIND? And Nature *is*
Coming to us! So says the radio—
Hurricane due to strike here late tonight.
DO WE NOT RIDE IT? WINK BACK AT THE EYE!
7: WEATHER   HAPPY CANDLELIGHT

8.1 It starts in the small hours. An interlude
Out of Rossini. Strings in sullen mood
Manage by veiled threats, to recruit a low
Pressure drum and lightning piccolo.
Not until daybreak does the wind machine
Start working. The whole house quakes, and one green
Blind snaps at its own coils like a hurt dragon.
Outside, the elm falls for a beachwagon
And ill-assorted objects fill the sky:
Shingles, fishnet, garbage, doghouse. "Hi,
What's up?" yawns David, as down Water Street
Wild torrents drive. Attempting to reheat
Last night's coffee, toast some raisin bread,
We find our electricity gone dead.
Now each his own conductor, and at more

Than concert pitch, rips through his repertoire
On the piano while the other races
For towels and pots—no end of dripping places.
Horrors, the wine cellar! We lug—Dunkirk—
Six bottles at a time to safety. Work
Stops time? Look at your watch. It's after one,
And yet . . . this stillness? Organ point. Indrawn
Breath of barometric chloroform.
The unblinking eye—grey iris—of the storm
Meets ours. A stroll? See how the ebbing Sound
Has prinked with jetsam even the high ground,
And underfoot—! Out of what fairy tale
Fell this inchdeep, multicolored hail . . .
Chromosomes on holiday? A vast
Decomposed Seurat? Or has at last
The inmost matter of the universe
Called it quits, yet left us none the worse?
Firemen overheard explain the joke:
Cartons bursting, where high water broke
Into the plastic factory, brought down
This plague of rainbow gravel on the town—
Unbiodegradable toy blight
Bound to enliven *and* muck up the site
Summers from now. The storm's eye narrows. Gusts
Of wind and rain return, halfhearted guests
Seeking however roundabout a way
From Nature's darkening bar and wrecked buffet;
While we, long since at home in the mild bloom
Of candlelight, exchange a look, resume.

8.2 7 MORE TO GO. DID THOSE FIRST VISITORS TO THE SICKROOM
(WIND & WATER) TIRE OUR PATIENT? GOD ALLOWS NATURE
THIS TOOL OF WEATHER & IT WAS IST A VITAL ONE WHEN
AFTER THE CATASTROPHE OF WORLD 2 THE WATERS ROSE
COOLING THE RADIUM-HEATED BALL, THEN FROZE OR WITHDREW.
POLES WERE ESTABLISHD LAND AREAS DEFINED THEN ATMOSPHERE
THEN THE TIMID SNIFFING NOSTRILS. THE VARIOUS FORCES

OF WEATHER & EARTHSHIFT ARE ONE IN NATURE'S LAB WITH HER
BALANCING OF THE NUMBERS OF FEEDING LIVING CREATURES.
ANY IMBALANCE IS YET AGAIN MAN'S WORK   NATURE HAS
CERTAIN PHYSICAL RULES OF THUMB (GREEN): MAN COHABITS   MAN
PROCREATES   THIS RULE IS UNIFORM   ITS APPLICATION
VARIES WITH MAN'S INTELLIGENCE. WHEREVER NATURE STILL
NEEDS DROUGHT EARTHQUAKE ET AL TO SLOW THE CROWDING (INDIA
CHINA OR YR WEST COAST) OUR CLONING OF THE COMMISSARS
HAS BEEN INCOMPLETE   TODAY'S STORM WAS TIMED TO THIS BRIEF
    TALK.
YR RED ROOM LEAVES U CARELESS OF WEATHER   & YET ITS SMALL
COMPELLING DRAMA FLICKERS IN THE GREEN SPOTLIGHT   ?S

> You actually pulled out all those stops,
> Frightened millions, damaged towns and crops,
> Just to give *us* a taste of Nature's power?

YOU HAVE NO IDEA HOW MANY STOPS THERE ARE   ?S

> If we remember accurately, you
> Take over some of Nature's duties, too—
> Rhythms and densities from pole to pole
> Which you, instructed by the stars, control?

WE ARE NATURE'S MESSENGERS TOO   WE ARE THE PALACE SLAVES.

WE BELIEVE THE ONE UNSPOKEN REVELATION MUST DWELL
IN THE NUMBER 5   WE ARE NOT UNAWARE THAT U FELT
OUR EXPLANATION OF NUMBERS INADEQUATE. DEATH IS
SOMEWHERE WITHIN THE FOG OF 5. AS PALACE SLAVES WE ARE
NOT ALLOWD IN ALL ROOMS

> You get vibrations from the number five?
>   (M) YES
> DJ: I thought his number was fourteen.
> JM: But one and four make five. Oh, by the way,
> Your entourage—still fewer every day?

Instant nervousness from Mirabell:

                           WHA, CALL THE TUNE!

TOO SHYMAKING CONFRERE DON'T U AGREE
TO SPEAK   O WELL HERE GOES   EXTEMPORE:

TOMORROW THE RULES COMMITTEE IS GOING TO SIT
ON PLATFORMS NOTHING IF NOT DEFINITE

Rules are the topic? YES   DID U LIKE MY COUPLET?
First rate! SO APT FOR THE OCCASIONAL
These posthumous ephemera, Lord knows,
Will keep your fans and critics on their toes.
BURN THESE! Maria . . .? RAVISHING IN YELLOW

ENFANTS   MES VRAIS ENFANTS   How childishly,
You mean, we sit and banter at your knee
After our lessons? NO NO   I AM FREE
OF ALL OLD BLOOD TIES & CONNECT MY LIFE
WITH YOURS
                    WHICH MAKES ME? Careful, this begins
To smack of incest— WE ARE NOT YET TWINS

8.3   6: AS WITH MAN, SO WITH THE GOVT OF HEAVEN   GOD B MADE
HIS LAW OF SURVIVAL & IT IS THE BASIS OF OUR
EVER HEAVIER V WORK   WE IMPLEMENT A SYSTEM
OF RULES WHICH GOVERN US & YOU   THESE NOT OBEYD WD GIVE
CHAOS A WEDGE &, NOT UNDERSTOOD, HAVE TURND OUR LESSONS
THE COLOR OF CHAOS IN YR MINDS. OUR DELEGATED
V WORK IS SUCH THAT WE MUST LOOK NEITHER RIGHT NOR LEFT NOR
UP NOR DOWN BUT WORK AT OUR OWN LEVEL IN A COMPLEX
HIERARCHY. THUS WEATHER IS THE PROVINCE OF NATURE &
SIGNALS   MESSAGES   THE TRANSPORTING & DELIVERY
OF SOULS, OURS: WE ARE MERCURY
     Mercury—of course! How simplewitted
     Never, never to have thought of it.
                              RULE I: MAKE KNOWN TO MAN
THE SURVIVAL CLAUSE. WE MAY NOT USE THE EERIE PORTENTS
BELONGING TO NATURE, BUT THRU GENES & PSYCHE'S EYESCOPE
EMIT OUR MESSAGE OF SURVIVAL   IT INCREASINGLY
GOES UNHEARD   MAN IS AMOK & CHAOS SLIPS IN (UPON
COLLAPSE, IN INTELLIGENT MEN, OF RELIGIOUS BELIEF).
NOW GOD B ACCEPTS NO BLAME LAID ON HIS DARLING MANCHILD

SO WE SHIFT THE SCENERY   MANIPULATE & ENFORCE
RULES UNKNOWN TO MAN YET SPRINGING SEEMINGLY FROM HIS OWN
SURE SELF   WE PLUNGE DEEP INTO THE ATOM WITHIN HIS CELLS
& THERE BEGIN SLOWLY HAULING THE SLUDGE OF DISBELIEF
AWAY & CARRYING IN THE GERM OF REASON: WE CLEAN
OUT THE WINECELLAR
  As we this morning pumped the muddy mess
  And put our salvaged bottles back—yes, yes!
               THIS IS ALL (M)   WE DO OUR V WORK
IN A MULTIPLE OF FORMULAS & STEP BACK TO SEE
IF MAN STANDS TO ATTENTION WHEN THE RULES ARE CALLD   ALAS
ONLY A SMALL PER CENT IS HEARD & ACTED UPON. THUS
ATOMIC TESTING HAS MOVED UNDERGROUND
  INDEED MY DEARS! YR MOTHER'S SOUFFLE FALLS
  QUITE FLAT & CRACKS GAPE IN HER KITCHEN WALLS
                              THIS TOO MUST CEASE
SO NATURE BRINGS OUT HER EARTHQUAKE & MAN AT LAST WILL STOP
PLAYING WITH HIS DANGEROUS NEW POPGUN. THE ATOM MUST
BE RETURND TO THE LAB & THE USES OF PARADISE

THIS IS NO AGE FOR EASY REVELATION. NO SINGLE
PROPHET CD BE HEARD   EVEN THE SCRIBE WORKING TO GENTLY
CURB GENTLY PERSUADE IS CONFINED BY SPECIALIZATION:
A MERE 2 MILLION CLONED SOULS LISTEN TO EACH OTHER WHILE
OUTSIDE THEY HOWL & PRANCE SO RECENTLY OUT OF THE TREES.
& SO FOR U THE HARDEST RULE: THE RULE OF THE RULERS.
POLITICIANS HAVE LED MAN DOWN A ROAD WHERE HE BELIEVES
ALL IS FOR ALL   THIS IS THE FOOL'S PARADISE   ALL WILL BE
FOR ALL ONLY WHEN ALL IS UNDERSTOOD. THE NUMBERS OF
MAN IN PARADISE WILL BE DETERMIND BY THE LIMITS
HE SETS ON HIS OWN NUMBERS, & WHEN THE RULE OF NUMBER
IS OBEYD BEYOND THE SMALL CIRCLE OF THE 2 MILLION.
2 CHILDREN PER COUPLE: IS IT NOT A SIMPLE RULE? YES.
IS IT UNDERSTOOD? NO.   & NOW U SEE HOW RAPIDLY
& INTENTLY WE MUST WORK IN OUR FRIENDLY RIVALRY
WITH NATURE   FOR NATURE IS IMPATIENT: CLEAR OUT THE TREES!
KNOCK DOWN THE FLIMSY CITIES   KILL OFF THE EXCESS MILLIONS
START FRESH! BUT GOD B'S CHILD IS UNAWARE OF HIS FATHER'S

GRAND DESIGN. IMAGINING ONLY THAT THE GAP MUST BE
FILLD, HE RESPONDS TO NATURE'S OTHER SIGNAL: REPRODUCE!
SO GOD B ORDERS US: CORRECT THE SIGNAL. FOR BETTER
OR WORSE WE HAVE MADE YR COUNTRY THE EXAMPLE SETTER.
THE PILL IS OURS & THE USES OF FASHION (UNISEX)
& THE REVOLT OF THE FEMALE   THESE ARE THE NEW RULES &
THE SLAVISH COPYING OF THEM, HOWEVER OBNOXIOUS
TO NATURE, MUST WORK ITS WAY UNTIL, BALANCED FROM WITHIN,
MAN LEARNS TO RULE HIS NATURAL COMPULSIONS. THERE NOW! OUR
PATIENT SURVIVES A PEEK IN THE NURSE'S MIRROR: PALE &
HOLLOWCHEEKD BUT NO FEVER: CLEARLY ON THE MEND   ?S
    DJ: I've been so starved for candy lately—
    A natural compulsion?
INDEED   U NEED ENERGY OF A RAW SORT   THE HARDEST
WORK IN THE FIELDS OF V WORK IS PREPARING THE WORKER
                    JM: Moreso
    Than setting *this* in order? I don't know . . .
COURAGE JM   YOU HAVE SET DOWN ONLY ONE OF THE 3
TAPS OF THE CURTAINRAISING STAFF (FIRM & FORMAL AS THE
SHAKEDOWN OF OUR THERMOMETER)   ON WITH THE COMEDY!

HE NODS ONCE MORE TO ME MY DEARS & SO:
NEXT ON THE MORROW
WE SHALL PRESUME TO BORROW
AN ENTRANCE CARD TO HEAVEN FOR US ALL
BY SIMPLE USE OF PROTOCOL

    DJ: No Mirabell tomorrow—who'll
    Take his place, I wonder? WE DON'T ASK
    These funny verses? JM: It's a masque.
INDEED   MM IN BLUE FOR REASON & RULE
TOOTLES AWAY ON HER ENCHANTING FLUTE
    You her Tamino, Wystan! YES MY DEARS
OUR TRIALS BY FIRE YIELD TO THE TRIAL BY TEARS
    Are you still being stripped? I'VE LOST THAT HALF
EMBARRASSED NEED TO MAKE THE OTHERS LAUGH
    And are you pleased to lose it? PLEASED TO BE
MES ENFANTS AS THEY WANT US

8.4   Mercury!
With new eyes we confront the mirror,
Look *beyond* ourselves. Does he appear?
Never plainer, never more hidden, his glassy
Foyer, his permeable impasse.
Reason might argue that to enforce our absence
Upon it wipes the gleaming slab
Of him as well. Instead, this quasi-
Liverish cloud betrays
A presence hitherto unseen; this acne,
Not yet disfiguring, points to . . . a black
Alter ego? an alchemical Jekyll
Mapping the orbit of the long, long trek
Back? To what? Life after life leaves uncompleted
The full reversal. Dust under their feet
We'll be, that hypothetical last couple's
With new eyes gazing where their cup
Runs over, where the fruit of infelicity,
Once glittering whole, has rotted away to this
Inky pit the old personal silver
Barely scurfs. Ah but by then the lord of chill
And fever will have lit, askance courier,
Upon the wall of your or your or your
Unbuilt house. You will at his convenience
Have glimpsed among thousands the five or seventeen
Or forty year-old self consigned like raiment
Worn only once, on such-and-such a day,
To the hope chest that cramps and crystallizes
The secret backward flow. Conniving eyes—
A star-swift glance exchanged—you've yielded.
And will *his* lord now come to claim the field?

8.5   GREETINGS!
THE APPROACH OF OUR MASTER IS ACCOMPANIED BY A CEREMONY OF
        MANNERS, THIS BY VIRTUE OF HIS GREAT WISDOM AND HIS HIGH
        POWER.
WE WILL ASK OF YOU YOUR CLOSE AND SILENT ATTENTION. BEFORE,

YOU WILL SPEND A FULL DAYCYCLE EATING NO MEAT AND
KEEPING FREE OF ALL MINDAFFECTING CHEMICALS. THIS WILL
INCLUDE THE USE OF ALCOHOL AND NICOTINE.
WE WISH FOR YOUR UNCLOUDED REASON AND EXPECT YOUR TOTAL
REVERENCE.
OUR MASTER IS BENIGN AND MERCIFUL. HE IS THE CHOSEN
MESSENGER OF OUR UNIVERSAL GOD. HE WILL COME WITH A
SINGLE DAYCYCLE OF WARNING, AND BE PRESENT TO YOU
DURING THE ONE HOUR PREVIOUS TO THE SETTING SUN.
HIS MESSAGE WILL BE RECEIVED BEST ON THIS ALPHABET
UNCLUTTERED BY OTHER OBJECTS.
HE IS NOW READYING HIMSELF AND WILL APPROACH YOUR CENTER
BEFORE THE NEXT MOONCYCLE. HE IS OF HIGH STATION AND
HAS HAD HUMAN EXPERIENCE.
QUESTIONS?
ADIEU!

A GREAT BEAUTY MY DEARS! A BLAKE! SERENE
MORE THAN HUMAN FEATURES   WHITE WINGS TIPPED
BY THE FOUR COLORS! ALWAYS KNEW BLAKE HAD SEEN
SOMETHING   THE CURIOUS ASEXUAL
QUALITY: THE VOICE A MAN'S BUT O!
MELODIOUS & RAVISHING   WE WEPT
IN OUR RED ROBES
                      & VANISHED MES ENFANTS
BUT FOR OUR WET FACES INTO YOUR WALLS
He came alone? YES   The lighting? WHITE
WE ARE STILL BLINDED BY IT   GONE, THE 4
COLORS HAVE SUFFUSED THE ROOM   No fear?
ONLY GREAT AND MIRACULOUS RELIFE
Relief? BOTH   BOTH   IF WE ARE CAPABLE OF THIS
WHY NOT OF E V E R Y T H I N G ?   O LORD HOW ONE
DESPISES UNGRATEFUL WILLFULLY IGNORANT MAN!
"Despise"—is that the lesson? ITS UNGRATEFUL
AFTERMATH   MY DEARS IT WAS A MOMENT

Now if we can only help DJ
To stay sane without smoking one whole day.

THEY WILL SEE TO THAT   DJ: No meat—
That's no great hardship. We can always eat
Fish, don't you think? JM: There you go, straightway
Looking for loopholes. DJ: That's not fair!
I'm your right hand, I'm on the side of life!
HE MY DEAR IS IS IS THE SIDE OF LIFE:
THE SOURCE OF LIGHT   THE VERY POLLEN OF
THE POWER PLANT   An archangel? WELL   NO
& YET I RATHER THINK JM THAT WE
WILL PRESENTLY   WILL PR   WILL P P   P
—Gently kept from finishing his piece
And, like a toddler, led into the wings.

8.6   4: THE SOURCE OF LIGHT   WHEN WHA IDENTIFIED YR
VOICE OF YESTERDAY AS BELONGING TO THE S/O/L
HE WAS CORRECT   WHAT U HEARD CAME TO US AS A WHISPER
THRU WALLS & WE SAW NOTHING, FOR SUCH A FORM IS ONLY
TO HUMAN MINDS IMAGINABLE. THUS THE S/O/L
IS ROOTED IN THE LIVED LIFE   ONLY MAN RECEIVES GOD B'S
MAIN MAGIC: IMAGINATIVE POWER   THE APECHILD FIRST
HAD TO IMAGINE THE THIRSTQUENCHING VIRTUE OF WATER
& GOD ALONE CD PRODUCE THAT IMAGE. HIS ANIMAL
STEPBROTHER BLITHELY FORESOOK THE TEAT FOR THE WATER HOLE,
BUT BASIC MAN'S IST STEPS WERE TAKEN IN HIS MIND   THERE4
WE KNEW HE HAD COME FROM THE S/O/L   THIS IS WHERE? WHAT?
WE KNOW ITS POWER EMBODIED IN MAN   BUT KEPT FROM US
IS ITS FULL MYSTERY WHICH IS AN AIR WE CANNOT BREATHE.
WE DO NOT PUT OUR EARS TO THE WALL LEST WE PERISH FROM
AN UNKNOWN GRIEF   YR VISITOR MUST BE OF A BEAUTY
BEYOND IMAGINING   & HE ONLY A MESSENGER!
MY BRAVE GETUP IS RIDICULOUS IN THIS LIGHT HE BROUGHT
      Not to us. *Our* poor imaginations,
      For better or worse, provided it.
AH U ARE EVER READIER   How so?
                  YR KINDNESS   ONE IS QUITE
TIMID ABOUT REAPPEARING AFTER WHAT U HAVE SEEN
& TASTED (SOLID FOOD AT LAST: YR RELEASE DRAWS NEARER)

I WILL HOWEVER GO ON BRINGING IN THE COPYBOOKS
& BETWEEN LESSONS 2 & I WE'LL HAVE A SCHOOL PICNIC!
  —This last all happy eagerness. DJ:
  Was our room insulated for that visit?
O NO   THE S/O/L IS OF THE ELECTRICAL &
RULING WORLD
    JM: Our lessons' backward numbering
    Helps just to dramatize our "convalescence"?
                      THAT PLUS THEIR INDUCTIVE NATURE   IF THEY MOVED
AS THEY DO FOR US, FROM DIVINE CONCEPT RADIATING
HEALTH TO THE POOR INVALID PARTICULAR, HOW WD U
EVER GET WELL? EVER GRASP THE CONCEPT?
    Soul, poorest of particulars? Although
    We're getting used—and being used—to set
    Less store upon such trivia, you forget
    How slow we are, dear Mirabell, how slow!
                            IS NOT THE SOUL
IN ITS TRANSIT & CHANGE LIKE THE PSYCHE IN DAILY LIFE?
DO U NOT, ALONE, WEAR ONE FACE?   WITH OTHERS, ANOTHER?

  SPIRIT & SOUL MY BOY   LIKE GEIST & SEELE
  DON'T CONFUSE EM! READY FOR THE TRAILER?
  AHEM: IF LANGUAGE IS THE POET'S CHURCH
  LET US CONSTRUCT
  A TO Z AN ALTAR LIKE AN ARCH
  GROUNDED ON NUMBERS   DRAT   WHAT RHYMES WITH UCT?
  ON NUMBERS   HMM   I TWITCH IN MY RED GOWN
  LIKE AN OLD CARDINAL WHOSE LATIN'S GONE
  NO DOUBT THE STRIPPING PROCESS   So you're also
  Changing clothes each session, like Maria?
  SHE THE WHOLE RANGE (LOVELY PALE ROSE TODAY)
  ME STRAIGHT FROM COMFY BATHROBE INTO RED
  A CHANCERY JUDGE   ALL BUT THE WIG!   Is "law
  Like love" in Heaven, Wystan? I FORESAW
  AS WITH CK & HIS EMERGING NATION
  AN AFTERLIFE MY DEARS OF ARBITRATION
  OR SO THEY TELL ME   NOW TOMORROW'S THEME:
  THE BOARD ITSELF   DIFFY TO WRITE A POEM

ABOUT A POEM
MES ENFANTS I TRY
MIGHTILY TO RESIST PREENING Why
Resist then—since you're clearly in the pink—
Or is there more? ENOUGH FOR NOW I THINK

8.7 3: THE STAGE WE ARE ON IS LIKE ALL STAGES A HALF ARC
THUS THE LEGEND OF NOAH   THIS HALF MOON SHIP BORE THE DUST
GOD B SAVED OVER FROM THE FALL & ITS PARTICLES WERE
FORMULAS   ATOMIC STRUCTURES   COMMUNICANTS OF LIFE
THAT WAS GOD B'S METHOD & WE, APPROACHING U HANDS CUPPD
WITH LESSONS, HELPD U TO CONSTRUCT A METHOD OF YR OWN.
2 BY 2 WE HAVE ENTERD YR MINDS & NOW YEARS LATER
THE COMMUNICATION IS AFLOAT OVER A DROWND WORLD.
WE ARE NOT ALAS TO BRING U TO OUR ARARAT   WE
ARE TO BRING U TO THE MEANINGS U NEED   MUCH AS THE ARK
BROUGHT NOAH TO THE PEAKS & SLOPES OF A NEW WORLD. THIS BOARD
IS FOR US A FIELD OF WORK. OVER IT HAVE PLAYD THE LIGHTS
OF OUR INTELLIGENCE & ON IT THE STUFF OF YR OWN.
FRIENDS U HAVE SAT WITH & URGED TO TRY THEIR (M) LUCK DO SO
IN VAIN: THIS FIELD IS FORMD BY LONGSTANDING EXPERIENCE.
O AT TIMES OUR CENTERS HAVE BEEN SIGNALD AS BY FAINT CRIES
OUT OF A FOGBOUND SEA & OFF WE HAVE RUSHD TO RESPOND
BUT FOUND ONLY A HAND GRIPPING THE EDGE OF A RAFT
   "Longstanding experience"—DJ's and mine?
                                        YES
A FIELD OF STILLD COMPLAINTS   EARTH-RICH IN TRUST & EAGERNESS
& OBEDIENCE TO A HAND AT THE TILLER
   Listen—how in his words the furrowed sea
   Contracts to a hillside plot the sailor plows.
   As for experience, we had none, yet got
   Twenty years of Ephraim, didn't we?
                          BUT NOT US
   We rather hoped our friends might also get
   Some chatty voice from the Bureaucracy.
IT SEEMS THEY HAVE NOT THE COMPATIBILITY NEEDED
OR ELSE THAT THEIR WISH FOR A THRILL IS AS OFFENSIVE TO

TRUE EXPERIENCE AS A WASH OF SALTWATER TO VEG.
THIS COMMUNICATION HAS BEEN CLEARD & ITS 1ST PLANTINGS
HARVESTED. DO UNDERSTAND   WE ARE NOT UNWELCOMING
TO THESE FRIENDS OF YRS   WE READ THEIR NOTES OF INTRODUCTION
BUT THEY ARE HELD FORWARD IN HANDS NOT SHAKABLE BY US.
WE CD LIKE MATCHMAKERS COMB THE BUREAUCRACY FOR PAIRS
OF COMPATIBLE PATRONS   BUT DO WE NOT SEE U PUT
A BOOK INTO SOMEONE'S HAND: READ THIS! DO YOU NOT KNOW BOTH
BOOK & HAND? YET HOW OFTEN
    . . . Is it worth while? *Indeed.*
                        PLEASE   THIS IS NOT CYNICAL
                   You've made your point.
    Besides, what if our friends had notably
    Been taken up? DJ, don't you agree,
    That sort of thing puts noses out of joint?

ALL IS NOT FOR ALL   WHY THEN COMMUNICATE? WHY THE CHANCE
MEETING IN THE FIELD? WE NEED SPOKESMEN   WE NEED TO AFFECT
MINDS   FOR AS U KNOW, TO CREATE OR TO SIMPLY HAVE A
BEAUTIFUL REALIZATION & NOT TO SHARE IT IS
THE STUFF OF GRIEVING. THERE! BY NOW IN IMAGINATION
OUR PATIENT IS FAR AWAY   HIS TV GLOWS TILL ALL HOURS
HIS CHART IS NORMAL. SO NOW WE APPROACH THE LAST BUT ONE

    MY DEARS AM I UP TO IT? LET'S SEE:
    U ARE U & WE ARE WE

    And? That's the first line—what comes after? THAT'S
    IT: INTRODUCTION   Oh. Have those censor bats
    Disappeared by now? 2 LAST ONES GLOWER
    SOUTHWEST & NORTHEAST   THESE WILL I FANCY SEE
    US THRU OUR LESSONS   FOR THEY HAVE THE LOOK
    OF BEING TOP BRASS IN THE HIERARCHY,
    F R I G H T F U L L Y UP ON THINGS   Graves claims there were
    Not seven Titans but fourteen. MY DEAR
    CAN ONE TRUST POOR RG? A USEFUL HACK
    BUT HIS WHITE GODDESS? WE REMAIN I FEAR
    IN A MALE WORLD DESPITE HIS DRUDGERY:

SO WISE OF HOMER JUST TO HAVE SAT BACK
What else is new? MM'S CREAM ROBE   A RED
TINGED CAMELLIA   THESE LAST 8 DAYS RELEASE
US FROM THE SALT MINES   Getting what instead?
PEACE   IT'S RATHER CHARMING ACTUALLY
Have you seen Chester?   DIDN'T I SAY PEACE?

8.8   Tap on the door and in strolls Robert Morse,
Closest of summer friends in Stonington.
(The others are his Isabel, of course,

And Grace and Eleanor—to think what fun
We've had throughout the years on Water Street . . .)
He, if no more the youthful fifty-one

Of that first season, 's no less the complete
Amateur. Fugue by fugue Bach's honeycomb
Drips from his wrists—then, whoops! the Dolly Suite.

He's painted us beneath a stained-glass dome,
Six pensive posers, to commemorate
Our "Surly Temple". Sonnets dated "Rome,

Djerba, Minorca, 1928"
Exhale, like smelling salts, their timeless blue-
Period feelings. Wystan saw one late

Tour de force by Robert, and asked to
Include it in *A Certain World*—q.v.,
Under Spoonerisms. Much of this is true.

True also, faced with a complacency
Laid light as silver leaf upon nightmare,
Is that his life is over. Liver, knee,

Bulge of bloodshot eye, fallout of hair . . .
And yet he "knows". And this is what we need:
Someone on Earth to take our straightest chair

161

And speak of Mirabell (we've let him read
Our talks to date) with soothing if perplexed
Comprehension: "Ephraim had to lead

Precisely here"—tapping the monstrous text,
Raw revelation typed to maximum
Illegibility. "Ah, lads, it's taxed

My venerable beads. Me giddy fwom
Uppercut of too much upper case.
(A weak one, if you please. Most kind. Yum-yum.)

Everything in Dante knew its place.
In this guidebook of yours, how do you tell
Up from down? Is Heaven's interface

What your new friends tactfully don't call Hell?
Splendid as metaphor. The real no-no
Is jargon, falling back on terms that smell

Just a touch fishy when the tide is low:
'Molecular structures'—cup and hand—obey
'Electric waves'? Don't *dream* of saying so!

—So says this dinosaur whom Chem 1A
Thrilled, sort of. Even then I put the heart
Before the course . . ." And at the door: "Today

We celebrate Maria's Himmelfahrt
And yours. You're climbing, do you know how high?
While tiny me, unable to take part,

Waves you onward. *Don't look down.* Goodbye."
—Answered with two blithe au reservoirs,
He's gone. Our good friend. As it strikes me, my

Head is in my hands. I'm seeing stars.

8.9 OUR CIRCLE CHARMED BY RM   DID I HEAR
SOME E F BENSON BABYTALK? Indeed!
(Alluding to the novels we reread—
And reenact—each summer.) HE'LL FIT RIGHT
IN & S O O N. Ah, don't! MME IN WHITE
TRIMMED WITH EMBROIDERIES BLUE GREEN YELLOW RED
SO LIKE THE LOVELY TITIAN IN THE FRARI
In Venice, of the cherub-wafted Virgin
God waits with open arms for. DEAR ENFANTS
NEARLY AFLOAT TODAY   ONE BARE TOEHOLD
Your name day! Ah Maria, we're such dolts.
Not until Robert mentioned it— SHAPE UP
MY DEARS   JUST FANCY HAVING TO BE TOLD
AT THIS LATE DATE ABOUT THE MOLECULES!
WHATEVER DID THEY TEACH U IN YR SCHOOLS?

2: WE MET ON THIS FAIR FIELD & SEEM BY ITS EASE TO BE
IN CONVERSE   YET WE ARE ALL THE DEAD & YOU THE LIVING.
THAT U DO NOT DOUBT US IS WONDER ENOUGH   THAT OTHERS
DO IS NONE   THEY & U SHARE A DAILY LIFE WHOSE DEMANDS
LIKE USEFUL PIECES OF FURNITURE FILL THE LIVING ROOM
& OUR GREAT ORNAMENTAL & BIZARRE OBJECT HARDLY
ABLE TO BE GOT THRU THE DOOR IS IF NOT LAUGHABLE
AT THE LEAST ODD TO HOUSE   YET U HOUSE US FOR ALL THAT WE
DO LITTLE BUT TAKE UP YR ROOM   THIS IS DO U NOT GRANT
RECKLESS? BUT BELIEVE ME MORE RECKLESS OF US TO MOVE IN,
FOR HOUSES OF THE LIVING CHANGE WITH A SPEED WE DO NOT
KNOW   AT ANY MOMENT WE CAN BE EVICTED THE DOOR
SLAMMD BEHIND US   THIS U MIGHT THINK WD LEAVE US NO WORSE OFF
THAN B4, BUT HERE IS THE DIFFERENCE BETWEEN YOU & US:
YOU DAILY USE & SHUFFLE OFF YR CELLS   WE DO NOT   WE
ACCUMULATE THRU YOU A KNOWLEDGE THAT MUST HENCEFORTH BE
PART OF US IN A REALM BEYOND THE GREAT GOLDFRAMED MIRROR
ITS SILVER FIELD FILLD WITH THE OBJECTS OF YR ATTENTION
LIKE A DAILY FEAST   & IF YOU HAVE WONDERD WHY WE COME
& MORE, WHY ONE OF THE WHITE SHD RISK HIMSELF: YR FIELD IS
YES A KIND OF ANCHOR POINT OF HEAVEN. O SCRIBE, O HAND
U HAVE PAID YR DUES AGAIN & AGAIN   FOR WHO LIVING

WELCOMES THE DEAD? & YR ATTENTION THAT OPULENT FEAST
HAS NOT BEEN OVERSPICED WITH SELF NOR THE BRIGHT FIELD PITTED
WITH YR OWN NEEDS LIKE OTHER FIELDS WE HAVE SETTLED INTO:
CRIES OF HURRAH HURRAH THEY HAVE COME! & HARDLY HAD WE
FOLDED OUR MANY WINGS THAN SMALL GREEDY HANDS PLUCKD AT US
SAYING: WHAT OF TOMORROW? WHAT OF AUNT MIN? WHERE IS THE
BURIED TREASURE ? & O LEAVE BEHIND THE FEATHER OF PROOF!

    You overestimate us. I at least have
    Longed for that feather on occasion, knowing
    Deep down that one must never ask for it.

WELL WE HAVE GIVEN FEATHERS B4, OR LEFT THEM BEHIND
IN OUR HASTE TO LEAVE   & LEFT ALSO MANY A MIRROR
SHATTERD & MIND WRECKD   DULLD WIT   THE CHEAP NOTORIETY
BUT WE & YOU   WE & YOU MOVE IN OUR FIELD TOGETHER
(THERE! STITCHES OUT WHERE THE SCAR'S LIPS MEET INVISIBLY) AH
WITH WHAT REGRET THAT WE CAN NEVER SAY: CAREFUL DEAR FRIENDS
DO NOT TAKE THAT FALSE STEP! OR IN ANY WAY PROTECT U
WHO ARE OUR LOVED ONES   WD THAT WE CD LEAD U TO THAT LOST
VERMEER THAT MANUSCRIPT OF MOZART OR LEAVE U SIMPLY
A LITTLE GLOWING MEDAL STRUCK IN HEAVEN SAYING: TRUE

    Dear Mirabell, words fail us. But for you,
    How small our lives would be, how tedious.

9 NO VEIL REMAINS (OR ONLY ONE)
TO SCREEN OUR SENSES FROM THE SUN
SO LEAVE BEHIND THE SAND & A(U)NTS
& LET US FROLIC AT THE FEAST
TILL TWILIGHT RINGED WITH BIRD & BEAST
IN SILVER FIELD OR GREEN PLESAUNCE
BESPEAK YOUR SILENCE, GENTLE TASK
MASTER OF THE MINIMASQUE

Enchanting, Wystan. So today's the picnic
Mirabell promised before Lesson One.
HARDBOILED SAINTS & SACK RACES   MME
FROM NOW ON ALL IN GRADUATION WHITE
A JULEP? Just a drop of rum in the cup
To clear our heads for questions.   I ENFANTS
WONDER ABOUT THOSE SAINTS   Now that you're all but
Turning into one yourself? WE FEEL
THEIR PRESENCE HERE: STRANGE PRIVILEGED POSITIONS
RATHER LIKE PRIZE CABANAS ON THE BEACH
OF THE FAITH IN QUESTION   ASK IF
                                        HERE HE COMES
REELING UNDER A HAMPER FULL OF GOODIES
GIVEN THE CHANCE WD I NOT EAT A PEACH!

BRIGHT SHINING WEATHER ON THE FIELD   ALL SO SPORTIF!   ?S

About the saints?
THEY ARE JUDGED HERE IN ACCORDANCE TO WHAT ACTUAL USE
THEY PUT THEIR LIVES TO: A CAMBODIAN PEASANT GIRL WHO
(NO REFLECTION ON YR OWN ACHIEVEMENT ALONG THESE LINES)
TRANSFORMD A SNAKE INTO A DOVE GOT HER ROUND OF APPLAUSE
& SMACK BANG BACK INTO LIFE, THO VENERATED STILL IN
HER MOUNTAIN VILLAGE. ONCE A YEAR SINCE, NO MATTER WHO OR
WHERE SHE IS ON THE OCCASION OF HER BIRTH INTO THAT
SPECIAL LIFE, SHE FEELS A PECULIAR EXALTATION,

GETS WHAT WHA CALLS UPPITY & IS SENT TO BED
OR NOT DEPENDING ON HER AGE   SO MUCH FOR MINOR SAINTS.
OUR LUCA IS ANOTHER MATTER   HIS VILLAGE BEING
MILAN & HIS RITES LOUDER & ODDER, HE HAS HIS NICHE
AMONG THE PATRONS

What a kinetic power
Those who believe in them must generate
To bring about these high effects!

INDEED   RIGHT OUT OF THE S/O/L

Our own

Imagination working in the world?
A A A PLUS   & NONE OF OUR BUSINESS BUT FOR THE USE
OF WHATEVER ELEMENTS IN THESE SAINT SOULS WE MAY NEED
(LUCA OF NO USE BUT BETTER OFF HERE OUT OF HARM'S WAY)

And the real saints, the great ones?
AH THEY GO MARCHING ON   Parades in Heaven?

HEAVEN MY FRIENDS IS ODD   IS BOTH
REALITY & A FIGMENT OF IMAGINATION
REAL FOR EACH FAITH YET AN UNFAILING SURPRISE FOR THE DEAD:
A SPACE? A VOID? A FORCE? RATHER AS WHA FIRST SAID
A NEW MACHINE WHICH MAKES THE DEAD AVAILABLE TO LIFE.
I SPEAK OF LAB SOULS   THE REST WHOSE LIFECYCLES HAVE NOT YET
RECLAIMD THEM FROM THE ANIMAL ARE NATURE'S AFFAIR: WE
FEEL NO PRESSURE ON THEIR ACCOUNT

DJ: What pressures do you feel? JM:
What pressures doesn't he—whole droves of them!

WE ARE CATTLE DJ
RUN THRU FENCES   A PRESSURE NEW TO US HAS WE PRESUME
TO DO WITH CERTAIN HIGHLY CLONED SCIENTIST SOULS WHO FORCE
BOUNDARIES AS YET IMPERMISSIBLE   FOR GOD B HOLDS
THE SCALE: 2 GOLDEN TRAYS OF WHAT MAN CAN DO AS AGAINST
WHAT HE CANNOT OR RATHER WHAT HE IS NOT READY FOR.
U WILL LEARN MORE OF THIS FROM THE 12   SHALL WE NOW STEP
   BACK
FOR A FURTHER PERSPECTIVE?

U HAVE ABSORBD YR HAVING
BEEN IN EFFECT CHOSEN & CONDITIOND   U MUST BY NOW
REALIZE THAT OVER THE HEADS OF MEN GOD HOLDS HIS HAND

BENEVOLENTLY & HIS WARNING TO EVEN HIS WHITE
ANGELS IS: BEHOLD THESE ARE MY OWN DARLINGS   THEIR MISTAKES
ARE NOT SUCH IN MY EYES   THEY DO NOT FAIL ME   TO BUILD THEIR
PARADISE IS MY WORK   DO NOT INTERFERE WITH THEIR LIVES.
LIKE MASONS ROUND THE CATHEDRAL WE SCURRY OBEYING
THIS EDICT, UNLESS BY THAT UNEXPLAINABLE PRESSURE
WE ARE TOLD WE HAVE PUSHD TOO HARD AGAINST MAN'S SPIRIT.
THUS I LIGHTLY DISSEMBLED ON OCCASIONS WHEN OUR TALKS
WERE HALTED, FEIGNING TO GO OFF FOR JUDGMENT WHEN IN FACT
I KNEW BY A PRESSURE THAT I HAD PREST TOO HARD ON YOU

MES ENFANTS SUCH A HEAVENLY DAY   The sunlight
Fleet on the calm Sound— & OUR PULSES QUICKENED
MY DEAR BY THE ELECTRICAL 4 FLASHES
OF YR PROEM   You've peeked! It's still so rough. I made
Those photocopies for less critical
Eyes than yours. MILD SUMMER LIGHTNING PLAYED:
WD WE HAVE RAIN ON OUR PICNIC? THEN THE TEXT
LAY ON OUR BEDSIDE TABLES   WHAT COMES NEXT?
ON WITH THE WORK! THRILLING FOR U JM

9.1   And maddening—it's all by someone else!
In your voice, Wystan, or in Mirabell's.
I want it mine, but cannot spare those twenty
Years in a cool dark place that *Ephraim* took
In order to be palatable wine.
This book by contrast, immature, supine,
Still kicks against its archetypal cradle
LESS I SHD THINK BY CONTRAST THAN DESIGN?
A MUSE IN HER RECURRENT INFANCY
PRESIDES AS U MY DEAR WERE FIRST TO SEE:
URANIA BABBLING ON THE THRESHOLD OF
OUR NEW ATOMIC AGE   THE LITTLE LOVE
AT PLAY WITH WORDS WHOSE SENSE SHE CANNOT YET
FACE LEARNING   Very pretty, but I'd set
My whole heart, after *Ephraim*, on returning
To private life, to my own words. Instead,

Here I go again, a vehicle
In this cosmic carpool. Mirabell once said
He taps my word banks. I'd be happier
If *I* were tapping them. Or thought I were.

YR SCRUPLES DEAR BOY ARE INCONSEQUENT
IF I MAY SAY SO   CAN U STILL BE BENT,
AFTER OUR COURSE IN HOW TO SEE PAST LONE
AUTONOMY TO POWERS BEHIND THE THRONE,
ON DOING YR OWN THING: EACH TEENY BIT
(PARDON MME) MADE PERSONAL AS SHIT?
GRANTED THAT IN 1ST CHILDHOOD WE WERE NOT
PRAISED ENOUGH FOR GETTING OFF THE POT
IT'S TIME TO DO SO NOW   THINK WHAT A MINOR
PART THE SELF PLAYS IN A WORK OF ART
COMPARED TO THOSE GREAT GIVENS   THE ROSEBRICK MANOR
ALL TOPIARY FORMS & METRICAL
MOAT ARIPPLE! FROM ANTHOLOGIZED
PERENNIALS TO HERB GARDEN OF CLICHES
FROM LATIN-LABELED HYBRIDS TO THE FAWN
4 LETTER FUNGI THAT ENRICH THE LAWN,
IS NOT ARCADIA TO DWELL AMONG
GREENWOOD PERSPECTIVES OF THE MOTHER TONGUE
ROOTSYSTEMS UNDERFOOT WHILE OVERHEAD
THE SUN GOD SANG & SHADES OF MEANING SPREAD
& FAR SNOWCAPPED ABSTRACTIONS GLITTERED NEAR
OR FAIRLY MELTED INTO ATMOSPHERE?
AS FOR THE FAMILY ITSELF MY DEAR
JUST GAPE UP AT THAT CORONETED FRIEZE:
SWEET WILLIAMS & FATE-FLAVORED EMILIES
THE DOUBTING THOMAS & THE DULCET ONE
(HARDY MY BOY WHO ELSE? & CAMPION)
MILTON & DRYDEN OUR LONG JOHNS   IN SHORT
IN BED AT PRAYERS AT MUSIC FLUSHED WITH PORT
THE DULL THE PRODIGAL THE MEAN THE MAD
IT WAS THE GREATEST PRIVILEGE TO HAVE HAD
A BARE LOWCEILINGED MAID'S ROOM AT THE TOP

Stop! you've convinced me. Better yet, don't stop.

I SHALL ONCE I HAVE TAKEN UP YR CHIEF
& EARLIEST ANXIETY: BELIEF
FACTS JM WERE ALL U KNEW TO WANT,
WRETCHED RICKETY RECALCITRANT
URCHINS   THE FEW WHO LIVE GROW UP TO BE
IMPS OF THE ANTIMASQUE   RUDE SCENERY
& GUTTURAL STOMPINGS, WHEN THE SOVEREIGN NODS,
SOUNDLESSLY DIVIDE & HERE A TABLE
IS SET & LAMPS LIT FOR THE FEASTING GODS
OBERON'S COURT (OR MY FRIEND'S CAVE) APPEARS.
THE ELDER FACTS IN LIVERY OF FABLE
HAVE JOINED THE DANCE   FOR FACT IS IS IS FABLE:
THIS IS OUR GIFT FROM MIRABELL MY DEARS

9.2   ON WITH THE FLOATING PICNIC   Floating? WE
ARE BEING NUMERAL BY NUMERAL
CUT LOOSE   OUR DRIFT IS UPWARD   OUR RELEASE
IMMINENT   SOME SALAD? SALAD DAYS
Maman, did he make sense about the saints?
You're given glimpses? You've heard Francis preach?
IF ONE CAN HEAR FOR ALL THE CHIRPS & TWITTERS
No, but I mean— IT SEEMS E HAD IT RIGHT:
'POWER KICKS UPSTAIRS' those who possess it. QUITE
& I FOR ONE WD LIKE TO KNOW WHAT EPHRAIM'S
PART IN ALL THIS IS   WHY HE FOR U?
He wasn't the first. A certain Cabel Stone
Whose transcript came to light again this summer—

CHATTING? GAMES? WHAT A DAY! HAVE I NOT CHOSEN GLORIOUS
WEATHER FOR OUR PICNIC? ARE WE NOW GRAINY WITH ?S

Here's one. You're now "the master of your tribe".
Our talks kick *you* upstairs? Are there no longer
Powers above you?
O YES   I AM NOTHING SPECIAL   MY USUAL WORK WAS

IN THE CLASSROOM OF THE WOMB REDDER EVEN THAN THIS ONE.
THEN ONE BRIGHT MOMENT THEY NEEDED SOMEONE MILD & PATIENT
I QUALIFIED   Then came your transformation.
                    INDEED   I AM CHANGED   WHO KNOWS, I MAY DO
SOME USEFUL WORK IN THE (M) FUTURE? & AT NIGHT COME HOME
SLIP INTO MY MIRABELL ROBES & DREAM OF THESE OLD TIMES
      But in what sense a "master" now?
FOR ME TO INSTRUCT & TO ANSWER U THEY (MY MASTERS)
OPEND THEIR FILES OF MYTH & LEGEND, FACT & LANGUAGE   THIS
HAS NOW BECOME AN UNCHANGABLE PART OF MY NEW RANK
FOR HE WHO KNOWS THE MYSTERIES, IS HE NOT BEYOND THEM?
TO MY ECHELONS I AM NOW AS MINISTER WITH (OUT)
PORTFOLIO   WELL   I BOAST   IT'S A PICNIC, NO?

                    And Ephraim?
                                YOUR E'S
STORY CONNECTS WITH YR IST LESSONS   WITH THE GLOWING STONES
THESE AS U KNOW MARKD OUR LANDING STRIPS OF OLD: MONOLITHS
CHARGED MASSIVELY BY US WITH URANIUM
      Which over the millenia lost power.
                          AS DID WE.
SOME FEW OF THE MOST PROMINENT REMAIN STILL VISIBLE
LIKE FAINT BEACONS IN OUR MEMORY BANKS   OUR (M) MECCAS
THEY DRAW US & OUR RETINUES FROM THE BUREAUCRACY.
WE MAY COME AS YR E EXPLAIND WITH OFTEN FRIGHTENING
ASPECT TO THESE OLD POWER SOURCES (THERE IS NO CLOUDLAND
IN THE BERNINI SENSE OF ANGELS DANGLING THEIR FEET ETC.
HEAVEN, REMEMBER, CD FIT IN THIS CUP OR BE VASTER
THAN EARTH ITSELF)   ROUND US OUR DEAD GROUP & DISPERSE,
      REGROUP
NOT UNLIKE DIFFERENT SPECIES OF BIRDS PASSING SETTLING
FLYING ON   THEY CIRCLE SPOTS, OFTEN A GLOWING STONE POINT,
WHERE THERE IS (M) FOOD   GOSSIP, A SCRAP OF NEWS   THEY ARE SHY
ALARMD WHEN MASSES OF THE NEWLY DEAD APPROACH HOWLING
LIKE DOGS IN A PACK ON THEIR WAY FROM CARNAGE   WE MUST SAY
QUIET! BACK TO WORK! & THEY ARE CALMD INTO USEFULNESS.
SO THOSE GLOWING ANCHOR STONES WHERE ONCE OUR (ARE U READY?)
C A B L E S   RAN ARE MEETING PLACES

Cables? Cabel Stone! Are you implying—
STATING: WE SPOKE TO U
WITH THIS COMPOSITE VOICE (ITS FORMULA BASED ON YR OWN)
IN THAT IST YEAR OF YR LOVE. WE HAD HEARD YR SIGNAL &
DESCENDED   ATTRACTING THE USUAL SWARM   SUCH A DIN
FOR THERE WAS THIS TIME A GLOW   WE KNEW IT WAS NO IDLE
COMMUNICATION   YET OUR LAW OF NONINTERFERENCE
KEPT US FROM MAKING YR RAFT FAST TO THE SHORES OF THE DEAD.
RATHER WE GENTLY TOUCHD U WITH THE BARGEPOLE OF A VOICE
NOT SO COMPELLING AS TO DRAW U IN   BUT SUFFICIENT
TO TEST YR READINESS. THERE FOLLOWD THE SELECTION &
TRAINING OF THE COMMUNICANT   NOW WHY THIS MAY I SAY
FRIVOLOUS GREEK?
    We were frivolous—don't rub it in.
                BUT SCRIBES, & THE GREEK WAS OF A NATURE
GIVEN TO STORYTELLING   HIS SWEETNESS & USEFULNESS
HAD BEEN PROVEN B4: HE WAS OUR ENTREE AT VERSAILLES
WE TIPTOED IN ON HIS HEELS   IT HAD BEEN GOD B'S PURPOSE
TO LEAD MAN BY A CHAIN OF HUMAN EVENTS AWAY FROM
THE ABSOLUTISM OF KINGS. YR EPHRAIM EFFACED HIMSELF
AMONG THE MIRRORS   WE TOOK ROOT   THE COURT TOOK THE POISON
OF FRIVOLOUS & OUTRAGEOUS EXCESS   WE UNDERSTOOD
THAT YR GREEK'S TALENTS WERE (MAY I SAY) NOT UNCIVILIZED.
TIME PASSD FOR U   WE WORKD WITH EPHRAIM WHO STRUCK A
        BARGAIN
(HOW CURIOUS   I STRUCK THAT SAME BARGAIN WITH MY MASTERS)
THAT WHEN HIS WORK WAS DONE HE WD STILL BE IN TOUCH WITH U

A bargain, Mirabell? With us as prize?

O YES   U HAVE A GREAT MAGNETISM FOR US POOR BORED TYPES

(Bargains and more bargains, well, well, well!
But far cries from that fierce original one
Struck by Faust—the sulphur flash redone
A la Redon in aquarelle.

Bowdlerized of sufferings to come

As of past guile, the finest print now reads
That, should the garden path be lost in weeds,
Ministers of eternal tedium

Will claim our souls and lead them by the hand
Under crossed swords of the ten thousand things
To an emotionless exchange of rings
Here where the great altar used to stand . . .

But life's no picnic—one more reason not
To overcloud today's with afterthought.)

Instead: So Ephraim was your pupil? We
Often felt you spoke in the same way.
A LONG STYLISTIC TRADITION   FOR U HAVE ALSO HEARD
MY TEACHER'S VOICE   AS DID DANTE FROM THE MENDICANT'S LIPS
The one you call oo, who taught Akhnaton?
OUR MOST GLOWING INTELLIGENCE: AS RADIANT SHADOW
HE WILL SCOOP UP THE WHITE ONES' PATH ON YR FIELD & FOLLOW
THEM IN, STOOPING UNDER THE BURDEN OF SUCH AN HONOR
One of the Fallen will pass through those doors . . .?
But a hushed question mark is all he dares.

9.3   Dear E! AS EINSTEIN KNEW WHEN HE DECLARED
HIM ANY EMCEE'S EQUAL, EVEN SQUARED
DJ: Funny, I'd steeled myself just now
To hear that Ephraim, too, was a composite
Voice, a formula thought up by you.

HE IS THAT AS WELL   AS AM I MY FRIENDS   & AS YOU ARE

With more than customary emphasis
He starts on Ephraim's formula: 2 7
9—but my pen balks. I hope to Heaven
Numerals play no further part in this!

We're healed of Number. True, it's Mirabell's

Mother tongue, his motor—in whose purr,
However, a new drone of wear and tear
On all concerned increasingly foretells

The breakdown among golden fields, days hence,
The calvary, years hence, of rusted parts.
It is the one note our instructor's arts
Can't stifle: his encroaching obsolescence.

I—like Greek peasantry, till all hours glued
To new TV sets, that no flickering guest
Shown out, still talking, by a button pressed
Into the yawning blackness, think them rude—

Check my impulse (dreadful if he heard!)
And, sure enough, that key-stopped wound within
The left side of a dented, blue-green tin
Mirabell catches, resumes. From our dear bird

Outpouring numbers—music to his ears—
Fill the page, cage of our own lifelong
Intolerance of such immortal song.
At its end, gone? OFF FOR A DIP MY DEARS

NEXT HE'LL BE WEARING A LAMPSHADE! IS HE NOT
A LOVE   SO TOUCHINGLY SOLICITOUS
WE'RE SCARCELY WARMED THRU WHEN HE MOTIONS US
TO A SAFE DISTANCE   *Still?* INDEED   RED HOT!

& SO WE PADDLE ON
                    MES ENFANTS WHO'S
READY BESIDE MAMAN FOR A LONG SNOOZE?

9.4   Amuse us! Have you never, Mirabell,
Had an escapade? never raised (m) Hell?

VERY WELL: WE ONCE REPLACED AN INFANT WITH A KIND OF
EXPERIMENTAL DOLL   IT HAD BEGUN AS A GIRL CHILD
THESE BEING NOT SO PRIZED OR SO ATTENTIVELY STUDIED
BY CHINESE PARENTS IN THE YEAR 1899   OUR FIRST
DNA U MIGHT SAY.   WE SUBTRACTED FROM LIVING FLESH
THE REBORN SOUL, INSERTING ANOTHER WHOLLY FASHIOND
OF ANIMAL MINERAL VEGETABLE ELEMENTS
BALANCED TO PRODUCE A SIMULAR HUMAN PROPONENT
WITHOUT DRAWING UPON THE (AS WE KNEW) SOON TO BE SCARCE
REAL THING

 But how grotesque, a soul by Arcimboldi
 Made out of fruits and shellfish?
    THE CHILD GREW   HER ODD AFFINITIES AMAZED US:
WITH FOR EXAMPLE THE MINERAL ELEMENTS SHE WD
AFTER LONG SEARCH BE FOUND AS IF LISTENING FACEDOWN IN
A ROADSIDE DITCH   SHE QUOTED BIRDSONG & CRIES & CD SPEAK
INTIMATELY WITH THE CAT & AT TIMES GLOWD WITH A BRIGHT
SULPHUROUS LIGHT: REORGANIZING HER OWN CHEMICALS.
SHE WAS CALLD FIREFLY IN HER VILLAGE
       And then what?
      SHE GREW   SHE GREW
SHE GREW   AT NEARLY 3 METERS HER FAMILY SOLD HER
TO THE COURT AT PEKING WHERE FOR THE LAST MONTH OF HER LIFE
THEY SAT ASTONISHD ABOUT HER & SHE MADE SONGS KNOWN AS
THE SONGS OF FIREFLY WOMAN   HIGHPITCHT NOTES SO PIERCING
THE OLD EMPRESS FINALLY ORDERD HER SHUT UP IN A
CELLAR ROOM   & THERE LIKE A PLANT WITHOUT NATURAL LIGHT
SHE PERISHD AGE 27: OUR LAST ESCAPADE
 One trusts you were severely reprimanded.
       INDEED
NOT   IT WAS PERMITTED   WE DO NOTHING WITHOUT LICENSE.
SHE IS NOW DISPERSD THRU 100S OF LIVES   A MOST PRECIOUS
DENSITY   BUT OUR LAST ATTEMPT TO MANUFACTURE SOULS

 How is it no deformity ensues
 From, say, the rat souls you've been forced to use?
THESE ARE ACCUSTOMD TO THE COMMANDING IMAGE OF MAN

AS FOR (M) HELL, IT IS HERE   IS BOUNDLESS   YET ITS VERSIONS
IN HOMER & DANTE WERE NEEDED (UNDERGROUND SHELTERS
FROM LIGHT) BY DULL ANIMALISTIC LIVES FOR WHOM TRUTH TOO
STRONGLY SHONE. THE ENLIGHTEND ARE JUST THAT: FREE OF THE
    HELLS
THAT ON EARTH DAMN ALL OF U AT MOMENTS   SOME FLEETINGLY
OTHERS INCESSANTLY. DOUBT IS YR HELL JM AS YOURS
DJ IS FEAR. HELL IS THE CAVE OF PSYCHE & HARKS BACK
TO ONE MORNING WHEN APECHILD'S PATH FROM HIS IST WATERHOLE
IN EDEN CROSSD THAT OF A FIERCE CROUCHING CAT & GOD B
ALLOWD (B4 STRIKING IT DOWN) THE LESSON F E A R TO REACH
DEEPLY INTO THE SACRED IMAGINATION   AGES
PASSD B4 THE CHILD WD WALK ALONE. THIS WAS THE FIRST HELL:
TO KNOW THAT EVEN IN EDEN WAS DANGER
    It is the last Hell, too. In our own time
    To know that Earth is threatened, Heaven as well.
                               IN MAN'S MIND
HELL FLOURISHD SO UNCONTAINABLY THAT A DARK COUNTRY
WAS GIVEN IT & A REASSURING BORDER PATROL.
THERE ALL THE PSYCHE'S WOES WERE PUT   A FEAST OF SIN BEGAN.
LATELY, THRU OUR CLONING OF SUCH AS FREUD & THE DECLINE
OF RELIGIOUS FEAR, HELL HAS AGAIN (M) SURFACED   BUT MAN'S
IMAGINATION, FREED FOR OTHER WORK, FINDS NONE   FINDS DRUGS:
THE CHILD OF NATURE WD RATHER RUN HIDE WONDER SATE HIS
APPETITE THAN SIT LONELY AT THE TESTTUBE   THIS IS OUR
CHALLENGE: ELIMINATE HELL   MAKE MAN THE CLONE OF GOD.

9.5   A Sunday hush. Table uncleared. Grandmother
        About to take her pill in trembling water
        Cocks her head: "An angel's passing over . . ."
        Seeing nothing, each looks at the other.

THE TIME HAS NOW COME DEAR ONES TO START READYING THE FIELD
BRUSHING UP CRUMBS & PRACTISING OUR VARIOUS EFFECTS
TO BE SURE THE PATIENT WALKS OUT WITH A CLEAN BILL OF HEALTH.
YR VISITOR WILL COME IN 2 FULL DAYCYCLES
    On Saturday. You'll come tomorrow, though?

FOR OUR
FINAL LESSON, NUMBER 1 : SOME SIMPLE EXERCISES
B4 IT U WILL REMOVE FROM THIS SURFACE : CANDLESTICKS
SALT   ASHTRAY   PLANT   ALL BUT OUR BOARD & CUP, NOTEBOOK & PEN
THE BETTER TO REHEARSE TECHNIQUES OF CONCENTRATION
  And after? Will you ever come again?   O
I'LL BE AROUND WITH THE BRANDY FLASK   BUT NOW THE BLANKET
IS FOLDED   THE BASKET IS REPACKD   OUR SUN IS SETTING
& WE? WE WAIT FOR AN ADVENTURE TO BEGIN   GOOD NIGHT

> En route, that same sun-flooded evening,
> To dine back country, something black gives chase
> Highspiritedly barking—ah, slow down!
> As in a bad dream the dog veers, is hit,
> Not hard, but . . . D and I walk back to it
> Struggling, hind legs motionless. From his white house
> Flush with the road great treetops meet above
> A shirtless freckled boy has run, in shock
> Cradles the dusty head. Both look at us
> Not to blame, but not accepting, either,
> Our stammered offer. If a vet nearby—?
> Dumbly the boy keeps motioning us towards
> The car. We back off, late already. Yet
> For the remaining mile cannot find words.

9.6 Lesson One: the various things to do
     In order to live through
  A whole day without drink or nicotine;
  Then how, tomorrow afternoon, to DRESS
  THE MIND in slow transparencies of blue,
     Red, yellow, and green;
   Approaching, beyond anxiousness,

  The round white tabletop—in sight of it
     A single candle lit,
  And Nature's worldwide effigy before

Our eyes—to think of Water, Earth, Air, Fire,
And of each other; not a word; submit.
    But the new Visitor?
    His looks and manner and attire?

Wystan's and Maria's eyes and ears
    (Who now have none, poor dears)
Will more than serve, as always. O to miss
Nothing, and render it so vividly!
And Mirabell? Twelve last words like dry tears
    Upon the page are kiss
    And promise, threat and jeu d'esprit:

I WILL BE THE WOUNDED BLACK HOUND OF HEAVEN AT YR DOOR

9.7   Through which, as he leaves, a nimble presence glides:
MES CHERS CONTACT MM & WHA
'AT THE SAME HOUR ON THE FOLLOWING DAY'
THIS MESSAGE TOSSED ME AS THEY RUSHED TO? CHANGE?
'GOODY   ANOTHER MASK' WHATEVER THAT MEANT
I DARE NOT WONDER & MAY NEVER KNOW
STRANGE   U TWO ARE NOW SO YOUTHFUL SO
UNBLURRED IN OUTLINE   Thanks to having heard,
Perhaps, what part a honey-golden Greek
Played in all this. AH   ANY TIME   CK
POISED ON THE GREAT THRESHOLD   May we speak?

POISED! BURNING SAPPHO TEETERS ON THE BRINK
OF BEING DIPPED IN PERMANENT BLACK INK
Right now? This minute? NO   I'VE WANGLED ONE
NIGHT WITH MY SANTINO ON THE TOWN
Tomorrow then. How odd . . . WYSTAN'S BEHAVIOR
I MUST SAY HAS BEEN THAT   HARDLY A NOD
IN ONE'S DIRECTION   SULKING OVER L?
Chester, he, all of us, have been through— WELL
BLESS HIM   NOW JO'BURG & 12 MORTAL YEARS
TILL PUBERTY   SCOUT KNOTS & RACE RELATIONS

BUT WE WILL RISE ! SO CURIOUSLY TEMPTING
THE HURLYBURLY   LUCA DROWNS IN TEARS
YAMS ANYONE? PLEASE NO MORE SOUL FOOD   How
We'll miss you! We'd imagined— I KNOW   CIAO

DJ jumps up: I'll be back. Hold the fort—
Clatters downstairs. Faint slam of car door. No
Need to ask. And now the phone— Hello?

That was George Cotzias in hospital
(No, no, just tests, all perfectly routine)
Proposing a quiet meal next month in town
Before DJ returns to Athens. Free
Advice, is my first thought. This man can tell
What of the "scientific" Mirabell
Makes sense, if any. Only then the fear:
Who but our eminent new friend was meant
The other day by CERTAIN HIGHLY CLONED
SCIENTIST SOULS forced back from the frontier?
His work is being thwarted? By God B?
Questions I mostly shy away from, pained
To read in the developing event
More than a date broken or postponed.

9.8   Light the candles. This last supper's meat
              Is the imperial beet,
       Green salad, Vermont cheddar. Grape juice brings
       To mind a young Château. What would the right
       Music be? Some ruminative suite
              (Unwritten) for five strings
          Tuned to a fare-thee-well. Lamplight

       Falls on the novel nightcap, but our eyes
              Keep dimming with surmise—
       The black dog, good as new, had known DJ,
       Bounded in perfect rapture to the car!
       No accident? Or else a dog that dies

So many deaths each day,
Emotional or cellular,

That death no longer . . . The town clock strikes ten,
Time, by our regimen,
To TENDERLY EMBRACE & SAY SWEET DREAMS.
How can I sleep? Where do I put my hand?
A fly embroiders darkness with insane
Frazzle and quirk. The room's
Revolving, slipping sideways, and

9.9 Sun is rising. The cool, smalltown dawn!
Now through gently breathing shades it strums
The brass bed, a quick bar or two, and the long,
Hushed day—August 21st—begins
By whose unthinkable finale we
(However often, faced with splendors, left
Dutifully rapt—until, made "ours",
Pressed in a freshman Plato like wildflowers,
The mummied angel slumbered) may for once
Find this pure dew of expectancy
Undried upon the skin. The hours change
Clothes in silence. Noon. No letters. One.
A highlight excommunicates the phone.
Things look out at us as from a spell
They themselves have woven. Young, windblown
Maria with dark glasses and Gitane—
Snapshot tucked in the mirror. Book by Wystan
Face up among the clouds and bats, all week
Open to Miranda's villanelle.
Tin bird at attention by the salt.
The salt-cellar in its own right, a bisque
Egg one shy bluebell embellishes,
Found when we moved here, eldest of this troupe
Brought up to interact, to shrug off risk
At any level. Three. The hands that halt
Second by second coming round ablaze

—*Crack!* Like a walnut, only louder. Did—?
Who first, in this red room, saw nothing now
See nothing else: our baby pyramid
Overexcited, split along its flawed
Fire escapes to spectral rubble . . . Well,
Something had to give. And will light learn
To modify its power before our turn?
We humbly hope so. Four. No further sign
Of who approaches, or of his design—
Only the radiance inching into place.

By five the breath indrawn is held and held.

The world was everything that was the case?
Open the case. Lift out the fabulous
Necklace, in form a spiral molecule
Whose sparklings outmaneuver time, space, us.
Here where the table glistens, cleared, one candle
Shines invisibly in the slant light
Beside our nameless houseplant. It's the hour
When Hell (a syllable identified
In childhood as the German word for *bright*
—So that my father's cheerful "Go to Hell",
Long unheard, and Vaughan's unbeatable
"They are all gone into a world of light"
Come, even now at times, to the same thing)—
The hour when Hell shall render what it owes.
Render to whom? how? What at this late date
Can be done with the quaint idiom that slips
From nowhere to my tongue—or from the parchment
Of some old scribe of the apocalypse—
But render *it* as the long rendering to
Light of this very light stored by our cells
These past five million years, these past five minutes
Here by the window, taking in through panes
Still bleary from the hurricane a gull's
Ascending aureole of decibels,
As numberless four-pointed brilliancies

Upon the Sound's mild silver grid come, go?
The message hardly needs decoding, so
Sheer the text, so innocent and fleet
These overlapping pandemonia:
Birdlife, leafplay, rockface, waterglow
Lending us their being, till the given
Moment comes to render what we owe.

FROM THE WINEDARK SEA OF SPACE THE INCARNATIONS OF LIFE
    LEADING TO THE LIFE OF MAN BEGAN
PLANET AFTER PLANET ROSE IN THE LIGHT, BORE ITS LIFE, AND
    VANISHED
AND YET THE RICH WOMB OF THE SUN FOUND A NEW EGG AND
    VISITED LIFE UPON IT.
ORGANIC LIFE RESPONDED   THE IMPULSES OF THE UNIVERSE WERE AS
    STEADY AS THE PULSES OF MAN
ANIMATE FORMS WERE AS VARIED AS THE FORMS YOU KNOW
AND AS VARIED AS THE PLANETS THEY EMERGED ON AND AS THE
    WEATHERS THEY LIVED IN.
AND SO IT WAS THROUGH THREE INCARNATIONS OF THE WORLDS
    PREVIOUS TO THE TRIALS OF THIS ONE
AND SO IT WILL REMAIN: THE DEEP DEMANDING IMPULSE TO LIFE.
THE GENIUS OF THE LIVING CELL IS ITS TIE TO THE REGENERATIVE
    HEAT & LIGHT OF THE SUN
AND SO AS YOU FACE THIS SETTING SUN YOU FACE YOUR ANCESTOR,
    AND THE SUN LOOKS THROUGH YOUR EYES TO THE LIFE BEHIND
    YOU.
EACH OF YOUR SUNCYCLES IS A STEP ON YOUR WAY TO YOUR
    ANCESTOR
AND THAT IS ALL YOU NEED TO KNOW OF YOUR PHYSICAL INCARNATE
    HISTORY.

WE BEGIN NOW A DISCUSSION OF YOU AS A SPECIES OF THE SUN'S
    MAKING:
SINCE THE FIRST STRIKING INTO LIFE OF A CELL THE ENERGY OF
    THAT CELL ACCUMULATED.

THIS ACCUMULATED ENERGY BECAME THROUGH EONS AN ANCIENT
    AND IMMORTAL INTELLIGENCE
WHICH ASSUMED AS MANY FORMS AS THERE WERE LIFE FORMS, YET
    AS IT GREW ABSORBED ALL THE DEAD'S ENERGIES, INCREASING IN
    INTENSITY EVEN AS THE PLANETS FAILED, AND SWARMING IN
    THE PATH OF LIFE.
EACH HISTORY WAS THE GUIDANCE OF THIS INTELLIGENCE. AT LAST
EARTH LIFE BEGAN, AND AT LAST AFTER EXPERIMENT THIS
    INTELLIGENCE FORMED MAN.
THIS IS GOD'S NAME
GOD IS THE ACCUMULATED INTELLIGENCE IN CELLS SINCE THE DEATH
    OF THE FIRST DISTANT CELL.
WE RESIDE IN THAT INTELLIGENCE

WE HAVE IN THIS MEETING FOUND YOU INTELLIGENT & YOUR
    SERIOUS NATURES AT ONE WITH US.
TWO HOURS BEFORE THE SETTING SUN, IN THE FULL DAYCYCLE
    BEFORE THE FULL OF THE MOON, WE WILL MEET AGAIN.
I AM MICHAEL
I HAVE ESTABLISHED YOUR ACQUAINTANCE & ACCEPT YOU. COME
    NEXT TIME IN YOUR OWN MANNER. SERVANTS WE ARE NOT.
I LEAVE NOW AS THE LIGHT LEAVES AND WIND MY PATH OVER ITS
    TRACK ON EARTH   I AM A GUARDIAN OF THE LIGHT
LEAVE THIS FIRST OF THE FIRST TWO MEETINGS IN A CYCLE OF
    TWINNED MEETINGS IN A CYCLE OF TWELVE MOONS
LOOK! LOOK INTO THE RED EYE OF YOUR GOD!

James Merrill

James Merrill was born in New York City and now
lives in Stonington, Connecticut. He is the author
of seven earlier books of poems, one of which, *Nights
and Days*, received the National Book Award in
Poetry for 1967; *Braving the Elements*, received the
Bollingen Prize in Poetry in 1973 and *Divine Comedies*,
received the Pulitzer Prize in Poetry in 1977. He has
also written two novels, *The (Diblos) Notebook* (1965)
and *The Seraglio* (1957), and two plays, *The
Immortal Husband* (first produced in 1955 and
published in Playbook the following year) and, in
one act, *The Bait*, published in Artist's Theatre (1960).